# The Early Shows

# The Early Shows:

## A Reference Guide to Network and Syndicated Prime-Time Television Series from 1944 to 1949

### by Richard Irvin

BearManor Media
2018

*The Early Shows: A Reference Guide to Network and Syndicated Prime-Time Television Series from 1944 to 1949*

© 2018  Richard Irvin

All rights reserved.

No portion of this publication may be reproduced, stored, and/or copied electronically (except for academic use as a source), nor transmitted in any form or by any means without the prior written permission of the publisher and/or author.

Photographs are from author's collection.

Published in the United States of America by:

BearManor Media
P. O. Box 71426
Albany, GA 31708

BearManorMedia.com

Printed in the United States.

Typesetting and layout by John Teehan

ISBN—978-1-62933-241-3

# Table of Contents

Acknowledgements ............................................................................... xv

Preface .................................................................................................. xvii

**Chapter 1: Family Comedy Series** ..................................................... 1
    *The Laytons* ....................................................................................... 1
    *The Growing Paynes* ........................................................................ 3
    *The Goldbergs* ................................................................................... 4
    *Mama* .................................................................................................. 6
    *The Ruggles* ...................................................................................... 8

**Chapter 2: Kid Comedy Series** .......................................................... 11
    *Wesley* ................................................................................................ 11
    *The Family Genius* .......................................................................... 12
    *The Aldrich Family* ......................................................................... 13

**Chapter 3: Couples Comedy Series** .................................................. 17
    *Mary Kay and Johnny* .................................................................... 17
    *Wren's Nest* ....................................................................................... 18
    *The Hartmans* .................................................................................. 19
    *Jackson and Jill* ................................................................................ 21
    *Mixed Doubles* ................................................................................. 23
    *Ruthie on the Telephone* ................................................................. 23
    *Easy Aces* .......................................................................................... 24

**Chapter 4: Central Character Comedies** ......................................... 27
    *Off the Record* .................................................................................. 27
    *The Billy Bean Show* ....................................................................... 29
    *The Life of Riley* ............................................................................... 30
    *That Wonderful Guy* ....................................................................... 31

**Chapter 5: Comedy, Drama & "Experimental" Anthology Series** ....... 33
   *The Kraft Television Theatre* ............................................................. 33
   *The Borden Show* ................................................................................ 35
   *Theatre Guild* ....................................................................................... 36
   *Television Playhouse* .......................................................................... 36
   *Dress Rehearsal* .................................................................................. 37
   *Variety* (aka *NBC Playhouse* or *The Players*) ............................ 37
   *Actors Studio* ....................................................................................... 38
   *The Chevrolet Tele-Theatre* (originally titled *Chevrolet on Broadway*) ....................................................................................... 38
   *The Philco Television Playhouse* .................................................... 39
   *Studio One* ........................................................................................... 41
   *Colgate Video Theatre* ....................................................................... 43
   *ABC Television Players* .................................................................... 44
   *Your Show Time* ................................................................................. 44
   *Believe It or Not* ................................................................................. 45
   *Fireside Theatre* ................................................................................. 46
   *Through the Crystal Ball* ................................................................. 47
   *Program Playhouse* ........................................................................... 47
   *Academy Theatre* ............................................................................... 49
   *Hollywood Premiere* .......................................................................... 49
   *Silver Theatre* ..................................................................................... 50
   *The Ford Theatre Hour* .................................................................... 51
   *Oboler Comedy Theatre* ................................................................... 51
   *Romance* (aka *Theatre of Romance*) ........................................... 52

**Chapter 6: Mystery, Suspense, and Crime Anthology Series** ............... 53
   *Suspense* ............................................................................................... 53
   *The Clock* ............................................................................................. 54
   *Volume One* ......................................................................................... 54
   *Armchair Detective* ........................................................................... 55
   *Lights Out* ............................................................................................ 56
   *The Big Story* ...................................................................................... 57
   *Mr. Black* .............................................................................................. 59
   *Your Witness* ....................................................................................... 59
   *Starring Boris Karloff* ....................................................................... 60
   *Hands of Murder* ............................................................................... 62
   *Famous Jury Trials* ........................................................................... 64

## Chapter 7: Continuing Character Crime Dramas ...... 65
*Barney Blake, Police Reporter* ...... 65
*Public Prosecutor* ...... 66
*Stand By for Crime* ...... 68
*Martin Kane, Private Eye* ...... 68
*Chicagoland Mystery Players* ...... 70
*Photocrime* ...... 71
*The Front Page* ...... 72
*The Plainclothes Man* ...... 72
*Man against Crime* ...... 74
*Mysteries of Chinatown* ...... 76
*TV Detective* ...... 77
*The Cases of Eddie Drake* ...... 78

## Chapter 8: Continuing Character Family and Romantic Dramas ...... 81
*Faraway Hill* ...... 81
*A Woman to Remember* ...... 83
*The O'Neills* ...... 85
*One Man's Family* ...... 85

## Chapter 9: Westerns ...... 87
*Hopalong Cassidy* ...... 87
*The Lone Ranger* ...... 88

## Chapter 10: Standard and Pop Music Series ...... 91
*The Swift Show* ...... 92
*Face the Music* ...... 93
*Musical Almanac* ...... 94
*Broadway Minstrels/ Broadway Jamboree* ...... 94
*Gabrielle* ...... 95
*Three about Town* ...... 95
*The Southernaires Quartet* ...... 96
*The Ted Steele Show* ...... 96
*The Earl Wrightson Show* ...... 97
*Song and Dance* ...... 97
*Young Broadway* ...... 98
*Chesterfield Super Club* ...... 98
*Arthur Godfrey and His Friends* ...... 99
*Music in Velvet* ...... 100

 The Skip Farrell Show ..................................................................101
 Sing-Co-Pation ............................................................................101
 Manhattan Showcase ..................................................................102
 Backstage with Barry Wood .......................................................102
 Vincent Lopez ..............................................................................103
 Delora Bueno ...............................................................................104
 Jack Leonard ................................................................................104
 The Fred Waring Show ...............................................................104
 The Sonny Kendis Show ..............................................................105
 Blues by Bargy .............................................................................106
 Mohawk Showroom ....................................................................106
 The Cliff Edwards Show ..............................................................107
 The Three Flames Show ..............................................................107
 The Meredith Wilson Show ........................................................108
 Capitol Capers .............................................................................109
 Words and Music ........................................................................109
 The Little Revue ..........................................................................110
 Al Morgan ....................................................................................110
 Sugar Hill Times ..........................................................................111
 Wayne King Show .......................................................................111
 Cities Service Band of America ..................................................112
 Paul Whiteman's Revue ..............................................................113
 Strictly for Laughs .......................................................................114
 Melody, Harmony & Rhythm .....................................................114

**Chapter 11: Classical and Jazz Music Shows** ................................115
 NBC Television Concert Hall .....................................................115
 Eddie Condon's Floor Show .......................................................115
 Adventures in Jazz .......................................................................117
 Penthouse Sonata ........................................................................117
 U.S. Marine Band ........................................................................118
 The Voice of Firestone .................................................................118
 Chicago Jazz (aka Sessions) ........................................................119

**Chapter 12: Country and Western Music Shows** .........................121
 America Song ...............................................................................121
 Village Barn .................................................................................122
 Hayloft Hoedown ........................................................................122
 Kobb's Korner ..............................................................................123

*Saturday Night Jamboree* ................................................................... 124
*ABC Barn Dance* ............................................................................ 124
*Sunday at Home* ............................................................................ 125
*The Paul Arnold Show* ..................................................................... 125

## Chapter 13: Themed-Variety Shows ........................................ 127
*Disc Magic/Musical Merry-Go-Round* ................................................ 127
*Brill's Playroom* ............................................................................ 128
*For Your Pleasure/Girl about Town* ................................................... 128
*At Liberty Club* ............................................................................. 130
*You're Invited* .............................................................................. 130
*The Alan Dale Record Shop* ............................................................. 131
*The Gay Nineties Revue* .................................................................. 132
*Club Seven* .................................................................................. 133
*Crystal Room* ............................................................................... 133
*Places Please!* .............................................................................. 134
*Fashions on Parade* ....................................................................... 134
*Champagne and Orchids* ................................................................. 135
*Captain Billy's Mississippi Music Hall* ............................................... 136
*Admiral Presents the Five Star Revue - Welcome Aboard* ..................... 136
*The Dennis James Carnival* .............................................................. 137
*The Fashion Story* ......................................................................... 138
*The Morey Amsterdam Show* ........................................................... 139
*Café de Paris* ............................................................................... 140
*School House* ............................................................................... 141
*Hotel Broadway* ............................................................................ 141
*Masters of Magic* .......................................................................... 142
*The Lambs Gambol* ....................................................................... 142
*Campus Corner (aka The Quadrangle)* .............................................. 144
*Rehearsal Call* .............................................................................. 144
*Benny Rubin Show* ........................................................................ 145
*Paradise Island* ............................................................................. 146
*Flight to Rhythm* .......................................................................... 146
*Versa-Tile Varieties* ....................................................................... 148
*Sunday Date* ................................................................................ 149
*Inside U.S.A. with Chevrolet* ........................................................... 150
*Studs' Place* ................................................................................. 151
*Hollywood House* ......................................................................... 152

## Chapter 14: Comedy Variety Series .................................................. 155
*Texaco Star Theatre*.................................................................................155
*Buzzy Wuzzy*...........................................................................................158
*The Arrow Show*.....................................................................................158
*Alice Pearce Show*...................................................................................159
*Jack Carter and Company*.......................................................................159
*The Henry Morgan Show*........................................................................160
*Cavalcade of Stars*...................................................................................161
*Fireball Fun-For-All*................................................................................162
*The Ed Wynn Show*.................................................................................163
*The Herb Shriner Show*...........................................................................165

## Chapter 15: Mixed Comedy, Music, & Novelty Variety Shows ........... 167
*The World in Your Home*........................................................................167
*Hour Glass* ..............................................................................................168
*Bristol-Myers Tele-Varieties* ...................................................................169
*Show Business, Inc.* .................................................................................170
*Toast of the Town* (aka *The Ed Sullivan Show*).....................................170
*The Gulf Road Show Starring Bob Smith*...............................................172
*The Bigelow Show*....................................................................................172
*American Minstrels of 1949* ....................................................................173
*Vaudeo Varieties*......................................................................................174
*Window on the World*..............................................................................174
*Admiral Broadway Revue* .......................................................................175
*Show Business, Inc* (aka *Danton Walker's Broadway Scrapbook*
   and *Broadway Spotlight*).................................................................177
*Front Row Center*....................................................................................178
*Garroway at Large*..................................................................................179
*Fifty-Fourth Street Revue* .......................................................................180
*This Is Show Business*..............................................................................181
*Let There Be Stars*...................................................................................181
*A Couple of Joes*......................................................................................182

## Chapter 16: Talent Shows ..................................................................... 185
*Doorway to Fame*....................................................................................185
*The Original Amateur Hour* ...................................................................186
*Hollywood Screen Test* ............................................................................187
*Arthur Godfrey's Talent Scouts* ..............................................................188
*The Jacques Fray Music Room* ...............................................................189

Paul Whiteman's TV Teen Club......189
Talent Jackpot......190

## Chapter 17: Children's Shows......193
Small Fry Club......193
Birthday Party......194
The Roar of the Rails......194
Tales of the Red Caboose......195
Child's World......196
Adventures of Oky Doky......196
Kukla, Fran & Ollie......197
Mr. I Magination......198
Judy Splinters......200
Captain Video and His Video Rangers......201
Science Circus......202
Going Places with Uncle George......203

## Chapter 18: Game Shows......205
Face to Face......205
Cash and Carry......206
Play the Game (aka *Let's Play the Game*)......206
Juvenile Jury......207
Party Line......207
Charade Quiz......208
Americana......209
Stop Me If You've Heard This One......210
Try and Do It......210
Winner Take All......211
Tele-a-Pun......212
Movieland Quiz......212
That Reminds Me......213
Quizzing the News......213
Break the Bank......214
Picture This......215
The Eyes Have It......215
Who Said That?......215
Draw Me a Laugh......216
Stump the Authors......217

Riddle Me This ..................................................................................218
Quiz Kids ........................................................................................219
Think Fast .......................................................................................220
Sparring Partners ............................................................................220
Ladies Be Seated .............................................................................221
Bon Voyage (aka *Treasure Quest*) ..................................................221
Blind Date .......................................................................................222
Stop the Music ................................................................................223
Hold It, Please .................................................................................223
It Pays to Be Ignorant .....................................................................224
Fun and Fortune .............................................................................225
Fun for the Money ..........................................................................225
Cut!/Spin the Picture .......................................................................226
Majority Rules .................................................................................226
Auction-Aire ...................................................................................227
Pantomime Quiz Time (aka *Stump the Stars*) ...............................228
Twenty Questions ...........................................................................229
Kay Kyser's Kollege of Musical Knowledge ......................................229

**Chapter 19: Informational Series** .................................................231
Serving through Science ................................................................231
Geographically Speaking ................................................................232
Television Screen Magazine ............................................................232
Eye Witness ....................................................................................233
The Nature of Things ......................................................................233
Author Meets the Critics ................................................................234
What's It Worth ..............................................................................236
Critic at Large .................................................................................236
Teenage Book Club .........................................................................237
Princess Sagaphi .............................................................................237
I'd Like to See .................................................................................238
Paris Cavalcade of Fashions ...........................................................238
Yesterday's Newsreel .......................................................................239
The Johns Hopkins Science Review ................................................239
Television Close-ups .......................................................................240
Photographic Horizons ...................................................................240
What Do You Think? ......................................................................241
And Everything Nice ......................................................................241
Action Autographs .........................................................................242

    *Crusade in Europe* ................................................................................ 242
    *Theatre of the Mind* ............................................................................. 243
    *The Amazing Polgar* ............................................................................ 244
    *Burton Holmes Travelogues* ............................................................. 244
    *Portrait of America* ............................................................................. 245
    *Kiernan's Kaleidoscope* ....................................................................... 245

**Chapter 20: Instructional Programs** ................................................. 247
    *I Love to Eat* ......................................................................................... 247
    *You Are an Artist* ................................................................................. 248
    *Let's Rhumba* ....................................................................................... 249
    *Dancing on Air* .................................................................................... 249
    *In the Kelvinator Kitchen* .................................................................. 250
    *The Wife Saver* .................................................................................... 250
    *To the Queen's Taste* (aka *Dione Lucas' Cooking School*) ............. 251
    *At Home and How* ............................................................................. 251
    *Dr. Fix-Um* .......................................................................................... 252
    *R.F.D. America* .................................................................................... 252

**Chapter 21: Sports Programs** ............................................................ 255
    *Campus Hoop-La* ............................................................................... 255
    *Sportsman's Quiz* ............................................................................... 256
    *Girl of the Week/Sportswoman of the Week* ................................... 256
    *Sports Album* ...................................................................................... 256
    *Identify* ................................................................................................. 257
    *They're Off* ........................................................................................... 257
    *Red Barber's Clubhouse* ..................................................................... 258
    *Practice Tee* ......................................................................................... 258
    *Fishing and Hunting Club* ................................................................ 259

**Chapter 22: Talk/Interview Shows** ................................................... 261
    *Tex and Jinx* ........................................................................................ 261
    *The Jack Eigen Show* .......................................................................... 262
    *Tonight on Broadway* ......................................................................... 262
    *We, The People* .................................................................................... 263
    *Key to the Missing* (aka *Key to Missing Persons*) ......................... 264
    *Kiernan's Corner* ................................................................................ 265
    *Mary Margaret McBride* ................................................................... 265
    *Pauline Frederick's Guestbook* .......................................................... 266

*Manhattan Spotlight* ..................................................................................267
*In the First Person* ....................................................................................267
*The Wendy Barrie Show* ..........................................................................268
*Maggi's Private Wire* ................................................................................268
*Leave It to the Girls* ..................................................................................269
*Broadway to Hollywood – Headline Clues* ............................................270

**Chapter 23: Public Affairs Shows** .................................................................271
*Meet the Press* ..........................................................................................271
*Court of Public Opinion* (aka *Court of Current Issues*) ......................273
*People's Platform* .....................................................................................273
*Operation Success* ...................................................................................274
*America's Town Meeting* .........................................................................274
*Newsweek Analysis* (aka *Newsweek Views the News*) ........................275
*On Trial* ....................................................................................................275
*Meet Your Congress* .................................................................................276
*Capitol Cloak Room* ................................................................................276

**Chapter 24: Reality Series** ..............................................................................279
*Candid Camera* ........................................................................................279
*They Stand Accused* .................................................................................280
*The Black Robe* ........................................................................................281
*The Crisis* .................................................................................................283

**Endnotes** .........................................................................................................285

**Index** ..............................................................................................................293

# Acknowledgements

**THE AUTHOR WOULD LIKE TO THANK** the following individuals and institutions for their help in completing this work: Syracuse University for information from the Gertrude Berg papers; University of Iowa Library for material from the Norman Felton Collection; Billy Rose Theatre Division, The New York Public Library for material from the Zero and Kate Mostel Collection; The New York Public Library for material from the *Studio One* Production Files, 1948 – 1955; The Southern Historical Collection, The Wilson Library, University of North Caroline for documents from the Kay Kyser and Georgia Carroll Kyser Papers; Sophia Smith Collection, Smith College for material from the Pauline Frederick Collection; American Heritage Center, University of Wyoming for material from the Larry Menkin Papers and the Edmund C. Rice Papers; Margaret Herrick Library, Academy of Motion Picture Arts and Sciences for *Celebrity Time* script from the Daniel Mann collection; Jeannette M. Berard for her assistance in summarizing material from the Broadcasting and from the Carlton E. Morse Collections at the Thousand Oaks Library in California; the Wisconsin Center for Film and Theater Research for material from its NBC collection; staffs at the Motion Picture and TV Reading Room at the Library of Congress and at The Paley Center for Media; Mark Matich for information on certain early television series from the UCLA Film and Television Archives and from the UCLA Script Collections; and Garry Settimi for proof reading and editing the manuscript.

# Preface

THE PHRASE "EVERYTHING OLD IS NEW AGAIN" applies in so many ways to television shows. The roots of most types of television series seen today can be traced back to the birth of network TV in the late 1940s.

Before Lucille Ball's pregnancy was made part of the story line of *I Love Lucy*, the comedy *Mary Kay and Johnny* did the same thing in the forties with its leading lady's pregnancy. Well before MTV premiered in the 1980s showing music videos, there was *Disc Magic* where a DJ played "soundies," the music videos of their day. Pre-dating "Weekend Update" on *Saturday Night Live*, *Admiral Broadway Review* presented a weekly satire, "Non-entities in the News." Prior to *Antiques Roadshow*, *What's It Worth* aired appraisals of various items highlighting their history; and long before *Judge Judy*, there were programs like *They Stand Accused* and *The Black Robe* that presented court cases involving real people.

Not only the subjects of TV programs but also much of the behind-the-scenes activities of the television industry were foreshadowed in the 1940s. Most TV fans are aware of the "two Darrin's" on *Bewitched*. How about the five different Henry's on the early television comedy *The Aldrich Family*? Other phenomena prevalent today on network television began occurring as early as the late forties with shows canceled after airing just one episode (e.g., *The Dennis James Carnival*), networks ordering series but not airing them (such as *Public Prosecutor*), and programs changing networks (*The Original Amateur Hour* was, at different times, on all four TV networks over its run).

American network television came into its own after the end of World War II. By April 1946, seven commercial television stations were in operation across the United States located in New York City which had three outlets, Chicago, Schenectady, Philadelphia and Washington D.C.

The four television networks in the 1940s were NBC, CBS, ABC, and DuMont. NBC was the largest and based many of its television series on programs that aired on its radio network. Likewise, CBS television broadcast TV versions of its radio series. ABC, which was created when the federal government forced NBC to sell one of its two radio networks – the Blue Network, lagged behind NBC and CBS in developing its own television programs. DuMont, created by scientist Alfred B DuMont, in order to sell his television receivers, had no radio network on which to base TV series. It struggled for a number of years to gain affiliates in major cities as well as to develop hit television programs before it folded in the mid-50s.

This book profiles the television series that debuted at the beginning of network and syndicated television. Unlike other guides describing television programs, this one focuses only on those prime-time shows that premiered on more than one TV outlet between 1944 and 1949. Also, this work goes into greater depth compared to other books by describing early episodes of most series as well as the personalities involved with the programs.

Since many of the early television shows were done live, few episodes exist today. For the small number that do, descriptions in the book are based on viewing certain episodes. Where no kinescopes or films exist, scripts or descriptions in show business publications such as *Variety* or *The Billboard* were used.

For the purposes of this book, "prime-time" refers to television series that aired, at least for part of their run, sometime between 7:00 pm and 11:00 pm Eastern time. Live news and sporting events, programs airing sports scores, and religious programs are excluded from the series profiled as are programs that aired on no more than one television station during their runs.

Shows are divided into the different genres that existed at the time. Surprisingly, most of these genres still exist today on network and cable outlets. Within each genre, the series are listed by the date they premiered on the network or in syndication. Keep in mind that the genre breakdown is not sacrosanct. Many programs, particularly variety shows, could easily be placed in more than one genre.

Although the beginning of early television is of fairly recent vintage, records of when a TV series began and when it ended are spotty as are, in some cases, the names of actors on many series. The information contained in this guide is based on the best data that is available but may not be 100% accurate.

The cast of *The Goldbergs*, from left to right: Gertrude Berg, Philip Loeb, Arlene McQuade, and Larry Robinson

# Family Comedy Series

**When referring to "family comedies,"** many people think of such iconic sitcoms from the 1950s like *The Adventures of Ozzie and Harriet*, *Father Knows Best*, and *The Donna Reed Show*. However, before those shows ever saw the light of day, there were several family comedies that appeared in the late 1940s. Most of these very early comedies had a mother or mother surrogate at the center as the family's problem solver.

### *The Laytons*
Premiered August 4, 1948 on DuMont Wednesday 8:30 pm; ran until October 13, 1948

>Cast of Characters: Martha (Amanda Randolph) – the Layton's black housekeeper
>Ruth Layton (Vera Tatum) – the mother of the family
>George Layton – the father who is a doctor
>Virginia (Ginny) Layton – the teenage daughter who lives at home
>Bill Layton –the Layton's son, a city official, who is married to Peggy and has a young daughter named Nancy
>Writer/Creator: Barbara Boothe
>Producer: O. Gordon
>Director: Pat Fay
>Sponsor: Bates Fabrics, Inc., maker of draperies and bedspreads

This comedy focused on the Layton family and its black housekeeper Martha who usually got the family out of its weekly predicaments. The only photo known to exist of *The Laytons*, published in the November 1948 issue of *Radio Mirror*, shows Bill, Jenny, and Peggy Layton sitting around a dining room table being served breakfast by Martha. As noted in the book, *The TV Writer's Guide*, two cameras, one or two sets, and four characters were the maximum allowed for each episode of the series. In a particular scene, Martha ordinarily appeared with two of the five family members and one of their friends or relatives. A simple story line, quick opening exposition, and a fast pace served as the standard formula for each show. The following episode description is taken from apparently the only published script for this series in existence.[1]

This live comedy initially emanated from DuMont's flagship station in New York beginning on May 19, 1948. *The Laytons* aired irregularly during the months of June and July often preempted for presidential convention coverage and other programming until August 4, 1948 when it started regular broadcasts running weekly until October 13, 1948. This no doubt explains why the script described below from early August was assigned #8.

"Uncle Charlie's Visit" or "The Moose Hangs High" aired live on August 11, 1948. Uncle Charlie Connery, Ruth Layton's uncle is visiting and keeps trying to help the family, particularly his niece. Among other things, he wants to repaint the Layton living room red with apple-green molding and hang a moose head above the fireplace. Everyone, including Martha, wishes he would leave. But they don't want to hurt his feelings by telling him to get out. Martha comes up with an idea to entice Charlie to leave on his own. She has Ginny tell Charlie that his sister, whom he dreads, is coming for a visit. He leaves quickly and takes his moose head with him.

Amanda Randolph, who played the maid, is the only cast member from this series that continued an active career in radio and television. After *The Laytons*, Ms. Randolph had a daytime series on DuMont called *Amanda*, which lasted until 1949, thus becoming the first African-American female with her own daytime show. Randolph subsequently became a regular on TV's *Amos 'n' Andy* from 1951 to 1953 and then starred on *Beulah* from 1953 to 1954. However, she is probably best remembered for her role as the maid Louise on *The Danny Thomas Show*.

Not known is who played the members of the Layton family other than the role of Ruth Layton. Vera Tatum, who appeared as Ruth, was a theater actress most notably acting for a number of years in the play *Kiss and Tell* on the road as well as on two USO tours in the South Pacific and in Korea and Japan. How she got the part of Ruth Layton is unknown, but, after the series ended, if not before, she apparently had a relationship with director Pat Fay. Newspaper reports in the 1950s indicated that she and Fay were weekend guests of Fay's father in Franklin, Pennsylvania and also attended the wedding of Fay's niece. Tatum was active in the theater world into the 1950s and had small roles on some TV shows such as a Martha Raye special in which she appeared as a woman passenger in a subway scene.[2]

## *The Growing Paynes*

Premiered October 20, 1948 at 8:30 pm Wednesday on DuMont; final episode August 3, 1949

> Cast of Characters: George Payne (John Harvey) – the father, an insurance salesman
> Larraine or Ellie Payne (Judy Parrish) – the mother
> John Payne (David Anderson) – their son
> Birdie (Ann Sullivan) – their maid
> Writer: A. S Guiness
> Director: Pat Fay
> Sponsor: John Wanamaker

Not to be confused with the 1980s comedy *Growing Pains* starring Alan Thicke and Joanna Kerns, the exploits of an insurance salesman, his not-so-bright wife, and their son were the subject of this 1940s comedy, which replaced *The Laytons*. Birdie, the Payne's maid often saved the Payne's from many awkward situations. The character also did the commercials for Wanamaker's products that were blended into each episode. The show's opening used a leather photo album with the series' title and subsequent pages containing photos of the cast.

The first episode involved George Payne inviting a wealthy life insurance prospect to stay overnight at the Payne's apartment, but Larraine has already arranged for other people to use their spare room. John Harvey and Judy Parrish, who first starred as the Payne's, were husband and wife in real life.

On January 19, 1949, Ed Holmes took over the role of George Payne, while Elaine Stritch became Larraine Payne. On that installment, a friend of George's, Jim Garson (Donald Curtis) persuades George to leave his job and go to South America to corner the market on car insurance on that continent. Their son overhears his dad telling his potential new employer that he is currently unemployed which leads Johnny and his mother to presume that George has been pretending to go to his office each day. Larraine gets a job from George's boss's brother to help out. In the end, George changes his mind when his wife points out that very few people have cars in South America.

A later episode of the series had George hiring a housekeeper, while his wife is away for a few weeks. The cranky housekeeper named Abigail Sneed (Georgia Simmons) redeems herself when she recognizes a man, Al Orwell (Blair Davies), with whom George is going to invest money, as a wanted felon and calls the police.

Elaine Stritch, who became the second Mrs. Payne, had a storied career on Broadway as well as on television. Among other credits, she played Trixie Norton on some of *The Honeymooners* sketches on Jackie Gleason's DuMont network series, *Cavalcade of Stars*. Later she was a regular on the television comedy *My Sister Eileen* and on the Peter Falk drama, *The Trials of O'Brien* as well as a semi-regular on the NBC sitcom, *30 Rock*.

## *The Goldbergs*

Premiered January 17, 1949 on CBS at 8:00 pm Monday, ran until 1956 on various networks and in first-run syndication.

> Cast of Characters: Molly Goldberg (Gertrude Berg) – a housewife who liked to gossip with her neighbors
> Jake Goldberg (Philip Loeb) – Molly's husband who ran a clothing business
> Sammy Goldberg (Larry Robinson) – the teenage son
> Rosalie Goldberg (Arlene McQuade) – the teenage daughter
> Uncle David (Eli Mintz) – the patriarch of the family
> Writer/creator: Gertrude Berg
> Producer: Worthington Miner
> Director: Walter Hart

This classic comedy, based on the radio show of the same name which ran for almost twenty years, presented the story of a Jewish family living in the Bronx dealing with their everyday problems. Born Gertrude Edelstein on October 3, 1899, Gertrude married Lewis Berg in 1918. She chose the name "Goldberg" for her radio series "because it sounded right."[3] The husband on the series was named "Jake" after her father.

With the exceptions of Gertrude Berg, Arlene McQuade, and Eli Mintz, the actors who played the other characters changed over the series run. Most notably Philip Loeb left the series in 1951 when its sponsor General Foods dropped its advertising in wake of accusations against Mr. Loeb for alleged left-wing associations. Blacklisted from the entertainment industry, Phillip Loeb committed suicide in 1955.

The series moved to NBC in 1952 where it aired three times a week in fifteen- minute episodes for six months. In July 1953, *The Goldbergs* resumed its thirty-minute installments until September 1953. It moved to Dumont in 1954. Its final 1955-56 season was syndicated to local stations.

On the January 17, 1949 premiere, Molly introduces herself to viewers and the Bronx apartment building where she and her family lived. She says, "In a big thirty-family house, you can well imagine that many things are happening at any time and the same time from morning until night . . ." The Goldberg family wants to find a larger apartment than their current four rooms since Sammy has to sleep in the living room and Molly would like Uncle David to come live with them. A neighbor, Mrs. Dutton, who currently resides in a two-room apartment, would like Molly's place. Rosalie finds an ad from a Mrs. Herman who wants to exchange a six-room apartment for two rooms. Molly works out an arrangement whereby Mrs. Dutton will lease her two rooms to Mrs. Herman, who, in turn will lease her six rooms to the Goldberg's with Mrs. Dutton then moving into Molly's four- room apartment. Moving day arrives, but Mrs. Herman's son-in-law comes by and informs his mother-in-law that he and his wife have to move in with her since his wife is having a baby and he can no longer tolerate living with his mother. Molly understands the problem and backs out of the lease on Mrs. Herman's apartment. When Molly explains the situation to Mrs. Dutton, however, Mrs. Dutton refuses to break the lease for the Goldberg's place. And so, the Goldberg's end up in a two-room apartment – more crowded than ever. (Summary from the "audition script" written by Gertrude Berg)

Another early episode dealt with the classic situation of wives and husbands playing games with one another. Molly thinks that Jake is spending too much time at work and would like him to take up a hobby. She suggests painting and buys him a set of artist materials. After painting a still life of apples, Jake is interrupted by work. To get her husband interested again in painting, she has the owner of the art supply store come by to tell Jake that he sold his painting of apples for $25. Subsequently, Jake finds his painting in the closet, realizes what Molly had done, and wants to get even with her. He pretends to become obsessed with painting, ignoring everything else. However, Molly learns from Uncle David that Jake is just putting on an act. When he returns from night school after supposedly painting a female model, Molly, feigning outrage, rips up Jake's latest work. Jake has to inform her that he borrowed the painting from the art store owner who was planning on selling it for $50.

As producer Worthington Miner recalled, *The Goldbergs* ". . . was Gertrude Berg's baby from the start. I created a style of camerawork to make Molly and her people come to life, but the characters themselves were hers. She was a great woman, no soap opera hack; she was a true writer."[4]

In the sixties, Gertrude Berg starred on another CBS comedy, *Mrs. C Goes to College* which later was called *The Gertrude Berg Show*. The series lasted only one season.

## *Mama*

Premiered July 1, 1949 on CBS Friday 8:00 pm; ran in prime time until July 27, 1956

> Cast of characters: Marta Hansen (Peggy Wood) – the mother of this Norwegian-American family
> Lars Hansen (Judson Laire) – the father of the family who was a carpenter
> Nels (Dick Van Patten) – the son
> Katrin (Rosemary Rice) – the eldest daughter
> Dagmar (Iris Mann) – the younger daughter
> Aunt Jenny (Ruth Gates) – the family's aunt
> Producer/Director: Ralph Nelson in association with Carol Irwin
> Writer: Frank Gabrielson

Sometimes referred to as the "Norwegian-American version of *The Goldbergs*," *Mama* was based on the book, *Mama's Bank Account* by Kathryn Forbes that was turned into the play, *I Remember Mama*, and into a movie of the same name. This live, gentle comedy-drama was set in turn-of-the-century San Francisco.

Each episode began with Rosemary Rice as Katrin leafing through an album of photos of her family and reminiscing, ending with the phrase, "But most of all, I remember Mama."

The initial episode dealt with Mama's efforts to help papa become an American citizen. Papa is too shy to attend school to receive training for taking the citizenship test, and so Mama attends in his place and teaches him at home. The entire family gathers in the kitchen to help papa study for the final test. He takes the test and passes to become an American citizen.

Another typical episode, "Mama's Bad Day," concerned Mama becoming overwhelmed with her household duties and not feeling appreciated by her family. Dagmar feigns illness every time she is asked to do something. Katrin doesn't want to practice the piano, and Aunt Jenny finds a pack of cigarettes in Nels' coat, while she is helping Marta make his bed. At the market, Marta is invited to play cards with the neighborhood women that evening but says that she doesn't have time. However, after spending five hours making a special meatloaf for dinner and receiving no compliments from her family, she decides to go to the neighbors for the card game. But she feels guilty leaving her family alone. When she returns home, she discovers everything is fine with Dagmar not really sick, Katrin practicing the piano, and her husband repairing a broken drawer and acknowledging how good the dinner was.

Ralph Nelson remembers directing this series.

> *Mama* scripts were mostly written by Frank Gabrielson, and very high quality scripts they were. But the pressure was always on him. The first day of rehearsal on a Tuesday morning, we might only have three pages of script out of thirty that we needed. It would sometimes be Friday, the day we were on the air, before we would get the final pages. The cast was accustomed to their characters, it was the same crew all the time, and we grew more and more easy with it. We eventually got to where it was so simple that we rehearsed about nine hours a week, went on camera, and were on the air that night at eight.[5]

Nelson also recalls a 1950 episode, "Along Came a Spider" featuring actor E.G. Marshall, that created some controversy. "... families trusted the show, there was always a kind of basic moral lesson in it, and suddenly Dagmar, the youngest child, alone in the house, was put into jeopardy by this man threatening her. In retrospect, it was so out of character for Mama that there were a lot of phone calls and letters afterwards denouncing us for having done it."[6]

Three actors who later became major film stars appeared in small parts on the series – James Dean, Paul Newman, and Jack Lemmon, as friends of Nels. When actor Dick Van Patten had to be away from the series for a few weeks to see if he was going to be recruited into the Army, James Dean played Nels in two episodes.

After the series ended, Judson Laire continued acting in episodic TV including playing a judge on several episodes of *The Defenders*. Peggy Wood co-starred in the 1965 film version of *The Sound of Music* as Mother Abbess; Dick Van Patten later appeared as the head of the family in *Eight Is Enough*. Iris Mann was featured in roles on *The Many Loves of Dobie Gillis* and *Tales of Tomorrow*, while Rosemary Rice performed on radio in several episodes of the *CBS Radio Mystery Theater* during the 1970s.

## *The Ruggles*
Premiered November 3, 1949 on ABC Thursday 9:30 pm; ran until June 19, 1952

> Cast: Charlie Ruggles – head of the family and an insurance salesman
> Margaret Ruggles (Irene Tedrow) – wife and mother
> Sharon Ruggles (Margaret Kerry) – teenage daughter
> Chuck Ruggles (Tommy Bernard) – teenage son
> Donna Ruggles (Judy Nugent) – twin daughter
> Donald Ruggles (Jimmy Hawkins) – twin son
> Writer: Fred Howard
> Director: George Cahan
> Producer: Bob Raisback

This family comedy began on ABC's Los Angeles station on October 23, 1949, Sundays at 9:00 pm. Soon after, it started airing on ABC's East and Midwest networks using kinescopes of the live LA show. The series portrayed typical home life of a middle-class family such as the family members waiting their turns to use the bathroom in the morning or the children getting dad to go square dancing with his wife. Irene Tedrow left the show in 1949 because of a time conflict with her starring on the radio show, *Meet Corliss Archer*.

Television episodes dealt with the problems encountered by the Ruggles' kids as well as by Charlie at work. One installment dealing with eldest son Chuck, written by Fred Howard and Irving Phillips, concerned the boy wanting to act sophisticated in order to attract a girl named Mary Ann. Charlie and the rest of the family prepare Chuck for a date with Mary Ann at the opera. However, Mary Ann decides that she wants to go to a jazz concert instead, and so Charlie and his wife attend *Rigoletto*.

On another episode dealing with work, Charlie thinks that he is in line for a promotion since he suggested that his boss, Mr. Williams, hire an efficiency expert. When he arrives at work, Charlie finds that one of the suggestions by the efficiency expert is to eliminate Charlie's position. After he informs his wife that he is out of a job, she comes up with a plan to help him. She invites the efficiency expert to dinner at the Ruggles so he can see how well Charlie has organized his family. Mr. Billings, the efficiency expert, is impressed on how everything at Charlie's house is timed to the second. Mrs. Ruggles explains that behind every efficient system is a key figure, but, if such a figure is removed, things can break down. Mr. Billings decides to change his recommendation about Charlie's job.

After its initial time slot on Thursdays at 9:30, ABC moved the series eleven times to virtually every night of the week until it ended in June 1952.

Actor Richard Tyler who played Henry Aldrich during the 1950-51 season of *The Aldrich Family*.

# Kid Comedy Series

# 2

**BEFORE ALL OF THE TWEEN** and teen comedies on Nickelodeon and the Disney Channel, there were a few such programs focusing primarily on young males in the 1940s.

## *Wesley*
Premiered May 8, 1949 on CBS Sunday 7:30 pm; ran until August 30, 1949

> Cast of Characters: Wesley Eggleston (Donald Devlin from May to July, Johnny Stewart from July to August) – the young boy
> Mr. Eggleston (Frank Thomas) – Wesley's dad
> Mrs. Eggleston (Mona Thomas) – Wesley's mother
> Grandpa (Joe Sweeney) – the boy's grandfather
> Elizabeth Eggleston (Joy Reese) – Wesley's teenage sister
> Alvin (Billie Nevard) – Wesley's best friend
> (Jack Ayres) – Elizabeth's boyfriend
> Writer: Samuel A. Taylor
> Director: Franklin Schaffner
> Producer: Worthington Miner

Before they made it big in the movies, writer Samuel Taylor who later scripted the Alfred Hitchcock film *Vertigo* and director Franklin Schaffner who later helmed motion pictures like *Planet of the Apes* and *Patton*, wrote and directed this early situation comedy centered on a typical twelve-year-old, freckle-faced boy, his friends, and family. The program was to show "the warmth of comfortable American life of twenty years ago."[7]

Little is known about the specific story lines of the episodes. Real-life husband and wife actors, Frank and Mona Thomas, played Wesley's parents. Mona Thomas remembers Samuel Taylor writing great scripts for the series. As she recollected, "I remember one scene in particular that I feel was semiautobiographical. It was a birthday party for a character I was playing. Her husband had saved his lunch money for months to buy some earrings she had admired. He had lost weight doing without lunch, and how the truth came out was a poignant and memorable piece of writing. To play the scene with my husband was an added joy."[8]

After the demise of *Wesley*, Mona Thomas appeared on the television version of *One Man's Family* (Chapter 8).

Reminiscing about the series, director Franklin Schaffner recalled that "It was essentially a Henry Aldrich setup. There was a young kid who was always getting into trouble, his mother, his father, his sister, and the kid next door. Unfortunately, we never got a sponsor."[9]

At the time, CBS was attempting to obtain sponsors for two of its comedies – *Wesley* and *Mama*. Maxwell House coffee ended up sponsoring *Mama*, but *Wesley* was canceled when no one wanted to sponsor the program.

*Wesley* was one series produced by Worthington Miner that was not a success. Miner was responsible for developing such early TV hits as *Toast of the Town*, *Studio One*, *The Goldbergs*, and *Mr. I Magination*.

## *The Family Genius*

Premiered September 9, 1949 on DuMont at 9:00 pm Friday; ran until September 30, 1949

> Cast of Characters: Tommy Howard (Jack Diamond) – the child prodigy
> Mrs. Howard (Phyllis Love) – Tommy's mother
> Mr. Howard (Arthur Edwards) – Tommy's father
> Hannah (Pat Hosley) – Tommy's sister
> Director: Jack Weiser
> Writer: Elwood Hoffman
> Producers: James L. Caddigan and Elwood Hoffman

Long before *Doogie Howser, MD* and *Young Sheldon*, there was the short-lived *The Family Genius* about a precocious boy named Tommy Howard who upsets the lives of friends and family. In the second episode of the series, Tommy wants to get rid of his sister's dumb boyfriend by making another girl named Hannah attractive so the boyfriend will date her. Tommy performs a Pygmalion-type transformation of Hannah turning her into a poised young lady. Not only did the transformation cost Hannah's dad a lot of money, but Hannah starts going out with a boy that Tommy's sister really wanted to date. In the end, naturally, everything is straightened out.

As DuMont's Director of Programming and Production, James Caddigan, who produced *Family Genius*, was the man behind many of that network's series including *Captain Video* and *Hands of Mystery*.

## *The Aldrich Family*
Premiered October 2, 1949 on NBC Sunday at 7:30 pm; ran until May 29, 1953.

> Original Cast of Characters: Henry Aldrich (Robert Casey) - the teenage boy
> Sam Aldrich (House Jameson) – Henry's father
> Alice Aldrich (Lois Wilson) – Henry's mother
> Mary Aldrich (Charita Bauer) – Henry's sister
> Homer Brown (Jackie Kelk) – Henry's best friend
> Writer: Clifford Goldsmith
> Producer: Ed Duerr
> Sponsor: General Foods

The trials and tribulations of a teenager interacting with his family, friends, and potential love interests were the focus of this comedy. The sitcom was adapted from the radio series of the same name which in turn was based on the play *What a Life*. The show always opened with the mother calling, "Henry, Henry Aldrich" with Henry's reply "Coming, Mother!"

On the first episode, when Henry seeks to avoid an English test at school by feigning a hand injury, he is sent to the doctor instead of to school. At the hospital, an attendant mistakes Henry for an accident victim and rushes him off for an X-ray. The X-ray reveals a small piece of metal lodged in Henry's shoulder. The situation is finally resolved when the piece of metal turns out to be a dime in Henry's pajama pocket. However, in the final scene, Henry really does sprain his hand.

On another first season episode, Henry wonders why everyone except him has been invited to his friend Rickie's costume dance party. His sister, mother, and father all try to find the reason he wasn't invited but to no avail. Despite his dad telling him not to go, Henry decides to attend the party anyway. He goes as the back end of his friend Homer's horse costume. They dance with every girl there but do not reveal themselves. When Henry returns home, his dad is ready to punish him for ignoring his advice but then finds Henry's invitation among his own unopened mail.

During its four season run, the cast members changed quite often. Robert Casey, who had been chosen from a field of forty-two actors that auditioned for the role, left the series after the first season to be replaced by Richard Tyler during 1950-51. For the 1951-52 season, Henry Girard replaced Tyler. Kenneth Nelson took over the role in 1952, and finally Bobby Ellis became Henry in the series final season.

The character of Mrs. Aldrich was played by Nancy Carroll for the 1950-51 season. Later, Ms. Carroll appeared mainly in live theater. Lois Wilson returned to the series in 1951, she later had roles on the soap operas *The Guiding Light* and *The Secret Storm*. Ms. Wilson was soon replaced by Barbara Robbins for the balance of the series. Movie actress Jean Muir was initially hired for the Alice Aldrich role for the 1950-51 season, but she was accused of being a Communist. The sponsor, General Foods, fired her – another victim of blacklisting during the 1950s.

Charita Bower who originated the role of Mary Aldrich on TV became more famous for appearing as Bert Bauer on the daytime drama, *The Guiding Light*. Mary was played by Mary Malone from 1950 to 1952. Malone subsequently played author Emily Kimbrough on the TV series, *The Girls*. June Dayton took over the role for the 1952-53 season. She would later portray a housekeeper on *The Young and the Restless*.

Robert Barry replaced Jackie Kelk in the role of Henry's best friend in 1951. He was replaced by Jackie Grimes in 1952.

House Jameson, who had played Henry's father on the radio series, was the only actor to star in all four seasons of the television comedy.

In the mid-fifties, there was an effort to resurrect *The Aldrich Family* on CBS with an all new cast. Network executive Harry Ackerman, who had worked for the advertising agency behind the original TV show, was the force behind this reboot. An actor named Bobby Trumbull got the lead role of Henry with Ann Doran playing his mother. House Jameson was again considered for the father along with actors Howard St. John and John Hoyt but the part eventually went to Vinton Hayworth, Rita

Hayworth's uncle. Jean Gal played Henry's sister Mary, and "Kip" King had the role of Henry's best friend. A pilot titled "The Blind Date," written by Budd Grossman and *Aldrich* creator Clifford Goldsmith, was shot on March 19, 1955. If the pilot had been picked up by CBS, the series would have been filmed by Desilu with a 7:30 pm time slot on Wednesday evenings.

From 1951, husband and wife, Paul and Grace Hartman, who had previously starred on their own situation comedy, *The Hartmans*.

# Couples Comedy Series 3

**THE SITCOMS PRESENTED** in this section began a genre of husband and wife comedies that have been seen throughout the history of television. Think *I Love Lucy, Burns and Allen, He & She, Mad about You,* and *Mike & Molly* to name a few.

## *Mary Kay and Johnny*

Premiered November 18, 1947 on DuMont Tuesday at 9:00 pm; ran until March 11, 1950.

> Cast of Characters: Mary Kay Stearns (herself) – pretty homemaker, something of a screwball
> Johnny Stearns (himself) – Mary's somewhat serious husband
> Howie (Howard Thomas) – Johnny's best friend
> (Nydia Westman) – Mary's mother
> Christopher Stearns (himself) (1949-1950) – the Stearns' young son
> Jim Stevenson - Announcer
> Writer: Johnny Stearns

First airing on DuMont as a fifteen-minute show, this live domestic comedy concerned New York newlyweds. The series moved to NBC in October 1948 in a thirty-minute format and subsequently to CBS in March 1949. On the move again and back to a fifteen-minute show, *Mary Kay and Johnny* went to NBC in June 1949, Mondays through Fridays from 7:15 to 7:30. In August of that year, it resumed as a thirty-minute program one day a week and remained that way until it ended in March 1950.

Typical episodes had Mary Kay preparing dinner for a visit by Johnny's boss and his wife, and Mary Kay pretending to play the harmonica to impress her husband, but the grocery delivery boy was actually playing the instrument.

An October 10, 1948 installment showed Mary Kay, years before Lucille Ball's pregnancy on *I Love Lucy*, making plans for her first baby and running into difficulties buying the right baby carriage. This story line, as would be the case with Lucy's pregnancy in 1952, was controversial at the time with some at NBC. The advertisers of the series assured the network in November 1948 that the subject of the pregnancy would not be a major continuing story line, ". . . but some mention would have to be made inasmuch as Mary Kay is getting pretty big and new viewers might wonder 'what gives?' They are going to have her sit down most of the time from here on in."[10] On a December 31, 1948 episode, one-week-old Christopher Stearns appeared on the show and became a regular character.

Foreshadowing plots of later husband and wife comedies, on a June 1949 program, Mary, who couldn't resist door-to-door salesmen, buys a whisk broom from a salesman for the Eager Beaver Company. Johnny says she is a "soft touch," but, when the salesman returns for his hat, Johnny ends up buying an electric vacuum cleaner from him.

In August 1949 when the show went back to being a half hour in length, the first episode focused on a visit from Uncle Leland (Jack Davis), a boxer, who stays at the Stearns home because the YMCA is full. He insists that Johnny begin an austere regimen and quit smoking and drinking. He persuades both Mary Kay and Johnny to do road work with him. Johnny responds to Uncle Leland's suggestions by saying "I'm run down and tired and I want to stay that way."

Johnny Stearns subsequently became a TV producer, while his wife continued acting for awhile after their sitcom ended.

## *Wren's Nest*

Premiered January 13, 1949 on ABC Thursday, Friday, and Saturday 7:15 pm; ran until April 30, 1949

>Cast: Sam Wren (himself) - husband
>Virginia Sale Wren (herself) - wife
>Christopher Wren (himself) – the Wren's son
>Virginia Wren (herself) – the Wren's daughter

Writer: Virginia Sale
Directors: Tom DeHuff, Charles Howard
Producer: Sterling Oliver Productions

Opening with a title card and birds decorating a nest, this was another comedy that looked at the home life of a suburban New York husband and wife and their twelve-year-old twins. The fraternal twins appeared only in one episode a week. The series was set in the Wren's home, and their children were supposedly at boarding school most of the time.

In one early episode, the couple, talking in one corner of their living room, discusses trying to ride the "Twentieth Century Limited" into New York City. On another installment, Sam, although lacking in culinary skills, tries to make fudge. Virginia is too busy to help him since she is working on a Red Cross drive and calling people to volunteer. Flipping through a cookbook to find a fudge recipe, Sam discovers that he has to use cocoa instead of chocolate and cries out, "How do you measure two squares of cocoa –it's impossible!" After being interrupted by his wife, Sam realizes that he forgot to put the cocoa in with the other ingredients. He fixes this but wonders why the recipe needs four cups of corn syrup. While stirring the concoction, Sam breaks the candy thermometer and pieces of glass end up in the mixture, and so he starts all over again. Smoothing out a new batch of fudge, he remarks that maybe he can make a canapé when the kids return from boarding school. As he is finishing the fudge, he accidentally starts following a chicken recipe. Predictably the fudge does not turn out well. He reluctantly admits that maybe he should have gone to the movies and allowed Virginia to do the cooking.

After the series ended, the Wren's continued acting mainly in the theater. Virginia also made several appearances on episodic television, most notably as the character Selma Plout on six episodes of *Petticoat Junction*.

## *The Hartmans*

Premiered February 27, 1948 on NBC Sunday at 7:30 pm, ran until May 22, 1948

Cast: Grace Hartman (herself) - wife
Paul Hartman (himself) - husband
(Harold J. Stone) – the handyman

(Bob Shawley) - nephew
(Gage Clark) - neighbor
(Valerie Cossart) – Grace's sister
(Loring Smith) – Grace's brother-in-law
Producer: Harry Hermann
Director: Gary Simpson
Writers: Frank Wilson, Ted Luce (Luce was the adult son of Paul and Grace Hartman)
Sponsor: Textron, Inc.

*The Hartmans* was yet another comedy starring a real-life couple, Paul and Grace Hartman, living in a New York City suburb. The first episode dealt with the Hartmans spending Sunday morning at home. The comedy appears to have offered a vision of married life similar to the radio series *Fibber McGee and Molly*.

In reviewing the premiere episode, *The New York Times* opined,

> Beyond being a married couple . . . the central figures never were detailed, and, as a result, it was difficult for the viewer to feel that he was meeting people and not merely stage personages. The main theme obviously is to revolve around a husband who is amusingly erratic and absent-minded and a wife who is never at a loss for a word or a deed, but it is not going to be sustained without the most meticulous regard for its credibility, which is what provides the basic fun in such domestic comedies.[11]

The most remarkable thing about this early comedy may have been its spacious set. As described by *Radio Mirror*,

> Callers enter through a gate in a white picket fence. The front door opens into a center hall, complete with a staircase. To the right, through an archway, is a spacious living room with built-in bookshelves and comfortable furniture. Separated from the living room by double doors is Paul Hartman's study. Beyond the study is Grace's kitchen, full-size, with complete electrical equipment. There's a bedroom with twin beds and a pretty dressing table for Grace.[12]

Paul and Grace Hartman had an illustrious career as dancers in Broadway shows before tackling television. Grace Hartman died from cancer in 1955. Paul Hartman continued acting, most notably as Emmett Clark on *The Andy Griffith Show* and *Mayberry RFD*.

## *Jackson and Jill*

Aired at various times on different stations; in New York, the series premiered on WNBT (now WNBC) on June 23, 1949 at 8:00 pm; ran for thirteen episodes

>Cast of Characters – Jackson Jones (Todd Karns) – salesman newly married to Jill
>Jill Jones (Helen Chapman) – newly married, scatterbrained blonde
>Mr. Gimling (Russell Hicks) – Jackson's boss
>Producer: Jerry Fairbanks

Originally ordered by NBC and filmed between April and August 1949, this comedy series presented the story of a young couple who had been married for six years and lived in an apartment. Each episode began with Jill writing in her diary about the latest misadventures involving her and her husband, Jackson.

The titles of the thirteen episodes that were made are: #1 "Nobody's Perfect," #2 "Strictly Wholesale," #3 "Ex-Cream Puff," #4 "Daises Don't Tell," #5 "It's Ridiculous," #6 "Model Mix-up," #7 "It's a Gift," #8 "Grand Lama Laughed," #9 "Let Them Eat Cake," #10 "Man's House," #11 "Parting Is Such Sweet Sorrow," #12 "Who's Who," and #13 "Trouble Is a Gift." When NBC failed to find a sponsor for the series, the network made it available to its affiliates. It premiered in summer 1949 on most of those stations. The network decided to air a preview of the series nationally on Thanksgiving night at 8:00 pm November 24, 1949, but the preview apparently sparked no interest from potential national sponsors.

The November 1949 preview episode was "Model Mix-Up" by D.H. Johnson. On the program, when Jackson learns that a big sugar plantation owner Jose Alvarado (Fritz Feld) is in town, he wants to try to sell him tractors for Alvarado's plantation. Meanwhile, Jill has her heart set on a necklace of cultured pearls and is hoping that her husband will receive a $200 bonus from the sale. Jackson finds that Alvarado is more interested in wine, women, and song than in purchasing tractors. When Jill learns this, she goes to see the plantation owner at his hotel. In the meantime, Alvarado has contacted a "modeling" agency to interview a female for possible marriage. When Jill arrives at his hotel room, Alvarado thinks she is the representative from the agency. She tells him about "models," and he thinks she is referring to women although she is really talking about tractors. But, as usual, in the end, things are resolved with Alvarado purchasing the tractors and Jill getting her pearl necklace.

Another episode, "It's Ridiculous," had Jill feeling that the magic has gone out of her marriage. She talks Jackson into reliving their first date when they were college students. At an ice cream parlor, the couple meets two college seniors whom they invite back to their apartment for a dance party. They are joined by the waitress from the ice cream shop. After the neighbors complain about all the noise coming from their apartment, the landlord threatens to evict them. After everyone leaves, Jill thinks that the evening was exciting.

The installment titled "Who's Who" was another predictable situation comedy mix-up. Jill is away visiting her mother, and Jackson sleeps in and is late for the office. While trying to put a shirt on over his head, a house painter comes by to look at repainting their kitchen. Jackson asks him to come back in the evening. While Jackson is at work, Jill arrives home early and receives a phone call from a grammar school friend who is in town with her husband, an artist. Jill invites the couple over to the apartment. The friend informs Jill that her husband will probably arrive before she does. One probably already knows what happens next. Jill confuses the house painter with the artist. When she and the painter step out for a moment, her friend's husband comes by, and Jackson, home from work, confuses him with the painter having not seen the house painter that morning because Jackson had a shirt over his face. He instructs the artist to begin painting the kitchen. Naturally more confusion ensues before everything is resolved.

The role of Jackson Jones was originally to be filled by Jack Laird, a young actor at the time. Laird went on to write, direct, and produce episodes of series like *Ben Casey*, *Night Gallery*, and *Kojak*. The actor who did land the role of Jackson Jones, Todd Karns, was the son of actor Roscoe Karns.

## Mixed Doubles
Premiered August 5, 1949 on NBC Friday 9:00 pm; ran until October 29, 1949

> Cast: Elaine Coleman (Rhoda Williams) – young newlywed
> Eddy Coleman (Eddy Firestone) – Elaine's husband
> Ada Abbott (Ada Friedman) – young newlywed
> Bill Abbott (Billy Idelson) – Ada's husband
> Creator: Carleton E. Morse

Created by the man who developed the soap opera *One Man's Family*, this comedy centered on two couples married for about six months and living side by side in one-room apartments where the husbands worked for the same company. The series evolved from a local Los Angeles TV show called *Slice of Life* which aired three times a week on station KFI.

The first episode introduced the couples. Both husbands are copywriters for the Minnick Advertising Agency. Bill Abbott is an introverted hypochondriac; while Eddy is an extrovert. Both compete with each other to receive a promotion at work. However, the promotion goes to someone else entirely. In the second episode, Bill is supposed to install some shelves for Ada but keeps making excuses not to do the work. Eddy is going to meet Elaine for a movie but is caught in a trap intended to catch a roaming lothario. He calls Bill and Ada to bail him out.

After the first two episodes, actress Rhoda Williams left the series to be replaced by Bonnie Baken. Bill Idelson, who appeared as Ada's husband, went on to produce the ABC comedy *Love, American Style*.

## Ruthie on the Telephone
Premiered August 7, 1949 on CBS Monday, Tuesday, Thursday, Saturday, and Sunday 7:55 pm; ran until November 5, 1949

> Cast: Ruthie (Ruth Gilbert) – the single lady
> Richard (Philip Reed) – an advertising executive
> Writer/producer: Goodman Ace

Not all "couples" comedies during the forties dealt with married partners. In this five- minute series, a young woman is in love with a man whom she has never met in person and tries to interest him in her. The idea began as a sketch on the Robert Q. Lewis radio show.

On the debut of *Ruthie on the Telephone*, using a split screen so viewers could see both characters, Ruthie, sitting on a divan with a bow in her hair, describes for Richard a date she had with a man who took her to a museum where, when she mentioned that she would like to look at the statue of Venus, he began to break off Ruthie's arms. She also told Richard about their relationship. "Let's not fight this, Richard, it's bigger than both of us."

Writer/producer Goodman Ace not only developed but also starred on the next comedy profiled in this chapter.

## *Easy Aces*

Premiered December 14, 1949 on DuMont Wednesday at 7:45 pm; ran until June 14, 1950

> Cast of Characters: Goodman Ace (himself) - husband
> Jane Ace (herself) - wife
> Dorothy (Betty Garde) – Jane's friend
> Writers: George Foster, Morris Green, and Jack Raymond
> Director: Jeanne Henderson
> Producer: Ziv Television

*Easy Aces*, a filmed fifteen-minute television series, featured husband and wife Goodman and Jane Ace commenting on film clips. Jane was a little eccentric or, to put it another way, somewhat confused in her thinking. The series opened with Jane reading a book titled *Brain Surgery – Self-Taught*.

Goodman Ace had a unique approach to television believing that he and his wife should not appear on the screen all that much. With his career as a writer, he preferred words to pictures and so developed the idea of showing old films with his wife and him providing audio commentary. Goodman was the straight man, while his wife was like Gracie Allen, usually misunderstanding or misusing a word or phrase, such as saying "Time wounds all heels."

On the premiere episode, in a facsimile of their living room, the Ace's view and talk about a film of New York City in the 1900's showing fashions, places, and people. The commentary went like this:

Goodman Ace: "Oh, that's the old pushcart district. You could buy anything on those pushcarts. Look, there's somebody buying food."

Jane Ace: "Food, my goodness. I guess that's what they mean by a la carte. I've heard of this section of New York. That's what they used to call the Ghetto – those old testament houses. Old testament, yes. Well, there's the famous Fulton Fish Market."

Goodman Ace: "Is that the Fulton they laughed at when he invented the fish market?"

Jane Ace: "Yes, he invented the first steam-fish."[13]

Ziv Productions, which syndicated *Yesterday's Newsreels* and *Sports Album* - both series using archival news film, provided the old newsreel film for this series as well. After *Easy Aces*, Goodman Ace continued his writing career most notably for Perry Como's variety series.

Jackie Gleason and Rosemary DeCamp from the initial TV version of *The Life of Riley*.

# Central Character Comedies 4

THE FIRST SITUATION COMEDIES involving a main character at work and at home were all centered around leading men.

## *Off the Record*

Premiered September 21, 1948 on DuMont, Tuesday at 7:00 pm; ran until at least September 28, 1948

>   Cast of characters: Zero Mostel - a disc jockey
>   Joey Faye – the DJ's assistant
>   Ken Roberts – announcer
>   Producer: Martin Gosch
>   Director: Tony Kraber
>   Writer: Vincent Curran

*Off the Record* was a situation comedy/variety series starring Zero Mostel as a millionaire disc jockey with comedian Joey Faye assisting him at the turntables. The setting for the show was Zero's lavish New York penthouse.

There is some confusion about when the program actually aired and for how many episodes. *The New York Times* on September 17, 1948 reported that *Off the Record* would have its premiere at 7:00 pm Tuesday (September 21) with guest star singer Georgia Gibbs.[14] Also, *Variety* reviewed a late September episode of the series, and so the show aired at least two episodes. After the episode with guest Georgia Gibbs, the second installment featured Mimi Benzell. Segments of that episode included Mostel scaring away a visiting Briton who offended him by telling unfunny jokes, and Zero, a gifted artist in real life, attempting to paint a portrait of a middle-aged Huck Finn with Joey Faye posing as Huck. Mostel repeatedly uses his thumb to gauge the correct perspective on his model and ends up painting a picture of his own thumb with a small drawing of Faye on the cuticle. Mostel, Faye, and Mimi Benzell then do a parody of the opera *Carmen* with Benzell flirting with both of them ending up in a duel between Zero and Joey with custard pies instead of swords.

*Off the Record* ended abruptly when producer Martin Gosch and Mostel complained that DuMont did not provide a live studio audience for the program since the Wanamaker studio from which the show emanated was too small to hold an audience.[15] Gosch and Mostel wanted to cancel the series right after its premiere claiming that the absence of studio reaction threw off the timing and performances. However, they were persuaded to do at least another episode. There also may have been a third episode broadcast on October 5, 1948, but no documentation, other than TV listings in newspapers at the time, could be found about that episode. The settlement with DuMont involved the network compensating the producer and star for the remaining ten weeks to go on the show. If one assumes that most series in the early days of TV were contracted for a minimum of thirteen episodes, then a third installment of the program may have been done.

The series itself was something like a "show within a show." Zero Mostel played himself as a fabulously wealthy disc jockey who spins records for his listening audience with the help of Joey Faye and announcer Ken Roberts, although very few actual recordings were played because of the various antics performed by Mostel. About the episode he reviewed in *Variety*, Herman Scheonfeld stated that ". . . the opening stanza . . . stuttered in confusion and failed to indicate a possible direction in which this series could move. It was virtually everything that an acceptable video program should not be, thereby becoming valuable in a way as a negative object lesson."[16]

In response to the review, Vince Curran wrote a script for an October 12 episode that had Zero Mostel depressed over the critic's opinion of the show. However, due to the illness of announcer Ken Roberts, the October 12 show was postponed to October 19, but apparently the episode never aired at all.

In the script for this presumably never-aired installment, found in the Zero Mostel collection at the New York Public Library, while Zero discusses the review in *Variety* with Joey, Mr. Snobby, the landlord of the building in which Mostel resides, stops by wondering if Zero is going to vacate his penthouse since Mr. Scheonfeld would like to rent the place. After the landlord leaves, Ken Roberts arrives to point out that his announcing job on the initial show received good reviews in the *Variety* article and thinks the title of the show should be changed to *The Ken Roberts Show with Zero Mostel*. Joey Faye confides to Roberts that, in addition to the bad review, Mostel is upset that he has depleted his "joke account." Supposedly, every year the "Comedian's Guild" allots so many jokes per performer, and Zero is overdrawn. If he can't get anymore jokes, he will have to (perish the thought) ad lib. Joey persuades Mostel to take a nap. While Zero is sleeping, he dreams that he has gone to "Comedians Heaven" where he is placed on trial to determine if he can be admitted on a permanent basis. He is defended by Herman Scheonfeld but before a verdict is reached, Mostel awakens.

While never a major success on television, Zero Mostel would later be acclaimed for his work on Broadway most notably for playing Tevye in the musical *Fiddler on the Roof*.

## *The Billy Bean Show*

Premiered March 22, 1949 at 9:00 pm Tuesday on ABC; appears to have ended in early April 1949. (Some sources indicate the show actually premiered in 1951. However, both *Variety* from March 30, 1949 and *Billboard* from April 2, 1949 contain reviews of the series and newspapers like the *Brooklyn Daily Eagle* list the show in its television section as of March 22, 1949).

> Cast of Characters: Billy Bean (Arnold Stang) – single, young man working at a corner drugstore's soda fountain
> Boss (Phil Tead) – Billy's employer
> Boss' daughter (Billie Lou Watt) – with whom Billy is secretly in love
> Producer: Jeffrey Hayden
> Director: Sean Dillon
> Writer: George Loring

This sitcom focused on a geeky soda jerk in love with his boss' daughter. In the first episode, Billy thinks his head is getting smaller when he, unwittingly, switches his hat with one that is several sizes larger. The boss' daughter is into psychology and split personalities and convinces Billy that he is schizophrenic. He tries to get help from a man he thinks is a psychologist but who is really the refrigerator repairman.

Originally, the character of Billy Bean was to have worked at "Grimble's" – the world's smallest department store.

Stang had a long career on TV appearing on early shows like *School House*, *The Texaco Star Theatre* with Milton Berle, and the comedy *Doc Corkle*. He later voiced the character Top Cat in the animated series of the same name.

## *The Life of Riley*

Premiered October 4, 1949 on NBC Tuesday 9:30 pm; ran until March 1950

> Cast of Characters: Chester A. Riley (Jackie Gleason) – blue-collar worker and family man
> Peg Riley (Rosemary DeCamp) – Riley's wife
> 'Digger' O'Dell (John Brown) – the friendly local funeral director
> Gillis (Sid Tomack) – Riley's coworker and best friend
> Junior (Lanny Rees) – Riley's son
> Babs (Gloria Winters) – Riley's daughter
> Writer/creator: Irving Breecher

The misadventures of Chester Riley, a Homer Simpson-type character, who often caused his own predicaments, were the focus of this comedy.

Irving Breecher's *Life of Riley* began on radio in 1944 with William Bendix in the lead, Paula Winslowe as his wife, and Conrad Binyon and Sharon Douglas as the kids. When the series went to television, Bendix was not available, and so Jackie Gleason got the role of Chester Riley.

Irving Breecher auditioned about forty actors for Riley including movie star Lon Chaney, Jr. And then he thought that comedian Jackie Gleason might be right for the part. Breecher relates his first meeting with Gleason, "He knew the radio show. Could he feel comfortable doing TV? He went right into character, improvising dialogue and falling over a chair. Physically, verbally, facially – instant funny. I told my agent to sign him if we could afford him. Jackie happily accepted five hundred bucks per show for twenty-six shows, with an option for thirteen more."[17]

The first episode of the series with Gleason titled "Tonsils" was written by Breecher, Reuben Ship, and Alan Lipscott.

Riley finds that he has to have his tonsils out but is afraid of the operation. Gillis suggests visiting a neighbor who underwent the surgery to convince Riley that it is a simple procedure. However, confusion ensues when the woman thinks Riley wants to know about her recent delivery of twin girls and not the tonsillectomy. At the hospital, the doctor has to postpone the surgery at the last minute when Riley is already under anesthesia. Riley wakes up feeling good thinking the surgery is over only to find out that he still has to undergo the tonsillectomy.

*The Life of Riley* was one of the few series from the 1940s that was filmed in Hollywood instead of being a live presentation from the East coast. The Gleason version lasted only a single season. The sponsor of the comedy, Pabst Blue Ribbon Beer, agreed only to finance six more episodes beyond the twenty-six already made. Breecher wanted them to do thirteen more for a total of thirty-nine. The company refused and instead put their advertising dollars into sponsoring boxing on TV instead of *The Life of Riley*. A reboot of the series with Bendix as Riley began in 1953 and ran until 1958.

## *That Wonderful Guy*
Premiered December 28, 1949 on ABC Wednesday 9:00 pm; ran until April 28, 1950

>Cast: Harold (Jack Lemmon) – bumbling valet for a pompous theatre critic
>Franklin Westbrook (Neil Hamilton) – the critic
>Harold's Girlfriend (Cynthia Stone)
>Producer: Charles Irving
>Director: Babette Henry
>Writers: Russell Begg and Charles Gussman

Originally conceived as a radio comedy, ABC asked the producer to make the series for television. Future movie star Jack Lemmon played a "brash young lad from Kalamazoo" just out of a Midwestern dramatic school who travels to New York City for a job in show business. While looking for employment, he becomes the valet for a drama critic played by future *Batman* co-star, Neil Hamilton. Cynthia Stone, who appeared as Lemmon's love interest, later married the actor in real life.

Typical episodes involved Westbrook romancing an old flame played by Doris Dalton who has a bratty twelve-year-old daughter (Laurie Weber) whom Harold and his girlfriend have to babysit. Harold's bumbling job as a babysitter breaks up Westbrook's relationship with the woman, but in the end, Westbrook realizes that Harold saved him from potentially marrying a shrew.

On another episode later in the series run, Harold becomes an excellent singer thanks to a flaw in a record player giving his voice a deep baritone resonance. He is an overnight singing sensation until the problem with the record player is discovered.

"This Westbrook is an opinionated, dour sort-of-chap. He doesn't care much for actors," said Neil Hamilton, commenting on the character he played. "There aren't many plays he likes. In short, he's a drama critic."[18]

The series ended after seventeen weeks due to lack of sponsorship.

Before becoming a major movie star, Jack Lemmon played many roles on anthology and other series during the early days of television. After *That Wonderful Guy*, he and Cynthia Stone starred on another situation comedy in 1952 called *Heaven for Betsy*.

# Comedy, Drama, and "Experimental" Anthology Series

# 5

**ANTHOLOGY SERIES,** which had a different story and cast each week, were very popular at the beginning of network television. Usually, such series consisted of dramatic presentations, but periodically a comedy or variety episode was aired. "Experimental" anthology programs refer to those that broadcast pilots for potential new series.

NBC led the way in introducing viewers to dramatic anthology programs. Beginning in April 1945 under the title of *NBC Television Theatre*, the network aired live presentations including a three-part adaptation of Robert Sherwood's *Abe Lincoln in Illinois*, classic plays like *Blithe Spirit*, and original teleplays like "Boy Wanted." These presentations were broadcast on NBC's New York station.

## *The Kraft Television Theatre*
Premiered May 7, 1947 on NBC Wednesday 9:00 pm; ran for eleven seasons until September 24, 1958

Cast: No regular cast members

The first live episode of this long-running anthology was directed by Fred Coe and Stanley Quinn. "Double Door" starred John Baragrey, Valerie Cossart, John Stephen, Romola Robb, and Eleanor Wilson in an adaptation of Elizabeth McFadden's play about three adult siblings living in a New York City mansion. The story was adapted for television by Edmund C. Rice. Since a complete description of this debut episode has apparently never been published, following is a synopsis taken from the May 7, 1947 script found in the Edmund Rice collection at the American Heritage Center.

The first scene of the episode shows a newspaper photo and headline – "Old Mansion to be Razed." The scene then shifts to inside the house in the 1880s where preparations are being made for the wedding of Rip Van Bret to Anne Darrow – a nurse who helped Van Bret recover from a recent illness. Rip, age twenty-five, has lived with his two older sisters – Victoria, fifty-four, and Caroline, forty-six, his entire life since their parents passed away. Imperious Victoria rules over her siblings with an iron-fist and is less than happy with the pending nuptials thinking Anne is beneath them and worrying that Rip will gain some independence. When a wedding gift of an expensive heirloom pearl necklace that had belonged to the siblings' mother is delivered for Anne, Victoria forbids that it be given to her. She substitutes a cheap pearl necklace and locks the heirloom in a hidden, soundproof room her father had built in the house so he could sleep away from the noise of the street.

After the wedding ceremony, Dr. Sully, who had been in love with Anne, warns her about Victoria potentially driving Anne out of her mind. When the newlyweds return from their honeymoon, Victoria puts the house off limits to the couple except for Rip's bedroom and the dining room. She also makes sure that during the day, Rip is away at their lawyer's office managing the Van Bret estate. Feeling very lonely, Anne begins visiting Dr. Sully in the park and at his apartment. Victoria hires a Pinkerton detective to follow them. She informs Rip that his wife has been seeing Dr. Sully intimating that the two are having an affair. Anne denies the affair and also says she never visited the doctor in his apartment which is untrue. Anne later confesses that she lied about the meetings, accusing Victoria of trying to drive her away from Rip. She demands that Rip choose between her and his sister. Rip decides to leave the house with Anne. However, while Anne is preparing to depart, unbeknownst to Rip, Victoria entices her into the soundproof room and locks the door. Victoria then tries to convince Rip that Anne has left him. The other sister Caroline, who heard Anne scream before she was locked away, eventually shows Rip where the hidden room is, and Anne is freed. Rip, Anne, and Caroline leave the house. All that Victoria has left is her mother's heirloom necklace.[19]

Other plays during the show's first season included Oscar Wilde's *The Importance of Being Earnest*, Horton Foote's *Only the Heart*, and Oliver Goldsmith's *She Stoops to Conquer*.

Fred Coe who directed the premiere of *The Kraft Television Theatre* went on to become one of the legendary producer/directors in early television. Among the late 1940s shows with which he was involved were *The Borden Show, The Philco Television Playhouse, Lights Out, The Clock, Girl about Town, Bristol-Myers Tele Varieties, Show Business Inc., Chevrolet Tele-Theatre,* and *American Song.*

## *The Borden Show*
Premiered July 6, 1947 on NBC Sunday 9:00 pm; ran until September 28, 1947

Cast: No regular cast members.
Director: Fred Coe

This "experimental" anthology presented several different types of programs - dramas, variety shows, and marionette shows - to attempt to determine what type of show and what type of commercials would work best on TV. The series started first on the local NBC affiliate in New York in March 1947 with episodes like "The Florist Shop," a one-act comedy; a dramatic film about the "Swiss Family Robinson;" and a public service program concerning the Boys Club.

When the series premiered on the NBC network, the first episode was a variety show called "The Borden Club" hosted by Wally Boag, who did a balloon act, and with other stars including vocalist Lisa Kirk, Pat Bright doing impressions of singer Hildegarde and actress Katherine Hepburn, and dancers, the Casinos. The show opened with a film clip of Broadway and then focused on a blinking electric sign, "The Borden Club." Viewers were brought right into the night club set with people at tables eating and drinking.

Other episodes of *The Borden Club* featured the Mary Chase puppets including a Bing Crosby puppet, a play called "The French Dilemma," and a musical titled "Ethel's Cabin," starring Ethel Waters living in a dilapidated house with the stereotypical lazy husband. Commenting on this installment of the series, *The Televiser* indicated that "Presenting the lazy Negro, supported by his wife, is objectionable as fostering color discrimination."[20]

## *Theatre Guild*

Premiered November 9, 1947 on NBC; presented on a monthly basis until June 6, 1948

Cast: No regular cast members

NBC advertised this monthly series presented by the New York Theatre Guild as the "Broadway of Television," declaring that if you live in a television area almost anywhere from Boston to Richmond, the new "Broadway" of television runs past your door.

The first presentation was *John Ferguson* by St. John Ervine – a play about a man with complete faith in God's will only to waver when he is met with misfortune after misfortune. Actor Thomas Mitchell starred in the work produced by Edward Sobel. The play had been the Theatre Guild's first success in 1919.

Other monthly plays included *The Late George Apley* by George S. Kaufman and John P. Marquand, *Angel Street* by Patrick Hamilton, *Mornings at Seven* by Paul Osborn, *Stage Door* by George S. Kaufman and Edna Ferber, *Great Catherine* by George Bernard Shaw, and *Our Town* by Thornton Wilder.


## *Television Playhouse*

Premiered December 4, 1947 on NBC Sunday 8:40 pm; ran until April 11, 1948

Cast: No regular cast members
Director: Fred Coe
Executive Producer: Richard Harrity

Originally titled *Rehearsal in 3H*, NBC aired live dramas every third Sunday night in cooperation with the American National Theater and Academy. The debut was Tennessee Williams' *The Last of My Solid Gold Watches*. The play, which takes place in a dingy hotel room, concerns the story of an old salesman living on past glories unwilling to accept the limitations of age or the changing world. To a younger salesman, the man, played by actor John Stuart Dudley, describes his faith in an unchanging world that appreciated manners and good quality.

## Dress Rehearsal
Premiered March 21, 1948 on NBC Thursday 8:00 pm; ran until August 31, 1948

Cast: No regular cast members

Experimental programs presented as "dress rehearsals," that is, pilots for potential series, served as the basis for this anthology. One of the episodes, titled "You're the Salesman," directed by Ira Skutch, was a giveaway show in which a man and a woman were selected from the studio audience and given a piece of merchandise like a tennis racket or coat to sell to another member of the audience. The "customer" was given $15 to make the purchase and told not to select an item until both salesmen completed their pitches. The sales people kept the money with which a purchase was made, and the "customer" got the merchandise.


## Variety (aka NBC Playhouse or The Players)
Premiered April 11, 1948 on NBC Sunday between 8:30 pm and 9:00 pm; ran until September 19, 1948

Cast: No regular cast members

As the show's title implies, *Variety* consisted of special programs ranging from music to comedies to dramas. The twenty-minute premiere presentation, which started at 8:48 pm, featured the "Jealousy Scene" from *Othello* by William Shakespeare.

The final program, "Heavens to Betsy," written by Ruth Roberts and Gene Pillar and produced and directed by Fred Coe, focused on two young actresses, Betsy (Elizabeth Cote) and her friend (Mary Best) coming to New York City with hopes of appearing on Broadway. With the help of a young male taxi driver played by Russell Nype, who also wants to break into acting, they rent a rundown apartment in the Village with a landlord (Nick Dennis) who acted like Groucho Marx. The episode apparently seemed like a pilot for a sitcom because some publications (e.g. *The Great Sitcom Book* by Rick Mitz) list this as an early TV series but no evidence could be found that indicated any episodes beyond this one installment were ever made.

## Actors Studio
Premiered September 26, 1948 on ABC Sunday at 8:30 pm; ran until June 23, 1950

> Cast: Marc Connelly – narrator beginning with the 1949-50 season
> Producer: Donald Davis

Produced live by the Actor's Studio, Inc., this anthology presented both original and classic dramas.

"Portrait of a Madonna" by Tennessee Williams, staged by Hume Cronyn, directed by Ralph Warren, and starring Cronyn's wife Jessica Tandy was the initial installment. The play concerned an aged Southern belle living in a cheap hotel who is convinced that a man she once loved named Richard is sneaking into her room every night and sexually assaulting her. After receiving a call from the woman, the hotel's manager sends a porter and an elevator boy to investigate. In the end, the woman is institutionalized.

Another installment was Rebecca Ward's "Salt of the Earth" about how a neurotic and domineering woman wrecks her own life and that of her family's. It starred Ann Shepherd and Hebert Nelson.

Beginning November 1949, the series moved to CBS on Tuesdays at 9:00; in February 1950, it became a one-hour drama on Fridays at 9:00 pm. In March 1950, the title was changed to *The Play's the Thing*.

## *The Chevrolet Tele-Theatre* (originally titled *Chevrolet on Broadway*)
Premiered September 27, 1948 on NBC Monday at 8:00 pm; ran two seasons until June 26, 1950

> Cast: No regular cast members
> Producer: Fred Coe
> Sponsor: Chevrolet Dealers Association

Original works written specifically for television along with adaptations were featured on this live, half-hour anthology series. The first episode, "The Home Life of a Buffalo," starred John McQuade and Virginia Smith. Written by Richard Harrity and directed by Gordon Duff, the story concerned Eddie, a dancer (McQuade), his wife (Smith), and son Joey (Kevin Matthews). Eddie refuses to believe that vaudeville is dead, but his wife is more realistic. Eddie wants his son to go into vaudeville instead of to school. Eventually, he faces reality and plans an elaborate suicide by turning on the gas in the hotel room where the family lives. However, he then conjures up a great idea for a new act. He turns off the gas, wakes up his wife and son, and prepares to rehearse the new act.

The second installment of the series, "Mirage in Manhattan," featured Jesse Royce Landis and Will Geer as husband and wife, Sam and Bessie Hobbs. The couple from Oklahoma registers at the Hotel Ritz-Plaza and becomes the one millionth guests at the establishment. The hotel offers to treat them to a special night on the town with a photographer in tow to document their experiences. Mrs. Hobbs wants to pretend that they are more sophisticated than they actually are. She takes samba lessons so they can go to a nightclub but is humiliated on the dance floor when she ends up falling into the base drum. The photo of the incident is printed in the newspaper, but she doesn't want copies of the paper sent to her friends in Oklahoma. In the end, the couple decides to pay the hotel bill themselves, leave the Ritz-Plaza, and attend a rodeo as Mr. Hobbs wanted to do in the first place.

Another notable episode titled "Whistle Daughter, Whistle" presented Gertrude Berg in her television debut. Berg starred as Mrs. Marks, a Bronx housewife, trying to arrange a marriage between her daughter Peggy (Lenore Lonergan) and Adam (John Harvey), the son of another Bronx housewife Mrs. Kalat (Minerva Pious). The story was based on *The Goldbergs* radio series and was a precursor to *The Goldbergs* TV series.

*Chevrolet Tele-Theatre* was one early series that filmed certain scenes and inserted them into the live presentations.

## *The Philco Television Playhouse*

Premiered October 3, 1948 on NBC Sunday 9:00 pm; ran until October 2, 1955

Cast: Bert Lytell – first season's host
Producer: Fred Coe

This live one-hour dramatic program featured major actors in both new and classic dramatizations. The Philco anthology was a successor to the *NBC Television Theater* which the network had aired on Sunday nights since 1945

From the October 23, 1949 presentation of the *Philco Television Playhouse*, Marjorie Gateson and Bramwell Fletcher in "Because of the Lockwoods," the story of a young English girl whose widowed mother has been cheated of her inheritance by an unscrupulous lawyer.

without a sponsor. The first season of the Philco series was produced under the auspices of the Actors' Equity Association. The premiere episode, "Dinner at Eight" (adapted from the Edna Ferber and George S. Kaufman play) was directed by Fred Coe and starred Peggy Wood as Mrs. Oliver Johnson, Dennis King, as her husband, and Mary Boland as Carlotta Vance. Although Oliver Johnson's firm is in financial trouble, his social-climbing wife wants to hold a small dinner party for a visiting British aristocratic couple. The guests include a faded theatre star, an over-the-hill alcoholic actor, a philandering doctor and his wife, and a powerful but disliked nouveau-riche couple.

*Dinner at Eight* aired in New York City, Philadelphia, Baltimore, and Washington D.C.as well as in Boston, Schenectady, and Richmond. Restrictions by movie studios at the time prohibited the network from sending kinescopes of the series to its other affiliates since they were deemed films to which the studios owned the rights.

Other dramas presented during the series first season included an adaptation of Daphne du Maurier's *Rebecca*, Alexandre Dumas' *Camille*, and Charles Dickens' *A Christmas Carol*.

Three presentations in early spring 1949 aired under the title of *NBC Repertory Theatre* or *NBC Dramatic Theatre* without Philco sponsorship. The plays were "Mr. Mergenthwirker's Lobbies," "Burlesque" with Bert Lehr, and "Macbeth" with Walter Hampden in the lead role.

For summer 1949, the program was known as *Arena Theatre*. Among the offerings was an original musical revue titled "Summer Formal" by Marty Donovan and Gerry Kenyon showcasing song and dance numbers presented by new talent.

Instead of relying solely on adaptations of plays and short stories for this series, producer/director Fred Coe encouraged original television plays done by writers like Paddy Chayefsky, A.E. Hotchner, and J.P. Miller.

## *Studio One*

Premiered November 7, 1948 on CBS Sunday 7:30 pm; ran for ten seasons until September 29, 1958

Cast: No regular cast members
Producer: Worthington Miner

Unique (for the time) camera work such as filmed montages to give the production scope and breadth was a hallmark of this sixty-minute anthology. The debut episode presented "The Storm" starring Margaret Sullavan as Janet Layton and Dean Jagger as Ben Willson. Written by McNight Malmor, adapted for television by Worthington Miner, and directed by Frank Schaffner, the premiere installment was a mystery about an aspiring actress in New York City who, not having succeeded at her craft, plans to go back to her home town in Virginia. However, when she attempts to purchase a bus ticket, she finds that her money has been stolen. Chronically frightened of people and the city, she is befriended by Ben Willson. Not knowing much about Ben's background, nevertheless, Janet eventually marries him. He takes her to a beautiful home in a remote location. Janet discovers that Ben has a brother David (John Forsythe) that he never mentioned. Injured in the war, David has mental and emotional problems. Janet also sees that Ben periodically receives mysterious letters that he never shares with her but which make him depressed and upset.

After a period of time, Ben suggests that Janet visit her ailing mother in Virginia for a week. She returns to the house she shares with Ben during a violent storm only to find that he is not there and that the phone line is dead. Going to the basement to obtain wood to build a fire, Janet sees that the cellar door is opened and notices a handkerchief hanging out of her old trunk. When she opens the trunk, she discovers the body of a woman. Hysterical, Janet believes that David may have murdered the woman, but, when Ben finally returns, he initially says there is no body in the basement. Janet checks and finds no body. In tears, she reaches into Ben's pocket for a handkerchief and pulls out the one that had been hanging out of the trunk. Ben confesses that he murdered the woman who had been his first wife because she wouldn't leave him alone. The woman kept sending him letters stating she would destroy his marriage to Janet. Janet runs away from Ben and leaves the house in his car presumably to contact the police.

The episode ends with the viewers wondering if Janet had imagined the murder and Ben's confession or if it was all real. The audience and critics alike were left dangling. Producer Worthington Miner claimed that he had deliberately sought to do a show that had no ending – that left viewers in doubt and indeed the script for "The Storm" ends in that fashion.[21]

Werner Michel, who oversaw the production of the episode for the network indicated, "The payoff was a handkerchief. That's how the detective accused the murderer, but they put the wrong camera on and you couldn't see the handkerchief. Nobody could figure the story out. A hue and cry went out in the press, so we decided to open the next week's show repeating that scene..."[22] However, in the script, while the handkerchief is key, there is no detective character. Viewers may not have been able to see the handkerchief that Janet pulled from Ben's pocket, but nonetheless, the ending is still vague and leaves the question of whether Ben really did murder his former wife or if an emotional Janet imagined that he did.

On October 17, 1949, *Studio One* repeated "The Storm" but with a new cast – Marsha Hunt, John Rodney and Dean Harens.

## *Colgate Video Theatre*
Premiered January 3, 1949 on NBC Monday at 9:00 pm; ran until June 25, 1950

    Cast: No regular cast members
    Sponsor: Colgate

*Colgate Video Theatre* presented thirty-minute comedies, dramas, and mysteries. The debut was titled "Funny Meeting You Here" from a story in *McCall's* magazine by Olga Moore adapted for television by William L. Stuart and starring Mary Wickes and Betty Garde. The final episode, "Satan's Waitin'" starred Jeanne Cagney and Pierre Watkin in a tale about a woman who has married for money rather than for love and then falls in love with a young executive at her husband's company. The woman and the young executive decide to murder her husband, but their plans are foiled when the husband learns of the plot.

Among other offerings during its first season, this anthology presented a pilot for the 1952 series *Mr. and Mrs. North*. The episode, airing on the 4th of July, 1949, starred Joseph Allen Jr. and Mary Lou Taylor. However, the comedy/mystery television series about a pair of amateur detectives starred Richard Denning and Barbara Britton.

Three installments of a try-out series *Vic and Sade*, based on the radio program, were aired in the time slot for *Colgate Video Theatre* on July 11 through July 25, 1949. Filmed by producer Frederick Ziv and written by Paul Rhymer, the show featured married couple Vic (Frank Dane) and his wife Sade (Bernadette Flynn) along with their son Rush (Dick Conan). Vic was an accountant; Sade - a homemaker. The debut of the three-episode series concerned Vic being sent out-of-town on a business trip on the same day that Sade is planning a big supper party. A subsequent episode had Vic and his arch rival Ike Kneesuffer competing to have their streets paved in order to prove their importance to their boss.

*The Billboard,* in reviewing the program, indicated that Paul Rhymer was better at writing for radio than for television since the latter requires comical action and not just funny dialog.[23]

The try-out was not successful enough for Colgate Palmolive to pick the series up as a regular feature for fall 1949.

## *ABC Television Players*
Premiered January 16, 1949 on ABC Sunday 9:30 pm; ran until October 30, 1949

Cast: Don Gallaher (sometimes spelled "Gallagher") – narrator

This anthology aired live dramas from Chicago featuring Midwestern actors and actresses. The series' title changed to *ABC Tele-Players* in April 1949 and then to *ABC Penthouse Players* in August of that year. The August 14, 1949 episode was titled "The Balacchi Brothers." Based on a short story, the play concerned a pair of trapeze artists – Zack and George, who were not really brothers. George is infatuated with his landlord's granddaughter and invites her to see him perform a stunt that he has never done before in public. The stunt involves leaping from a trapeze to a rope in the middle of the theater. He attempts the feat but fails. Seriously injured, one of George's legs is amputated and Zack leaves the act. Eventually, Zack sees George performing as a strong man in a circus and learns that he has married Suzy – the landlord's granddaughter.

## *Your Show Time*
Premiered January 21, 1949 on NBC Friday at 9:30 pm; ran for twenty-six episodes until July 15, 1949

Cast: Arthur Shields – host

*Your Show Time* presented filmed adaptations of classic short stories. Arthur Shields introduced each episode seated behind a desk in an old book store. The first episode, "The Necklace" adapted from the Guy de Maupassant story, starred John Beal and Maria Palmer. It related the tale of a young

French married couple who worked and saved to replace what they believed to be a valuable necklace which they had borrowed and then lost only to discover that the original necklace had been made of paste. The drama won the first Emmy award for a network broadcast.

"The Real Thing," the March 11, 1949 edition of the series, was based on a Henry James story and adapted and produced by Elihu Winer. The episode opens with artist John Gloucester (John Archer) working on a drawing of his model Sybil Churm (Marjorie Lord) dressed as a housekeeper. He has been commissioned to do a set of illustrations for a book by popular author Philip Vincent. A sophisticated-looking elderly couple Major Monarch (Robert Warwick) and his wife (Sally Corner) arrive at John's door looking for work as models. Mr. Monarch explains that they have fallen on hard times and need the work. Mrs. Monarch mistakes Sybil for a maid and asks her to fetch some tea. John thinks they would be excellent for the illustrations he is doing since they look like "the real thing." However, the Monarch's become increasingly overbearing critiquing John's work and then taking over and drawing themselves. John's boss rejects the illustrations and gives John more time to complete the project. John decides to use a delivery man named Joe (Michael Browne) and Sybil for the illustrations and, after Mr. Monarch pleads with John for a job, John hires them as his housekeepers. In the end, John marries Sybil declaring that she is "the real thing."

## *Believe It or Not*

Premiered March 1, 1949 on NBC Tuesday 9:30 pm; ran until September 28, 1950

>   Cast: Robert L. Ripley – host
>   Director: Joe Cavalier
>   Producer: Victor McLeod

Robert Ripley showed clips of the unusual people, places, and things he had uncovered on his travels around the world on this show. A weekly feature was a dramatization of an actual "Believe It or Not" incident. Mr. Ripley passed away on May 27, 1949 from a heart attack at age fifty-five. Guest hosts filled in until Robert St. John was named permanent host in July 1949. The series left the air for a few weeks starting in December of that year. It returned on January 4, 1950 with a new format as a true anthology program presenting stories based on Ripley's tales.

The January 4th episode, titled "Murder in Duplicate," was set in Victorian England. A wife, whose husband is missing along with their savings, contacts Scotland Yard. The inspector encounters a drunken lawyer who seems to know that the husband has been murdered. The inspector subsequently finds the husband's body in a freshly spaded plot in the backyard of the couple's apartment building. The lawyer then divulges who the murderer is. The "Believe or Not" factor was that the lawyer knew the facts of the case because a similar crime, down to the last detail, had been committed 250 years earlier and was already part of legal history.

Another episode late in the series run concerned a man from Britain who has murdered his wife in Hong Kong just before the Japanese took over the city during World War II. The man is never convicted of the crime but winds up in the same prison camp as the inspector who has been investigating the case. His Japanese guards force the murderer to dig a pit in the same spot where he has buried his wife and, unable psychologically to do so, he is murdered by the guards.

## *Fireside Theatre*

Premiered April 5, 1949 on NBC Tuesday at 9:00 pm; ran for ten seasons until May 22, 1958

> Cast: Win Elliott - announcer for the first eight telecasts
> Frank Wisbar – host 1952-53
> Gene Raymond – host 1953-55
> Jane Wyman – host 1955-58
> Sponsor: Proctor & Gamble

*Fireside Theatre* began as a showcase for potential series pilots during its first three months. The program switched to more traditional dramas in fall 1949. The debut episode, "Friend of the Family," starred Virginia Gilmore and Yul Brynner, (married in real life) and Peter Barry who wrote the story which dealt with husband and wife actors and their best friend and author. An April 26, 1949 episode was a musical satire called "What's New in the News" written by Leslie A. Cramer and starring Happy Felton, Joan Diener, and the Song Spinners. *The Billboard* called this episode ". . . the most atrocious production in many a moon" and went on to say: "As if all of this was not bad enough, the show stooped to a low in taste in its final sketch, which was set in a police station and dealt with wringing a confession out of a criminal by replaying a particularly obnoxious record, certainly one of showbiz's oldest gags. The desk sergeant, stepping down to congratulate the brilliance of the examining officer played by Felton, proved to be a midget. The taste exhibited was not questionable, it was putrid."[24]

## *Through the Crystal Ball*
Premiered April 18, 1949 on CBS Monday 9:00 pm; ran until July 4, 1949

>Cast: Jimmy Savo – host
>Producer/director: Paul Bellanger
>Writer: Ed Rue
>Sponsor: Ford Dealers

A unique approach to presenting dramas, this show dramatized classic fables through dance. Jimmy Savo, a pantomimist, was the original host and narrator, and also played a role in each story. Savo had difficulty memorizing a new script each week and left the program in May.

The first presentation was a dance dramatization of *Robinson Crusoe* choreographed by Michael Kidd. The second show presented "Humpty Dumpty." Other fables dramatized were "Cinderella," *Alice in Wonderland*, and "Casey at the Bat." In *Alice in Wonderland*, actor Arthur Treacher played the Cheshire cat.

The series was to air for thirty-eight weeks but was canceled after eleven weeks.

## *Program Playhouse*
Premiered June 22, 1949 on DuMont Wednesday at 9:00 pm; ran until September 14, 1949

>Cast: No regular cast members

Trying something different at the time, DuMont came up with the idea of airing potential series pilots on an anthology show. The series began with an announcer saying: "DuMont Presents . . . each Wednesday at 9 *The Program Playhouse* . . . bringing you new program ideas especially designed for television. Out of thousands of scripts (picture shows a rain of scripts) we have selected (a hand picks out one script) comedies, drama, mystery, romance, adventure, quiz and participation ideas."[25]

The first episode, "The Timid Soul," produced by Stark-Layton Productions, directed by Jack Hurdle, and based on H.T. Webster's comic strip, starred Ernest Truex in a live comedy as Casper Milquetoast, a man subject to life's misfortunes. Sylvia Field, Truex's real-life wife, played his spouse on this installment.

A July 27 broadcast of "Trouble, Inc." concerned a private eye played by Earl Hammond and his Girl Friday (Carol Hill) in a light mystery taking on a case of an ex-con (Maurice Gosfield) and his girl (Elaine Williams) wanting to dispose of $2 million. The private eye and his assistant find themselves in trouble when the money disappears, and the ex-con wants the money back.

An August 3, 1949 installment titled "Dead of Night," written by Michael Sklar, dealt with a couple moving into a new apartment. They are warned by their rather eccentric landlord that the woman may be murdered by her spouse and indeed she is. When the husband prepares to hide his wife's body behind a brick wall, the landlord comes upon him and divulges that he too had killed his wife and walled her in the same place whereupon the husband kills the landlord.

In an August 17 episode, actor Roscoe Karns starred in and produced "Roscoe Karns and Inky Poo"- a comedy in which the actor played a family man who almost wrecks his teenage daughter's (Sally Kester) chances with her first boyfriend (Jimmy Goodwin). When the boy comes to visit, Karns monopolizes the boy's time by playing checkers with him. After his daughter sends the boy home, Karns tries to make things right by sending his daughter flowers in the boy's name, but she sends them back, making the boy's wealthy father mad thinking she is trying to ensnare his son. Karns' conscience, dressed as a clown called "Inky Poo," appeared by way of super-imposition to set him back on the right course.

The only episode of *Program Playhouse* which led to an actual series was "Hands of Murder" – another anthology series premiering on DuMont in September 1949.

At the end of each installment of *Program Playhouse*, viewers were given an address to write in and indicate if they wanted the episode they had just watched to become a weekly series.

## Academy Theatre

Premiered July 25, 1949 on NBC Monday at 8:00 pm; ran until September 12, 1949

    Cast: No regular cast members
    Producer: Curtis Canfield, Professor of Dramatics at Amherst College

An NBC vice president, a graduate of Amherst College, had the Amherst College Masquers perform in a production of "Julius Caesar" in April 1949. The play was the first production of a full-length Shakespearian work on television. It was directed by Curtis Canfield, Director of Amherst's Kirby Theatre. During the summer of 1949, NBC had Canfield present *Academy Theatre*, a series of one-act plays on the network as a temporary replacement for *Chevrolet on Broadway*.

    The first episode, a Chinese romantic fantasy, "The Stolen Prince" by Dan Totheroh, starred Shirley Dale, Ivan MacDonald, and Collins Bain and was directed by Mark Hawley. The story dealt with a Chinese monarchy headed by Emperor Lang Moo whose wife gave birth to twins – a boy and a girl. Since females are considered worthless in the kingdom, the baby girl is to be killed. However, Wing Lee and Long Fo, the children of the royal cook, steal the baby they think is the female but who is really the male. They put the baby in a tub which floats down the river where poor fisherman Hi Tee and his wife rescue the baby and name him Joy. Time passes, and Joy grows up. Hi Tee's pet duck whom he has taught to fish for his family catches a valuable red fish. Hi Tee, his wife, the duck, and Joy are all arrested for the theft of the fish and are due to be executed. However, Wing Lee recognizes the jade chain around Joy's neck which the baby was wearing when the child was put in the tub. She confesses what happened years ago, and Joy becomes the new emperor after his father dies.

    Other one-act plays aired on *Academy Theatre* included "Drums of Oude" by Austin Strong, "In the Shadow of Glen" by J.M. Synge, and "Aria da Capo" by Edna St. Vincent Millay.

## Hollywood Premiere

Premiered September 22, 1949 on NBC Thursday 8:00 pm; ran until November 17, 1949

    Cast: No regular cast members

A series of programs starring established entertainers and actors in comedy and dramatic roles was the concept of this anthology. The first installment, "Pardon Mr. Pinky," featured comic Pinky Lee in a program written by Phil Shuken and Ed Tyler and directed by John E. Gaunt. Just out of drama school, Lee is mistaken for a millionaire interested in backing a Broadway show.

An October 20, 1949 episode presented two fifteen-minute comedy stories. The first one titled "A Doctor's Patience" concerned a physician's wife (Arlene Harris) who finds that her husband is unable to attend the theater with her because he has to care for a patient. The other story "Hey, Sweeney" starred Bob Sweeney in the title role as a not-too-bright dad with a precocious son. The dad brings home a canine as a watchdog. He begins training the mutt, but his son, appropriately called "Lucifer," starts to train his father. Dad gets up on a chair in terror as Lucifer commands "up, up."

## *Silver Theatre*

Premiered October 3, 1949 on CBS Monday at 8:00 pm; ran until June 26, 1950

    Cast: Conrad Nagel, host
    Producer/director: Frank Telford
    Sponsor: International Silver Company

This live, thirty-minute anthology, which had begun on radio in the 1930s, featured stories about romance.

The debut episode, "L'Amour the Merrier" by Richard Steele and Sid Sloan, concerned a young real estate agent played by Burgess Meredith who, wanting to buy a yacht, starts a relationship with his boss' daughter (Gloria McGhee). However, his plan becomes complicated when a man (Louis Van Rooten), who had befriended him overseas while he was in the military, arrives with his beautiful French daughter (Eva Gabor).

Every month, the series presented the "Silver Award" to a supporting actor who had appeared in one of the stories and was determined as deserving special recognition by a panel of drama critics.

## *The Ford Theatre Hour*
Premiered October 7, 1949 on CBS Friday 9:00 pm; initial run lasted until June 29, 1951

Cast: No regular cast members

This anthology began as a monthly series of live dramas on CBS in October 1948 but didn't become a regular series until a year later. The premiere episode of the monthly series was "Years Ago," a play written by actress Ruth Gordon and directed by Marc Daniels. Starring Raymond Massey as Clinton Jones and Eva LaGallienne as Annie Jones - father and mother of a young girl played by Patricia Kirkland who wanted to be an actress.

For its October 7, 1949 premiere on alternating Friday nights, the anthology presented the classic Hecht-MacArthur-Millholland play *Twentieth Century* with Frederic March as a bankrupt Broadway producer trying to entice Lilli Palmer as the temperamental stage and screen star into appearing in one of his productions.

During its initial season, this anthology shared its time period with *Fifty-Fourth Street Review* and the *Actor's Studio*.

After the CBS run ended in June 1951, NBC picked up the anthology as a thirty-minute filmed presentation in October 1952 where it ran until September 1956. Its final season (1956-57) aired on ABC.

## *Oboler Comedy Theatre*
Premiered October 11, 1949 on ABC Tuesday at 9:00 pm (Premiered on the West coast in September 1949); ran until November 1949.

Cast: No regular cast members
Writer/director/producer Arch Oboler

The first episode of this live comedy anthology series was titled "Ostrich in Bed." A married couple, played by Olan Soule and Frances Rafferty, returns home to find an ostrich in their bedroom. They need to get rid of the bird before a prospective client for the services of the husband's advertising agency arrives for dinner. The husband calls the police, but the desk sergeant is too busy reading the Kinsey Report to be interrupted and so passes the call off as from a drunk. The humane society doesn't help either because the couple can't determine if the bird is a male or female.

With the ostrich in their bedroom closet, the couple tries to entertain the potential client played by Hans Conried. To cover the bird's noises, the husband keeps breaking dishes while the guest gets drunk on his own product, "Grandmother Bedila's Elixir" which is 90 – proof. The client wants to be excused from the table, but the couple, fearing he will find the bird, ignores his pleas. When the guest can no longer contain himself, he departs only to be encountered by the ostrich and runs from the house almost hysterical. Finally the wife is able to drive the bird from the house.

## *Romance* (aka *Theatre of Romance*)

Premiered November 3, 1949 on CBS Thursday at 8:30 pm; ran until December 29, 1949

Cast: No regular cast members
Producer/director: Robert Stevens

Airing on alternate weeks with *Inside U.S.A. with Chevrolet* and replacing *Sugar Hill Times*, this anthology series featured love stories. Its premiere presentation was "Camille" adapted from the Alexandre Dumas story starring Ruth Ford, Richard Hylton, and Malcolm Keane. "Camille" was the sad story of a lower-class Frenchwoman who rises to Parisian high society thanks to money from a wealthy man. Camille falls in love with a handsome, young man, but their relationship is not to be. For the television adaptation, the story was set in 1920s New York City.

The final drama for the series was "The Afternoon of the Faun" starring Steven Hill and Lilia Skala.

# Mystery, Suspense, and Crime Anthology Series

**6**

**WELL BEFORE *AMERICAN HORROR STORY*,** several anthology series that premiered in the mid to late 40s were built around a central theme of mystery, suspense, or horror. These programs are profiled in this chapter.

## *Suspense*
Premiered: March 1, 1949 on CBS Tuesday 9:30 pm; ran until August 17, 1954

> Cast: No regular cast members
> Producer/Director: Robert Stevens

Aired live from New York, this television version of the radio drama, which had premiered on CBS radio during the early 1940s, presented stories of people in dangerous, threatening situations.

The first episode titled "Revenge," directed by Robert Stevens and based on a story by Cornell Woolrich, starred Eddie Albert and his wife Margo. In another early episode, Ernest Truex and his spouse Sylvia Field starred as a suburban couple who just hired a new maid. An arsenic poisoner is loose in their neighborhood with suspicions falling on the maid. The husband sips some cocoa only to find in it a large amount of poison. The real culprit turns out to be the wife. Apparently, she didn't like the crunching sounds her husband made when he ate.

## The Clock

Premiered May 16, 1949 on NBC Tuesday 8:30 pm; ran on NBC and then on ABC until January 9, 1952

Cast: Larry Semon, narrator
Creator: Lawrence Klee
Producer/director: Fred Coe

Based on an ABC radio series which commenced in 1946, *The Clock* featured stories of mystery and suspense with the passage of time playing an important part in each episode. The radio program opened with: "Sunrise and sunset, promise and fulfillment, birth and death ... the whole drama of life is written in the sands of time."

An early episode of the television series concerned a woman visiting her aunt in the country and suspecting the aunt has killed a traveling tie salesman. It turns out that the woman herself is psychotic. In another episode, a clerk, who is cheating on his wife, robs his employer and strangles his boss. The man subsequently has his face and hands altered by plastic surgery, and then he poisons the doctor, only to find that his boss is considered to have died from natural causes and that he has been left $100,000 in his boss' will. Due to the plastic surgery, he cannot prove his identity and is convicted of his own murder.

## Volume One

Premiered June 16, 1949 on ABC Thursday 9:30 pm; ran until July 21, 1949

Producer/writer: Wyllis Cooper, who also introduced the episodes

From the man who created *Lights Out* came the provocative drama *Volume One* – a six-part series of psychological thrillers. Originally the title was *Quiet, Please!* named after Wyllis Cooper's radio series of the same name.

"Number One" starred Jack Lescoulie as Floyd and Nancy Sheridan as Georgie - a couple who rob a bank of $40,000, kill an elderly man, and go to a seedy hotel to get away from the authorities. Milty, a bellhop played by Frank Thomas, Jr., shows them to their hotel room. After the bellhop leaves, they find their stolen money and gun missing. The bellhop seems to be able to control their situation. He leaves them without food and water and without the possibility of escaping. The bellhop could be some supernatural being or the personification of the couple's conscience. The TV screen was treated as a mirror above a dresser in the hotel room. As Floyd begins to crack up, he asserts that people are looking at him through the mirror. After Milty gives Floyd the missing gun not saying where he found it, Floyd hurls the gun at the mirror cracking it with the remainder of the episode played with crack marks between the viewers and the characters. When Floyd and Georgie find they can't escape the room through the doorway, the bellboy opens a "door" in the dresser and mirror, and then locks it leaving the couple to their fate which viewers are left to decide for themselves.

The same cast and story line were used in an installment of Cooper's next series *Escape* which premiered on January 5, 1950. This was another anthology series showing characters in fantastical situations. *Escape* ended its run on March 30, 1950.

"Number Six" of *Volume One*, the final show, starred Happy Felton, Abby Lewis, and Alex Segal in a tale of the inventor of a time machine who tries to outsmart the businessman who financed it. However, they both end up being foiled by a newspaperwoman.

## *Armchair Detective*

Premiered July 6, 1949 on CBS Wednesday at 9:00 pm; ran until September 28, 1949

> Cast: H. Allen Smith – Crime authority who provides the final answers about the crime
> John Milton Kennedy – Crime interrogator who asks the questions

Each week, two plays involving acts of criminality were presented to viewers with clues pointing to answers to questions posed beforehand about the crime. The answers were explained at the end of the show. The half-hour series stated at the beginning that it was 'a new kind of mystery that challenges your imagination." On one episode, the first case is about a stockbroker blinded in a train accident who is accused of murdering his wife on the train. He exchanges suits with a hobo to elude police. The stockbroker had $50,000 on him before the train wreck and his valet, who is accompanying him, wants to know where the money is. The police find the stockbroker after questioning a hobo wearing an expensive suit and arrest the valet for attempted robbery. The stockbroker isn't arrested since the train accident caused the death of this wife. In the second case, a gangster, drummed out of the mob, goes to a warehouse to find what his ex-boss has been smuggling. His girlfriend and his boss show up. He murders his girlfriend but tries to place the blame on his former boss. Through clues left by the gangster, the police know that he is the real murderer.

## Lights Out

Premiered July 19, 1949 on NBC Tuesday at 9:00 pm; ran until September 29, 1952

> Cast: Jack La Rue, host and narrator until April 1950 when Frank Gallup became the host
> Producer: Fred Coe
> Director: Kingman T. Moore
> Writer: Wilson Lehr

This live anthology focused on stories of suspense, mystery, and the supernatural. Each episode began with a close-up shot of eyes and a bloody hand turning off the lights, followed by a spooky laugh and the words "Lights out, everybody..."

The series began on local Chicago radio in 1934 and then aired on the NBC radio network in 1935. Wyllis Cooper created and wrote the radio episodes until 1936 and was then replaced by Arch Oboler.

The television version of *Lights Out* was first seen on the New York NBC station on June 30, 1946 in a fifteen-minute episode titled "First Person Singular" written by Wyllis Cooper, directed by Bill Stales, and produced by Fred Coe. The story concerned a husband who strangles his wife on a hot summer evening sick of his spouse's constant nagging and sloppiness. The episode is shot entirely from the point of view of the killer who is never seen. His thoughts are voiced by an actor (Carl Frank) off-screen. In the end, the killer is caught, convicted, and sentenced to hang. A black cloth covers the camera lens signifying the hood placed on the murderer as he is about to be hanged.

"Episode One" of the network version of the series with Francis Reid, Phil Arthur, Anita Anton and Gladys Clark dealt with a jealous and overpossessive wife played by Reid who thinks that her husband (Arthur) is having an affair. She decides to murder the woman with whom she perceives her husband has been unfaithful. The wife lures the woman to her country house and sits back while a rattlesnake bites and kills the girl. When her husband finds what she has done, she commits suicide hoping to implicate him as her murderer. However, she survives the suicide attempt and suffers the consequences.

In reviewing an episode of *Lights Out* from November 1949, *The Billboard* pointed out the limitations of television compared to radio in presenting the type of drama for which this series was known.

> In radio, there was no limit to the macabre story it could tell, for radio places no limit on imagination. That doesn't go for tele. The minute tele shows an actual set and an actual character, it establishes confines. Thus, the idea, on this show (November 14, 1949), of having a spectre walk out of the ocean to destroy the woman who's just murdered her husband is faced with a physical and visual limit which does not exist in radio. And so far, all *Lights Out* has tried to do is to move the camera in on radio scripts, rather than seeking and establishing its own purely video techniques. [26]

A June 12, 1950 episode of the series was different from the usual fare. The installment titled "Determined Lady" combined comedy with suspense. A crotchety old woman, a widow, fakes her own death to outwit her attorney who is after her estate. However, she then does actually die. The old lady returns as a ghost to make certain that her fortune goes to her niece and not to the attorney.

## *The Big Story*
Premiered September 16, 1949 on NBC Friday at 9:30 pm; ran until June 28, 1957 with an additional season in syndication.

> Cast: Bob Sloane – narrator (1949-1954)
> Norman Rose – narrator (1954-1955)
> Ben Grauer – narrator (1955-1957)
> Burgess Meredith – narrator (in syndication 1957-1958)
> Director: Charles E. Skinner

Producer: Bernard J. Prockter
Sponsor: Pall Mall cigarettes while series was on NBC

This docu-drama, which aired on radio originally, was based on actual stories of reporters who solved crimes or rendered significant public service. The original series combined live drama with filmed segments.

The first episode, written by Arnold Perl and directed by Charles E. Skinner, featured the story of Frank Shenkel of the *Pittsburgh Sun Telegraph* investigating the murder of a woman shot in her sleep. The reporter breaks open the case by tracking down a witness willing to testify against a powerful racketeer.

A January 4, 1957 episode hosted by Ben Grauer from the "Big Story Newsroom" was a repeat of a September 11, 1953 installment that featured actor James Dean. Based on the experiences of journalist Rex Newman of the Joplin, Missouri *Globe and News Herald*, the show opened with a scene of juveniles robbing a store and stealing a camera. The juveniles grow up to be adult criminals behind a crime spree in Joplin with witnesses too afraid to identify the culprits. One of the culprits, Todd Ingalls (James Dean) is about to marry his childhood sweetheart Julie (Wendy Drew). To get a ring for the ceremony, Todd's friend Howie Madden (John Kerr) suggests they rob a jewelry store. Newman thinks he knows the suspects and eventually recalls the culprits from the camera theft. Madden is arrested, but Todd and Julie get away. The two try to break Howie out of jail but find that he has already been transferred to the state prison to serve a twenty-five year sentence. In the process, Ingalls shoots a jail guard. He and Julie are arrested. Todd gets a fifty-year sentence; Julie ten years.

During the series final season in syndication, actor Burgess Meredith introduced and closed each episode from the so-called "Big Story News Stand." One such program titled "The Toy" (aka "Make Believe Bandit") dealt with reporter Emil Slaboda from the *Trentonian* newspaper, Trenton, New Jersey. Slaboda had been doing a series of articles on how toy guns, looking very much like the real thing, were being used to commit crimes. Danny Logan (Robert Brown), who has been discharged from the Navy after receiving a head wound in combat, has lost his job but leaves his wife under the impression he is still working. He purchases a toy gun and uses it to commit two robberies. Danny's wife reads the articles Slaboda has written and learns that her husband is no longer employed. A friend of Danny's brings the reporter to Danny's apartment. He turns himself into the police and undergoes psychiatric care.

## *Mr. Black*

Premiered September 19, 1949 on ABC Monday 9:30 pm; ran until November 7, 1949

> Cast: Mr. Black (Andy or Anthony Christopher) – host who appeared in character at the beginning and end of each episode.
> Writer: Bill S. Ballinger
> Director: Tony Rizzo

Originating from Chicago, the Devil's representative on Earth sees that bad guys get what's coming to them on this anthology series. Mr. Black takes particular satisfaction in crime and violent death.

On the debut, four racketeers play a game of Russian roulette to determine how to divide up the town among them. During the game, one of the gangsters is murdered. The other three fight and kill one another.

A few weeks after the series premiered, the show moved from 9:30 to 9:00 pm on Mondays.

While little is known about the actor who played Mr. Black including whether his first name was "Andy" or "Anthony," the man who wrote the series, Bill Ballinger became a noted mystery/suspense novelist and screen writer. Ballinger's first book in 1948 was titled *The Body in Bed*, a detective novel. He also wrote numerous teleplays for series such as *Alfred Hitchcock Presents*, *The Outer Limits*, *Ironside*, and *Cannon*.

## *Your Witness*

Premiered September 19, 1949 on ABC Mondays at 8:00 pm; ran until September 26, 1950

> Cast: Edmund Lowe - host
> Writer/producer: Ashmead Scott
> Director: Phillip Booth

Each week, a particular crime was dramatized on this show with the studio audience questioning the suspects in hopes of identifying the culprit. A character named "Lieutenant Burke," played by the program's writer/producer Ashmead Scott, acted as a conduit between the audience and the story, sitting in his office assembling evidence about the crime. He also appeared from time to time in the dramatization itself.

On the first episode, "Murder in White," a political figure is murdered in the hospital. Among the suspects are two doctors, a nurse, an errand boy, and the dead man's wife. The homicide detective has each suspect reenact the crime and then gives the audience a chance to question the suspects.

A January 12, 1950 installment concerned a nightclub singer Lily Claire (Florence Lake) whose brother has been killed in a failed illegal alien smuggling operation by one of the criminals behind the scheme. She believes she knows who murdered her brother since she has been hiding one of the fugitives in her house. The fugitive is Peter Jackson, a boxer, who is trying to evade the man who killed Lily's brother. He knows that "Mr. Big," the leader of the failed operation, wants to rid the gang of all of its small-time members along with the illegal aliens themselves to avoid being incriminated. Both Lily and Pete are shot. At this point, Burke addresses the studio audience asking them to question the remaining characters – Tony Moreno (Frederic Lazarro), a male singer at the El Toreador nightclub; Bert Carson (Tom Holland), the owner of the club; Trixie (Victoria Faust), another female singer at the club; and Wally Bannister (Jay Barney), Lily's lawyer in whom she confides information about her brother and the smuggling operation. After audience members question Bertie, Tony, and Bannister, Lt. Burke reveals that Wally Bannister is "Mr. Big," the murderer.

## *Starring Boris Karloff*

Premiered September 22, 1949 on ABC Thursday at 9:30 pm; ran until December 15, 1949

> Cast: Boris Karloff, host and star
> George Gunn – announcer
> George Henniger – organist
> Director: Alex Segal

During the 1950s, many movie stars, such as Robert Montgomery, Loretta Young, and Ronald Reagan, became hosts of their own anthology series. Boris Karloff was one of the first motion picture stars to undertake this task hosting tales of mystery and suspense on this half-hour series.

Boris Karloff, famous for playing Frankenstein's monster, was one of the first motion picture stars to host his own anthology series.

The initial episode, titled "Five Golden Guineas" by Robert Stephen Brode, featured Boris Karloff as a hangman who received five golden guineas for each hanging. He loved his work – the snap of a neck, the dangling of feet. But he kept his profession a secret from his wife played by Mildred Natwick. When his pregnant wife learns the truth, she leaves him. Twenty years later he has to hang a young boy who murdered his sweetheart. He receives a letter revealing that the boy is innocent. However, not wanting to lose the five guineas, he hangs him anyway. His wife reappears and tells him that the boy he hung was his son. Knowing that he is responsible for his son's death, the hangman goes out of his mind and strangles his wife. Naturally, he is convicted and hanged by another hangman who collects five guineas.

The day before each TV broadcast, the episode was heard on ABC radio.

In October 1949, the program's title was changed to *Mystery Playhouse Starring Boris Karloff*.

## *Hands of Murder*

Premiered September 30, 1949 on DuMont Friday 8:00 pm; ran until December 11, 1951

    Cast: No regular cast members
    Producer: James Caddigan
    Creator: Larry Menkin
    Writers: Larry Menkin and Charles Speer

This fast-paced anthology series featured stories of murder and suspense using deft staging and inventive camera work. The TV camera used a series of dissolves, cuts, fades, pans, focuses, and montages to show continuous action.

The pilot that aired as part of DuMont's *Program Playhouse* told the story of Fred Holt, a factory-worker and former veteran, who has a bad turn of luck. The furniture from the apartment he shares with his wife Marge has been repossessed because all of their money had gone for medical bills to treat their baby who eventually died. Fred borrows $100 from a loan shark named George but can't afford to pay back the funds plus interest. On his way to work one day, Fred is beaten up by thugs hired by George to make an example of him. Fred vows revenge, and, after he recovers from his injuries, he tracks down George, beating him up. George falls to the curb hitting his head which kills him. The police locate Fred, who refuses to surrender, and is mortally wounded by the cops.

Each scene in the production lasted only a minute with over thirty scenes and 100 shots in the pilot.

As the creator of the show, Larry Menkin, recalled, "A lot of the plots were the same. You can do the homicidal maniac and the girl a thousand times. He wants to kill girls, and the detective finds out. Who will get their first, the detective or the maniac? One week the killer works in a beauty parlor, maybe the next week a record library, or maybe he's a cutter in the garment industry with one of those big knives."[27]

*Hands of Murder* opened with an off-screen narrator saying: "Look at my hands. Now look at yours. Go on. Look at them! Look at my hands! (as the hands pick up a revolver and point it directly to the camera) These are the hands of murder! Yes, hands commit murder. But why? Is murder a disease that can be prevented and cured?"[28]

The October 21, 1949 episode of the series titled "Memo to a Killer," written by Larry Menkin and Charles Speer and directed by Frank Bunetta, concerned a taxi driver who has been murdered in the course of a mugging. Before the man dies, he is able to give a description to the police of his assailant, a man with a bandaged hand. The victim's brother, Louie, works for the same cab company. He and his fellow cabbies want to find the suspected killer based on a sketch printed in the newspaper. Harry Marvin, who works at a newsstand, is upset because the sketch resembles him. Louie comes to the restaurant where Marge, Harry's wife, works and notices Harry leaving the place. Louie concludes Harry is the culprit and believes if he follows Marge, she will lead him to Harry. Harry is about to leave town when Louie spots him and begins beating him up. The police arrive and arrest Harry who proclaims his innocence. The police end up catching a guy holding up the newsstand where Harry worked. The guy confesses that he murdered Louie's brother.

The program's name changed to *Hands of Destiny* in April 1950 and then to *Hands of Mystery* in August 1950 at the beginning of the program's second season. For the abbreviated third season, the title was again *Hands of Destiny*. Apparently, every time a new sponsor for the series came on board, the title changed.

## Famous Jury Trials

Premiered October 5, 1949 on DuMont Wednesday at 9:30 pm; ran until March 12, 1952. (Many sources cite October 12, 1949 as the start date for this series, but, as with *The Plainclothes Man*, noted below, the October 12, 1949 issue of *Variety* stated that the initial stanza of the series aired October 5.)

>Cast: No regular cast members
>Directors: Charles Harrell and Frank Nunetta
>Producer: John Clark for Trans-American and DuMont

Reenactments of real criminal trials constituted this thirty-minute program. The series was adapted from a radio version that began on the Mutual Broadcasting System in 1936 and later moved to ABC.

In the first episode, written by John L. Clark and titled "The People versus Frank Johnson," the case involves a man on trial for murdering his mistress. It unfolds in the courtroom through witnesses telling their version of events. In this case, the defendant is found guilty.

By November, 1949, the program incorporated flashback scenes about the crime so that the narrative did not totally take place in a courtroom.

# Continuing Character Crime Dramas 7

**CRIME DRAMAS HAVE BEEN A MAINSTAY** of television since the early days. From *Dragnet* and *The Untouchables* to *Columbo* and *CSI*, Americans love shows about the police and private detectives. Here are some of the earliest such programs.

### *Barney Blake, Police Reporter*
Premiered April 22, 1948 on NBC Thursday 9:30 pm; ran until July 8, 1948

> Cast: Barney Blake (Gene O'Donnell) – ace crime reporter
> Jennifer Allen (Judy Parrish) – Barney's secretary who started at the newspaper working in the want ads department.
> Producer: Wynn Wright Associates
> Director: David Lewis
> Sponsor: The American Tobacco Company (Lucky Strike cigarettes)

Barney Blake helped by Jennifer, his secretary, solved various murders in this thirteen-week series. "Matrimony Is Murder," "The Case of the Curious Corpse," and "Never Use Bullets" were just some of the episode titles. Each show opened with a close-up of Barney Blake's typewriter with his hands visible typing at full speed.

On the premiere, written by Max Ehrlich titled "Murder Me Twice," Barney becomes involved in a situation concerning Jennifer's twenty-four-year-old brother Tommy who has a case of hero-worship for gambler Deuce Duval. After Tommy convinces Deuce to bet on a horse named "Two Bells," he is cheated out of his portion of the winnings.

The third episode, which was also scripted by Max Ehrlich called "The E-String Murder," concerned the case of Schuyler Van Raalt and his wife Genevieve played by Clare Luce, a patroness of classical musicians. With her husband's knowledge, Mrs. Van Raalt takes more than a professional interest in young musicians. Currently, she is sponsoring a recital for violinist Pedro Valdez. Mr. Van Raalt contacts Barney about a story he is doing on a police raid of a gambling den. He says that his wife and Valdez were at the gambling house when it was raided and wants Barney to keep their names out of his story because he is concerned that undue publicity might cause his wife to lose interest in sponsoring Valdez and, if she does, Valdez could murder her. Genevieve does become disinterested in Valdez's recital but not because of any publicity about their relationship. She is now enamored with a young pianist named Paul Fedor. When Valdez learns that Mrs. Van Raalt wants the money she invested in the recital returned, he loses all confidence to perform. Meanwhile, Fedor overhears a phone conversation Genevieve has with another of her protégées and becomes concerned. Later that night, someone takes the top string from a viola in the Van Raalt music room and uses it to strangle Genevieve. Blake and police sergeant Toohey question both Fedor and Valdez about the murder. Barney finds that Mrs. Van Raalt was strangled by the A-string from a viola and not by an E-string from a violin as the police thought. He subsequently finds a viola in the Van Raalt music room with an E-string where an A-string should be, meaning that the murderer could not have been a musician and that Mr. Van Raalt is the real culprit in his wife's murder.

Gene O'Donnell broke into acting doing summer stock, and, after military service, he returned to the stage and television. He subsequently appeared on series like *The Lucy Show*, *Gunsmoke*, and *Perry Mason*.

## *Public Prosecutor*
Supposed to have premiered September 1948 on NBC but was delayed until 1951

> Cast of Characters: Mr. Allen (John Howard) – the public prosecutor
> Patricia Kelly (Anne Gwynne) – Allen's secretary

Det. Lieut. (Walter Sande) – police lieutenant who helped Allen
Producer: Jerry Fairbanks

This series explored the workings of a district attorney who, speaking directly to the camera, would discuss a criminal case he was investigating. In the course of the investigation, he would interview likely suspects and at the end ask the audience to decide who perpetrated the crime before revealing the true culprit.

In the pilot episode, "The Case of the Missing Bullets," Allen interviews three suspects for the murder of a police officer. The murder weapon has been found but not the bullets used. Witnesses say that three shots were fired in rapid succession. Willy Spencer, a petty crook, is interrogated first. Spencer confesses that he was near the murder scene but was just taking a walk. Helen Ferris, whose brother had been sent to prison based on testimony from the murdered officer, says she was at the movies when the murder occurred but then admits that she was in the neighborhood around the time of the incident. Mike Costello, a gangster, stole a car which was seen near where the cop was killed. Allen learns that Willy Spencer's fingerprints were on the gun. Willy explains that indeed he and Mike were planning to rob a jewelry store and that he fired warning shots when he saw the cop but says he was using blanks in the gun. After a commercial, Allen reveals what actually happened. He points out that one cannot fire blanks rapidly and thus Willy is the murderer.

Producer Fairbanks filmed twenty-six episodes each twenty minutes in length. NBC attempted to obtain a sponsor for the series in 1948 but its asking price for potential advertisers was deemed too high and so the producer shelved the series.[29] At one point in 1949, NBC and Motorola were in negotiations for the company to sponsor the program as a replacement for *Believe It or Not*, but those talks never came to fruition.

Beginning in February, 1951, episodes of *Public Prosecutor*, edited to fifteen minutes in length, aired in syndication. Subsequently, DuMont showed the series starting on September 6, 1951 Thursdays at 9:30 pm under the title *Crawford Mystery Theater*. Crawford Clothes sponsored the show. To make each episode run thirty minutes, the format was changed to that of a type of quiz program with detective-fiction writers and celebrities guessing the perpetrator, before the actual culprit was revealed. Warren Hull hosted the series. On the first episode aired, the panel was made up of actress Glenda Farrell, ventriloquist Doug Anderson, and actor John Derek.

## *Stand By for Crime*
Premiered January 11, 1949 on ABC Saturday 9:30 pm; ran until August 27, 1949

   Cast: Inspector Webb (Boris Aplon) – the lead investigative detective
   Producer/director: Greg Garrison
   Writers: Nancy Goodwin, Jane Ashman

A fifteen-minute version of this series aired live from Chicago on January 11, 1949 as part of a demonstration of the new coaxial cable linking New York and the Windy City at the time. Playwright Marc Connelly introduced the episode from New York. The series had aired on the local ABC Chicago affiliate beginning in late 1948.

*Stand By for Crime* told a murder story in flashbacks with Inspector Webb describing the clues to the perpetrator but not the identity of the murderer which was left to the viewers to guess whodunit. In the debut show, Connelly had to guess the murderer.

Boris Aplon, who played the Inspector, left the series in April 1949. According to producer Greg Garrison, Aplon, a radio actor, had great difficulty remembering his lines. Since the actor got worse every week, Garrison fired him.[30]

After being off the air for several weeks in April, the series returned on May 7 with Myron "Mike" Wallace as Lt. Anthony Kidd and George Cisar as Sgt. Kramer. The premiere show with Mike Wallace (later to become a legend in TV news) involved a murder done through an Indian poison injected into the victim by a scratch from a cigarette lighter.

## *Martin Kane, Private Eye*
Premiered September 1, 1949 on NBC Thursday 10:00 pm; ran until June 17, 1954

   Cast: Martin Kane (William Gargan) – the two-fisted, wisecracking private investigator
   Happy McMann (Walter Kinsella) – a former cop and the proprietor of the tobacco shop where Kane hung out
   Sponsor: United Tobacco

Based on the radio series also starring Gargan that debuted three weeks before the television show, each episode started with a silhouette of the Kane character lighting a pipe as a plug for the series sponsor. The initial episode of the television program, written by Frank Wilson and directed by Edward Sutherland, had the detective helping a friend's son who is accused of murder by a blackmailer and his girlfriend who had wooed the boy. Kane romances the girl and exposes her as the real killer to clear the young man.

In another early episode, Kane investigates the disappearance of a lawyer who last visited with three sisters – Sara, Agnes, and Lydia, living in an old house bequeathed to them by their father. Agnes is severely mentally disturbed; the other sisters seem to be simply "eccentric." The lawyer had informed the sisters that because their trust fund has been depleted, he has to mortgage their house and now they are facing foreclosure. When Kane goes to the house accompanied by Capt. Burke (Frank Thomas) and Sgt. Ross (Nicholas Saunders), they find the lawyer dead in the basement. Lydia says that Agnes killed him, but the autopsy shows he was poisoned before being knifed. Kane discerns that Lydia actually poisoned the man in order to collect on his life insurance policy which the sister's father had taken out on the attorney with the sisters as beneficiaries.

Referring to the series, Gargan reflected that:

> ... Very soon in the game, I realized our stories were nothing to rave about. How much well plotted story line and genuine character development can you accomplish in a half-hour? So I made the program a showcase for me. After all, that was what we were selling – Martin Kane. I developed a tongue-in-cheek style, a spoof of the hard-boiled detective, a way of silently saying "Don't blame me for the lousy stories, I didn't write them. And anyway, what's the difference? Relax"[31]

William Gargan left the show in 1951 and was replaced by actor Lloyd Nolan. Nolan stayed for one season. Beginning in 1952, Lee Tracy appeared as Kane. Mark Stevens then played Kane during its final network season, 1953-54. In 1957, a syndicated version of the series appeared titled *The New Adventures of Martin Kane* with William Gargan reprising his role, but this time his character was based in London.

## Chicagoland Mystery Players
Premiered September 18, 1949 on DuMont Sunday 8:00 pm; ran until July 30, 1950

> Cast: Det. Jeffrey Hall (Gordon Urquhart) – a criminologist working on the police force.
> Sgt. Holland (Robert Smith) – his detective partner
> Writers: George Broderick, George Anderson
> Director: Bruno DeSota
> Producer: J.E. Faraghan

This Chicago-based dramatic series initially focused on a criminologist and his partner solving crimes. The series had aired locally in Chicago from 1947 to 1949 sometimes under the title, *The Jeffrey Hall Mystery Theater*.

Examples of stories from the series before it aired on the DuMont network included "The Torch Song" about a cocktail lounge pianist and a torch singer each suspected of murder and "The Adventures of the Incriminating Manuscript" concerning a dead man's manuscript that reveals three motives for his murder, three suspects, and a blackmail plot.

The premiere presentation on Chicago's WGN on September 22, 1948 did not get off to an auspicious start. Aired live, one actor, whose character had just been knocked out, got up and nonchalantly walked off the set unaware that he was still on camera. Later, the same actor, whose head was heavily bandaged, went into a flashback, and, when the scene changed to the present, his head was without bandages.

Beginning in June 1949, the *Chicago Tribune* began sponsoring the series with the solutions to the crimes printed in that newspaper the day after each episode aired.

When the program began broadcasting on the network, the first episode dealt with the case of a circus trapeze artist who is murdered by someone who sawed through his equipment. A special needs girl provides the testimony that identifies that a clown committed the crime. The solution to the crime on the network episodes was provided at the end of each installment by the Jeffrey Hall character.

Another early network episode titled "Fool There Was" dealt with a young man and girl who attempt a robbery. The girl persuades the man to rob an elderly pawnbroker. During the robbery, he murders the old man. Frightened and bewildered, the two go into hiding but are found by Det. Hall and his partner.

In March 1950, the format of the series changed from an ongoing crime drama story line to a dramatic anthology series and the word "mystery" was dropped from the title. The series simply was called *The Chicagoland Players*.

After the series ended, Gordon Urquhart wrote screenplays for B-pictures like *Female Jungle* (1956) and *The Brain Eaters* (1958).

## *Photocrime*

Premiered September 28, 1949 on ABC Wednesday 8:30 pm; ran until December 14, 1949

> Cast: Hannibal Cobb (Chuck Webster) – police inspector
> Producer: Murray Burnett for Mildred Fenton Productions

Produced in association with *Look* magazine, the debut of this program involved a female free-lance investigator played by Diana Douglas. She receives some information about a big-time crime boss and attempts to sell it to a mayoral candidate. Inspector Cobb investigates when the woman's informant is shot. He sends the woman's fiancé (Lyle Sudrow) out with papers that the gangster wants as bait to trap the criminal.

The *Look* feature "Photocrime" appeared in most issues of the magazine during the 1940s. It presented pictures and brief text of a fictional crime that readers were challenged to solve. The solution to each crime was printed in the back of the magazine.

For example, one "Photocrime" feature titled "The Jewel Robbery" was about a divorcee who loved jewelry and planned to wear her most expensive gems to an afternoon tea and later to a dress ball. However, a masked man steals her jewels. Hannibal Cobb is brought in to solve the crime. Cobb discovers that the divorcee planned the theft with her chauffeur since she needed the insurance money to cover her gambling losses.

The television series did not last as long at the magazine feature. It ended after thirteen weeks because of failure to find a sponsor. However, its star, Chuck Webster continued to act on episodic television during the 1950s and 1960s with roles in series like *Highway Patrol*, *Bat Masterson*, and *Perry Mason*.

## The Front Page

Premiered September 29, 1949 on CBS Thursday at 8:00 pm; ran until January 26, 1950.

> Cast: Walter Burns (John Daly) – the editor of the *Center City Examiner*
> Hildy Johnson (Mark Roberts) – Burns' friend and reporter
> Producer: Donald Davis for World Video
> Director: Franklin Heller
> Writer: Alvin Sapinsley

From the classic play by Ben Hecht and Charles MacArthur, this half-hour program presented stories about a small-town newspaper editor and his star reporter. The series had a brief run on ABC radio from May 6, 1949 until September 16 of that year with actor Dick Powell as Hildy Johnson and William Conrad (later to play Frank Cannon on TV) as editor Walter Burns.

The first episode of the television program dealt with an assassination attempt on the life of the Mayor (Cliff Hall) of Center City. Assuming that the assassin would repeat his plan to kill the mayor, Burns and Johnson come up with a plan to let the killer shoot at the mayor again and then capture him.

Primarily a newsman, John Daly is better known for having hosted the game show, *What's My Line?* for several years. Mark Roberts had a long career as an actor appearing on such shows as *Dan August*, *The FBI*, and *The Bold and the Beautiful*.

## The Plainclothes Man

Premiered October 5, 1949 on DuMont Wednesday at 9:00 pm; ran until September 19, 1954

(Although many sources indicate that this series premiered on October 12, 1949, the *Brooklyn Daily Eagle* lists the series as premiering on October 5, 1949 with an episode titled "Wally Hudson." Also, *Variety* dated October 12, 1949 includes a review of the series. Since a review would not have been published on the same day the series premiered, a safe assumption seems to be that indeed *The Plainclothes Man* debuted on October 5.)

Cast of Characters: The Lieutenant (Ken Lynch) – the unnamed head of police investigations
Sgt. Brady (Jack Orrison) - the lieutenant's assistant
Producer: John Clark
Directors: William Marceau, Charles Harrell, Larry White
Writer: Len Finger

Seen from the viewpoint of the New York City lieutenant in charge of homicide investigations with the television camera acting as his eyes, each installment of this series would begin with an off-screen narrator saying: "Hero without uniform. Unknown, unsung, but always on guard, protecting you against crime. Now see another criminal brought to justice through the eyes of the plainclothes man." On screen, viewers would see an overhead shot of a desk with a gun and a badge with hands examining the gun and placing it into a holster. The hands then pick up the badge, show it to the camera and then put it down. As director Larry White remarked about the show, "If he (the Lieutenant) got something in his eye we made the camera blink by flicking it on and off. If he got hit, we would spin the camera up, and quickly out and into focus, or the guy would just wobble the camera."[32]

The series would also film certain complicated sequences and then insert them into the live broadcast in order to heighten the action.

In the premiere titled, "Wally Hudson," a young underworld operator (Bob Readich) is persuaded by his greedy girlfriend (Sally Gracie) into becoming a full-fledged gangster. He undertakes a number of robberies and murders on his way to the big money until he is trapped by the police. In reviewing the episode, *Variety* indicated that, "Directionwise, the production made telling use of extreme close-ups –nervous hands, a stolen pin atop the photo of the dead moll, fingers turning a revolver barrel, etc. There was a sharp contrast between close-ups of the detective's shoes on his desk followed by the feet of a victim on a morgue slab. Shots, besides giving the tale impact, overcame the limitation of studio space."[33]

An episode airing December 21, 1949 concerned a beachcomber who steals a valuable gem in the East Indies to use as bait in buying his way back to the United States. Conflict to gain possession of the gem ensues among the original thief, the ship's captain and his wife, and a cockney galley boy. In the end, the jewel is found to be paste.

## Man against Crime
Premiered October 7, 1949 on CBS Friday at 8:30 pm; ran until July 1954.

> Cast of Characters:  Mike Barnett (Ralph Bellamy) – the private eye
> Pat Barnett (Robert Preston) – Mike's brother who filled in for him during summer 1951 when Ralph Bellamy was on vacation
> Producer/Director: Paul Nickell
> Creator/Writer: Lawrence Klee
> Sponsor: R.J. Reynolds

This half-hour series featured the exploits of a tough private investigator who put "his brain and often his brawn against the underworld." The program moved from CBS to NBC and DuMont in October 1953 and was simulcast on both of those networks. Ralph Bellamy was one of the first movie stars to venture into television with his own series.

On the first episode of *Man against Crime*, Barnett becomes involved in solving the murder of a woman who has given him the key to her hotel room. He finds that a ventriloquist, who is in love with his dummy, is the killer and that the money he stole from the woman is inside the dummy.

*Man against Crime* started out as a live production. Bellamy was starring in the Broadway play *Detective Story* when *Man against Crime* premiered. The starting time of the play was delayed twenty minutes until 9:00 pm so that a police escort could rush Bellamy from the television studio to the theater.[34]

The program went to film in October 1952. An August 7, 1953 filmed episode, "Hide and Seek," had Barnett hired by a law firm to find a woman named Julie Matthews, a model, who owes department stores after making purchases but failing to pay for them. Barnett finds that Matthews used to work for racketeer Danny Martin, but now is missing. The police think that she committed suicide since her personal affects were found on the George Washington Bridge. However, Matthews' former roommate, Gloria, a friend of Barnett's, says that Julie left behind a Chinese music box that may contain some clues as to her disappearance. From a pawn ticket found in the box, Mike retrieves a camera with film that contains incriminating evidence of Martin's dishonest bookkeeping. Mike and Martin get into a fight. Suddenly, Julie reappears and shoots Martin.

An episode late in the series run airing March 17, 1954 and written by De Witt Copp concerned UFO sightings. Mike Barnett and journalist Ed Butler investigate a reported sighting of an unidentified flying object.

Ralph Bellamy and Gloria McGhee in a scene from *Man Against Crime*.

They find that two men – Phil Rice (Phil Lipson) and Tom Gorman (Jim Boles) were attempting to prank a professor into thinking he witnessed a UFO.

The filmed episodes of the series were syndicated under the title *Follow that Man* since R.J. Reynolds held the rights to the series original title.

*Man against Crime* was resurrected by NBC during the summer 1956 for a brief run. Frank Lovejoy played Mike Barnett during that incarnation of the series.

## *Mysteries of Chinatown*

Premiered December 4, 1949 on ABC Sunday 9:30 pm; ran until October 23, 1950

> Cast: Dr. Yat Fu (Robert Bice) – amateur sleuth and owner of a herb and curio shop in San Francisco
> Ah Toy (Marya Marco) – Yat Fu's ward who sometimes helps him solve crimes
> Yee Wai (Wong Artarne) - Ah Toy's love interest who spends a lot of time sycophantically trying to learn investigative techniques from Yat Fu
> Lt. Lear (Edmund MacDonald) – Yat Fu's contact at the police department
> Producer/writer: Ray Buffum
> Director: Richard Goggin

Each episode of the adventures of this Charlie-Chan-like detective began with a title card stylized with a dragon design stating "American Broadcasting Company Presents," followed by the series title. Viewers see the shadowy figure of a man walking up to a door where he is interrupted by a piece of paper bearing the show's title being pinned to the door by a thrown knife.

In an episode airing December 28, 1949, Yat Fu receives a phone call from Spencer Sung (Spencer Chan) saying he is being threatened and wants to meet with Fu. While on the phone, Sung is shot by an intruder who snatches a piece of paper from Sung's office and leaves. Sung published a magazine that was in the business to receive money not to print stories. Fu goes to Sung's office where he finds powder burns on the victim. Rubbing a pencil over a blank page of the notebook on Sung's desk, he sees the imprint of a message reading to call Shanghai 8448 at 10:00 pm. Fu calls Lt. Lear (Edmund MacDonald) to report the murder.

As 10:00 pm approaches, Fu calls the phone number and finds that the person on the other end is Chin Ahn (Philip Ahn), a disreputable lower-class figure who had married the beautiful and wealthy Chin Meng (Mari Young). Yat Fu, accompanied by Ah Toy, questions Chin Ahn at his home about his involvement in a blackmail scheme with the murder victim. As Fu leaves the premises with Ah Toy, he is shot by an unknown assailant who kidnaps Ah Toy. Later the kidnapper contacts Yat Fu to tell him to abandon the Sung case if he wants no harm to come to Ah Toy. Fu returns to the Chin residence to pressure Chin Ahn into revealing whether he hired someone to kill Sung. Ahn confesses that he did hire a hit man to murder Sung who was blackmailing him because he knew Ahn was a bigamist. Ahn advises Fu where the hit man and Ah Toy are. Fu arrives at the location, apprehends the killer, and frees Ah Toy.

Actor Marvin Miller (*The Millionaire*) is often credited with portraying Dr. Yat Fu, but that appears to be incorrect. Long-time TV actor Robert Bice played the character.

## *TV Detective*
Premiered December 2, 1949 on NBC Friday 9:30 pm; ran until January 6, 1950 in New York

> Cast: Detective Steve Black (unknown) – private detective who investigated criminal cases
> Director: Carl Degen
> Producer: Vance Hallack

*TV Detective* incorporated elements from *The Plainclothes Man* in its use of the television camera as well as from *Armchair Detective* in incorporating a viewer participation concept. The series presented mysteries with the TV camera serving as the "eyes" of fictional Detective Steve Black who was never seen. The camera registered all the clues in solving the mystery. At the end of each episode, viewers were told who the culprit was and the guest sleuths attempted to solve the case.

"Death Scores a T, K, O" was the premiere episode in which Det. Black is contacted by fight manager Toby Slade who is working with boxer Billy Dykes for an upcoming fight. Racketeer Vinnie Cooper wants Billy to throw the fight in favor of a boxer Cooper is grooming for a title bout. The racketeer is trying to distract Billy by having an ex-show girl, Kitty Dean, hook up with the fighter and have him ignore training. Dean's boyfriend, Duke Diamond, one of Cooper's henchmen, is jealous of the arrangement.

Black meets with Cooper to tell him to lay off Toby which Cooper refuses to do. Black informs Toby of this. When Billy and Kitty return to the apartment that Billy shares with Toby, he and Toby get into an argument over Kitty, and Billy punches him. Later, when Steve goes to Toby's apartment, he finds Billy there and Toby dead from a blow to the right side of his head. Black questions Billy, who says he just found the body upon entering the apartment. Black also questions Vinnie Cooper, Kitty Dean, and Duke Diamond at Cooper's office and then tells the viewers he knows who killed Toby.

On a "secret" microphone so the guest sleuths don't hear, the announcer informs viewers that Cooper killed Toby based on the following clues that the TV audience could discern if they had followed the story closely enough – Cooper was the only left-handed character in the mystery and Toby was killed with a blow to the right side of his skull, a pen lying by the phone in Toby's apartment matched a pen Cooper wrote with in his office, a cigar wrapper was found lying near Toby's body and Cooper was the only character who smoked cigars, and when Black was questioning Cooper he didn't mention where Toby was killed yet Cooper said, "What makes you think any of us were up in Toby Slade's apartment. . .?" The announcer then asks each guest whom they thought was the murderer.

The series was to alternate with NBC's *The Big Story* on Friday nights, but it ended in New York City on January 6, 1950. However, in other TV markets the program appears to have aired until March 1950. Those airings may have simply been repeats of the New York episodes.

## *The Cases of Eddie Drake*
Supposed to have premiered on CBS or in syndication during 1949, but did not premiere until 1951

> Cast of Characters: Eddie Drake (Don Haggerty) – private detective working in New York City
> Dr. Karen Gayle (Patricia Morrison) – psychiatrist to whom Drake related his investigations

Dr. Joan Wright (Lynne Roberts) – criminologist who took over for Dr. Gayle in the final four episodes
Lieutenant Walsh (Theodore Van Eltz) – the police detective whom Drake helps to solve cases
Writer: Jason James
Director: Paul Garrison
Producers: IMPPRO (Independent Motion Picture Producers Releasing Organization) - Herb Strock, Harlan Thompson, and Paul Garrison

Like the series *Public Prosecutor*, *The Cases of Eddie Drake* was filmed in the late 40s (from September 1948 to January 1949) but didn't premiere until the early fifties. The series concept was that Drake would periodically stop by a psychiatrist's office to relate his cases to her for a book she was writing on criminal psychology.

The program was adapted from a 1945 to 1947 radio program called *The Cases of Mr. Ace* starring George Raft. Eddie Drake always drove a fancy car. For example, on the episode, "Shoot the Works," Drake drove a 1948 three-wheeled D-2 Divan car.

In the opening episode titled "The Brass Key," Dr. Gale arranges for Drake to meet with her weekly to relate his cases. A Frenchman, Pierre Fore hires Drake to hold a key for him. He confesses that he just killed a lawyer named Frederick Miller because Miller would not stay away from his wife Sally. Fore thinks he will not have to serve time for the killing, but says, if he does, to give the key to Hogan, his attorney who will be defending him. A man steals the key from Drake. Drake follows the man to a locker which explodes when the man inserts the key. Drake learns from Det. Walsh that Fore has killed himself in his cell. Drake visits Fore's wife and finds $50,000 in her possession along with an envelope that contains a letter. He learns that Hogan actually killed Frederick Miller because Miller knew that Hogan was not really a lawyer. Hogan had paid Fore $50,000 for the Frenchman to confess to the murder, but Fore also insisted that Hogan write out a confession which was in the envelope. Hogan also murdered Fore while he was in jail. In the end, Det. Walsh shoots Hogan before the latter has a chance to kill Drake.

In an episode titled "Shoot the Works," Drake is hired by a woman who was at a gambling establishment when it was robbed and a man was killed. Her watch was stolen, and she wants Drake to retrieve it before her husband returns from a business trip. The club's owner meets Drake at a penny arcade. He is of little help with the case and wants Drake to find a peep show girl with whom he says he is infatuated. Later, a bartender Drake knows helps him arrange to get the watch back, but the robber doesn't show up at the appointed time. Instead, the peep show girl is found murdered. Back at his office, the robber appears advising Drake that he didn't kill anyone during the robbery. A sniper then shoots the robber through the window of Drake's office. Lt. Walsh arrives at Drake's office telling him that the man who was killed during the robbery was a private eye. Drake invites both the club's owner and the woman whose watch was stolen to his office. He accuses the owner of arranging the robbery and killing the peep-show girl, who was the robber's girlfriend, after the robber had turned over the stolen money to the owner but not the jewelry which he gave to his girlfriend. The owner also shot the robber. The woman whose watch was stolen actually killed the private eye at the club during the heist since he had been hired by her husband to keep an eye on her.

After nine episodes were made, Patricia Morrison left the series for a role in the Broadway show *Kiss Me, Kate*. Four other episodes were produced with actress Lynne Roberts playing the doctor to whom Drake related his stories.

When CBS was not able to sell the series in syndication, the producers attempted to offer movie theaters the episodes as part of a double bill. Beginning in 1951, the program was sold into syndication. It finally aired in 1952 in New York City on the local DuMont station.

# Continuing Character Family and Romantic Dramas

ANOTHER STAPLE OF NIGHTTIME television since its beginning has been soap operas or "continuing dramas." The earliest of such programs are highlighted in this chapter.

### *Faraway Hill*
Premiered October 2, 1946 on DuMont Wednesday at 9:00 pm; ran until December 19, 1946

> Cast of Characters: Karen St. John (Flora Campbell) – the young widow
> Charlie White (Mel Brandt) – the man with whom Karen falls in love and the adopted son of her rural cousins
> Louise Willow (Ann Stell) – the Willow family daughter to whom White has been promised
> Mrs. Willow (Lorene Scott) – Louise's mother
> Mr. Willow (Frederic Meyer) – Louise's father
> Jud Clark (Melville Galliar)
> Writer/Creator/Director: David P. Lewis

A young woman, newly widowed, moves to the country to visit relatives and falls in love with a man already promised to another in this first prime-time soap opera.

Creator David Lewis worked for the Caples Company, a travel agency serving railroad and resort clients. The company wanted to experiment with television as an advertising medium, and so Lewis devised *Faraway Hill* to determine the types of series that make good television.

On the debut episode, Karen St. John leaves New York City after her husband's death to visit her cousin's country estate in Kansas. She finds that the Willow's family house is not quite what she thought it would be. For example, it had outside plumbing. However, she becomes attracted to Charlie White, a young man who has been adopted by the Willow's and who Louise Willow intends to marry.

The series used an "all-seeing voice" to bridge gaps in the action and to permit viewers to be able to turn away from the screen while still being able to follow the story. As an example,

Louise Willow: "Dad didn't mention it when he wrote because he said you had your own dead to bury; and besides, he was afraid you might not come if you knew how Mother was and he wanted you to come."

Karen: "I almost feel . . ."

Louise: "Oh, please don't feel that way, we really wanted you. I just wanted to warn you about Mother. She's all right, only the war and Buddy are two things we never mention at Faraway Hill!"

(A musical interlude fades to the voice)

The Voice: "Turn back, turn back, Karen St. John! Something inside you is sounding a warning: This is no place for you! What you are seeking is surcease of trouble, not sharing the wearisome burdens of others. Where is the country estate you were dreaming of? How can you stay? You must leave in the morning . . . you cannot stay a summer!"[35]

*Faraway Hill* was done live in the cramped John Wanamaker-DuMont Studio in New York. Other production details related to this series included the use of "special effects." After Karen arrives in Kansas by train, to show the locomotive leaving the station, the program used recorded sound of a train and waved a pillow in front of the floor lights causing a series of shadows to simulate sunlight being cut-off by the motion of the moving train. A painted farmhouse backdrop and a dolly-in sequence were used to give locale and added motion as well as for a transitional sequence.

After ten episodes, the series ended. "When it was clear that the tenth episode would be the last, writer-producer Lewis matter-of-factly wrote the death of Karen St. John. There was a savage outcry from the show's four hundred fans . . ."[36]

Flora Campbell who played Karen St. John continued acting on television, in the movies, and on Broadway for a number of years. Her final television appearance was on the daytime drama *Love Is a Many Splendored Thing* in 1969. Mel Brandt, the love interest on the series, later became an announcer for NBC uttering the famous phrase "The following program is brought to you in living color on NBC" from 1962 to 1975.

## *A Woman to Remember*
Premiered May 2, 1949 on DuMont Monday through Friday at 7:30 pm; ran until July 15, 1949

> Cast: Christine Baker (Patricia Wheel) – star of the radio soap opera and engaged to Steve Hammond
> Steve Hammond (John Raby) – director of the soap opera
> Charley Anderson (Frankie Thomas) – the sound man for the radio series
> Bessie Thatcher (Ruth McDevitt) – actress on the soap opera and a friend of Christine's
> Carol Winstead (Joan Catlin) – Christine's scheming rival
> Writer: John Haggart
> Producer/director: Bob Steele

This continuing drama about the cast of a radio soap opera was performed live from an actual radio studio. The series had originally premiered in the daytime on February 21, 1949. On the initial prime-time episode, conflicts arise in the company of actors due to the director's replacement of one of the cast with a newcomer detested by the other actors.

The star of the series, Patricia Wheel, subsequently appeared on programs like *The Guiding Light*, *Naked City*, and *The Adams Chronicles*.

Frankie Thomas, who starred as the sound man on the show, was the son of actors Mona and Frank Thomas. Mona Thomas became a featured actress on *Woman to Remember*. In her memoirs, she recalled working on the program, "There was no special place for rehearsals. Any vacant room or office served. We had no makeup man and the actresses dressed in the ladies' room. The studio was postage-stamp size and the sets were so close together that you had to curtail your movements so that the camera, in following you, did not suddenly show you in the kitchen when you were supposed to be in the living room."[37]

Patricia Wheel who played Christine Baker in the DuMont series *A Woman to Remember*.

## The O'Neills
Premiered September 6, 1949 on DuMont Tuesday 9:00 pm; ran until January 10, 1950

> Cast: Peggy O'Neill (Vera Allen) – widowed dress designer with two children
> Janice O'Neill (Janice Gilbert) – Peggy's daughter
> Eddie O'Neill (Oliver Thorndike) – Peggy's son
> Uncle Bill (Ian Martin)
> Mrs. Trudy Bailey (Jane West) – neighbor
> Morris Levy (Ben Fishbein) – family friend who was a hardware dealer
> Trudy Levy (Celia Budkin) – Morris' wife
> Producer: Ed Wolf Associates
> Script Supervisors: Rubin and Jane West

Based on a popular radio serial that began on June 11, 1934 and ran until June 18, 1943, this thirty-minute weekly series told the story of a single mother attempting to raise her two children. A real-life Irish-American family was the inspiration for the radio serial. Producer Ed Wolf lived next door to the family in Far Rockaway, NY, and the family matriarch related her stories to him.[38] Janice Gilbert, who played the daughter on the TV series, was Wolf's real-life daughter.

On the first episode, Peggy O'Neill is fired from her job as a dress designer because she talked back to her boss. Mrs. Levy is having a birthday party. For a gift, Peggy makes her a gown that she designed herself. Her ex-boss sees the creation, likes it, and rehires her.

In addition to *The O'Neills*, Ed Wolf also produced other early television shows like *Break the Bank*, *American Minstrels of 1949*, and *Talent Jackpot*.

## One Man's Family
Premiered November 4, 1949 on NBC Friday at 8:00 pm; ran until June 21, 1952

> Original Cast of Characters: Henry Barbour (Bert Lytell) – a banker and father of five
> Fanny Barbour (Marjorie Gateson) – Henry's wife who was more liberal in dealing with her children than was her husband

Paul Barbour (Russell Thorson) – the oldest son who had served in World War II as a pilot and to whom his siblings turned for advice

Hazel Barbour (Lillian Schaaf) – the oldest daughter who was looking to marry

Claudia Barbour (Nancy Franklin) – a student at Stanford University who had a twin brother

Cliff Barbour (Billy Idelson, James Lee, Frank Thomas Jr.) –Claudia's twin brother also a student at Stanford

Jack Barbour (Arthur Cassell) – at ten years of age, the youngest sibling

Writer/creator/producer: Carlton E. Morse

Director: Clark Jones

*One Man's Family* focused on a large San Francisco family headed by a conservative father. The original radio series was one of the longest-running in history, premiering April 29, 1932 on three stations on the West coast. In 1933, the show was broadcast by the full NBC network becoming the first West coast show to be heard in the East. Changing from a thirty-minute format to a fifteen-minute series in 1950, *One Man's Family* ended on radio in 1959.

Carlton E. Morse, who created the series, started out in radio writing mysteries but decided that listeners were getting their fill of that genre and so elected to tell the story of life as it was to average Americans, well, at least, to upper-middle class Americans.

On the television premiere, Paul introduces the family to viewers and narrates the episode. Family secrets are revealed. Ten-year-old Jack is a member of a secret boys' society of women haters. Cliff and Claudia attend a party hosted by Johnny Roberts. In his parents' absence, Johnny corners Claudia and tries to kiss her. She reaches into a display cabinet and grabs a gun to scare him. He says it is not loaded. Claudia pulls the trigger, and the gun discharges causing Johnny to be moderately injured. Paul rescues Cliff and Claudia and keeps their secret about attending the party and Claudia's secret about the shooting. From the morning paper, Henry learns about the incident and takes Claudia and Cliff to his study. Fanny defends Jack's right to keep his friends' secret about where his society meets. The mother also covers for Hazel who is too tired to come to breakfast. The family saga continues. (Summary from Carlton E. Morse script)

From 1954 to 1955, the series aired on daytime television.

# Westerns

**WESTERNS ARE A RARE SIGHT** on television nowadays, but such was not always the case. In the late 1950s and early 1960s, Western dramas were at the peak of their popularity. Two Westerns premiered in the late 1940s. Although only one – *The Lone Ranger* – aired original episodes for television. The initial presentations of *Hopalong Cassidy* were edited versions of movies that William Boyd had made in the 30s and 40s.

## *Hopalong Cassidy*
Premiered June 24, 1949 on NBC Friday 8:00 pm; ran until December 23, 1951 and in first-run syndication until 1953

> Cast: Hopalong Cassidy (William Boyd) – cowboy hero dressed all in black whose horse was named "Topper"

The first *Hopalong Cassidy* film was produced in 1935 for Paramount Pictures starring Boyd along with a young actor named Jimmy Ellison. Simply titled *Hopalong Cassidy*, Bill Cassidy returns to the Bar 20 Ranch and becomes involved in a conflict over cattle grazing and water rights between the ranch and the neighboring Meeker family spread. Cassidy is made line foreman of the Bar 20. Rustlers intervene between the two ranches to cause trouble with each ranch owner thinking the other is responsible. Despite Cassidy's warning, Johnny Nelson (Ellison) goes to a party at the Meeker ranch and is blamed for the death of one of Meeker's cowpunchers. Cassidy rescues Johnny from a hanging party but is shot in the leg and is nicknamed "Hopalong." Cassidy figures out that the rustlers are behind the problems, tracks them down, and has a shoot-out with them. He discovers that Meeker's foreman headed the rustlers unbeknownst to the Meeker family.

The first Hopalong Cassidy movie to appear on TV was *Twilight on the Trail* made in 1942 and aired on the local NBC station in New York in 1948. William Boyd starred along with Andy Clyde as his sidekick California and Brad King playing Johnny Nelson. The Jimmy Wakely Trio provided musical interludes during the movie including the song "Twilight on the Trail." The plot was similar to the very first Cassidy film with Hopalong, California, and Johnny Nelson fighting rustlers. Jim Brent (Jack Rockwell) hires the three to find out who is stealing his cattle. Hopalong, California, and Nelson pose as private detectives dressed as dandies from the East with Boyd using a British accent. Eventually, the real identity of the three is revealed. Between songs and shootouts with the rustlers, Cassidy finds that the foreman at Brent's ranch is behind the rustling.

Commenting on the Cassidy movies when they first appeared on the local NBC station in New York, *Variety* noted that "Wide sweeping chase scenes have been almost entirely eliminated with most of the actors confined to scenes that can be viewed without eyestrain on the standard small-sized video screen."[39]

Due to the popularity of the movies on television, new half-hour episodes made expressly for TV were syndicated to local television stations beginning in 1952. On the syndicated shows, Edgar Buchanan as Red Connors appeared as Hopalong's sidekick.

## *The Lone Ranger*
Premiered September 15, 1949 on ABC Thursday 7:30 pm; ran until September 12, 1957

> Cast: Lone Ranger (Clayton Moore) – the masked hero
> Tonto (Jay Silverheels) – his Indian companion
> Producer: Jack Chertok
> Creator: George W. Trendle and Fran Striker

"A fiery horse with the speed of light, a cloud of dust and a hearty Hi-Yo Silver! The Lone Ranger!
With his faithful Indian companion, Tonto, the daring and resourceful masked rider of the plains led the fight for law and order, in the early western United States. Nowhere in the pages of history can one find a greater champion of justice. Return with us now to those thrilling days

The Lone Ranger (Clayton Moore) and his Native American companion Tonto (Jay Silverheels.

of yesteryear. From out of the past come the thundering hoofbeats of the great horse Silver! The Lone Ranger rides again!"

Such was the opening of this Western series that was first heard on radio in 1933 broadcast on eight stations in Michigan. The program formed the cornerstone of the Mutual Broadcasting System before moving to ABC in 1942.

ABC brought this Western to television in 1949 – the first such show to premiere with made-for-TV episodes. The debut, titled "Enter the Lone Ranger," presented the back story of how the Lone Ranger came to be. Six Texas Rangers, tracking a group of outlaws known as the Cavendish gang, are led into an ambush by a man named Collins. The outlaws think that they have killed all the Rangers, but one, John Reid, survives. Nursed back to health by a friendly Indian named Tonto whom Reid had helped a long time ago, Reid vows to seek vengeance on the gang and preserve law and order. He tells Tonto that he will never shoot to kill anyone, only to wound. Reid dons a mask to protect his identity so that people will still think he is dead.

Before trying to find the Cavendish gang, the Lone Ranger and Tonto go to Wild Horse valley where the Ranger finds a silver-white stallion to become his steed. The two then visit Jim Blaine, a retired Texas Ranger and an old friend of the Ranger's. Blaine agrees to work an abandoned silver mine so that the Lone Ranger can obtain the needed mineral for his silver bullets. Tonto and the Lone Ranger eventually track down the Cavendish gang and capture them with the help of people from a town named Colby.

Clayton Moore played the Lone Ranger in every season of the series except for fifty-two episodes in 1952 when John Hart took over the role.

Actor Dick Jones, who starred on the early TV Western *Buffalo Bill Jr.*, also worked on some of the *Lone Ranger* episodes. According to Jones, "Their whole system was in a station wagon. The front had a camera platform. On the tailgate was a guy with the sound equipment. They would do two shows at once. We would chase one way up a dirt road at Iverson's Ranch. When you'd get to the end, you'd turn around and get on a spotted horse that had been painted with white paint, change hats, and go shootin' the other way for the second film."[40]

# Standard and Pop Music Series 10

THE READER WILL NOTE that in this and succeeding chapters on music series, most premiered in 1948 or after. In 1944, James C. Petrillo, the head of the American Federation of Musicians, prohibited his union members from performing live music on any television program. This prohibition lasted until 1948. Until then, television shows had to use pre-recorded music or else have amateur musicians.

The artists on many of the shows described in this chapter are mostly long forgotten except for one – Perry Como whose singing career in television lasted into the 1990s. Unless otherwise noted below, most of these

Entertainer Arthur Godfrey does a commercial during a special hour-long CBS color telecast in 1951 that was relayed to New York City, Boston, Philadelphia, Baltimore, and Washington D.C. Standing with her back to the camera is actress Faye Emerson.

music variety programs were only a quarter hour in length. At the time, the networks broadcast the early evening news for fifteen minutes, and they needed shows to fill out the remaining quarter hour. Musical series were easy to make any length the networks wanted.

### *The Swift Show*

Premiered April 1, 1948 on NBC Thursday 8:30 pm; ran until August 4, 1949

> Cast: Lanny Ross – tenor/host
> Martha Logan – home economist who provided meal-planning advice in the Swift kitchen
> Sandra Gable – modeled fashions and provided home decorating ideas
> Eileen Barton – singer/actress
> Susan Shaw - actress
> Martha Wright (1949) – soprano/actress
> Dulcy Jordan (1949) - actress
> Max Showalter (1949) – actor/singer
> Ricki Hamilton (1949) - actress
> Frank Fontaine (1949) – comedian/singer
> Writer: Edith Evans
> Director: Tom Hutchinson
> Producer: Lee Cooley

Initially this show combined music with a quiz called the "Eye-Cue Game." Contestants were asked to identify people, places, or events from visual clues. The quiz segment was eventually dropped and the format changed to a variety series with a theme for each episode.

For example, the May 13, 1948 program's theme was a look at musical favorites in the first five decades of the twentieth century featuring the fashions of each decade. For the 1900s, Lanny Ross sings "She's Only a Bird in a Gilded Cage" with the camera showing a woman framed in a circular enclosure decorated with floral designs. The next song, sung by the Swift Trio, salutes the 1910s career girl. For the 1920s, the flapper style is highlighted. One of the featured songs is "Japanese Sandman" about the passage of time. The musical number for the 30s is "Body and Soul" done by a pianist. The commercial break presents Martha Logan in her kitchen showing viewers how to make a ham and asparagus recipe that includes Swift Margarine and a biscuit mixture with the margarine. Back to the musical favorites, for the 1940s, the American glamour girl is highlighted. Lanny Ross performs "Intermezzo." Sandra Gable talks about the "petticoat fever" sweeping the country and introduces a series of petticoats. For the 1950s, Ross prophesies that one of the singing sensations will be Patti Page who appears and performs "You Turn the Tables on Me."

Later in the series evolution, a story line was developed set in Lanny Ross' penthouse apartment, with friends and special guests dropping in to entertain. Lanny's girlfriend was played by Eileen Barton, but subsequently Lanny would go on dates with various girlfriends and have dreams set to music. In March 1949, the story line was dropped altogether and the show became a straight musical variety series.

Lanny Ross, whose main singing career was on radio, hosted only this one television series.

## *Face the Music*
Premiered May 3, 1948 on CBS 7:15 pm Monday and Wednesday; ran until May 19, 1949

>Cast: Johnny Desmond – singer/host
>Shaye Cogan – singer/co-host
>Tony Mottola Trio
>Producer: Ace Ochs
>Director: Ralph Levy

This early evening musical series, that began airing twice a week and then expanded to five nights a week, never aired later than 8:00 pm. Baritone Johnny Desmond and soprano Shaye Cogan were the initial stars of the program with the Tony Mottola Trio (guitar, piano, and base) providing back-up. Johnny Desmond had sung with the Bob Crosby, Gene Krupa, and Glenn Miller bands before appearing on *Face the Music*.

Pop and standard songs were presented with Cogan and Desmond performing solo and as a duet. In fall 1948 to add "sparkle" to the program, Sandra Deel replaced Cogan, and the show was given a new look with different backgrounds reflecting the theme of the particular episode. For example, Latin songs were done against a Mexican backdrop. On

December 13, 1948, both Deel and Desmond were replaced with singer Carol Coleman and the name was changed to *Make Mine Music*.

Tony Mottola continued to appear with his trio on *Make Mine Music*. On an episode from 1949, blonde Carol Coleman opens with "Somebody Loves Me" accompanied by Mottola on electric guitar. After the song, she speaks with Tony about not being able to find the right man and then introduces guest Johnny Thompson who performs "You Walk By." Mottola, his pianist and bass player then do an instrumental number before Carol talks with Thompson about being from a large family in North Carolina. She sings "I Want to Be a Country Girl." Johnny does a medley of "Smile" songs and sings "Love Is Just around the Corner" with Carol to close out the show.

## *Musical Almanac*

Premiered May 10, 1948 on NBC Monday through Thursday between 7:30 and 8:00 pm; ran until April 30, 1949

Cast: Harvey Harding – baritone singer/pianist

The original format of this series appears to have been built around recalling news events of yesteryear and relating them to ballads and other songs popular at the time.

After Harvey Harding left the show, various entertainers appeared such as Ted Steele, Barbara Marshall, Verle Mills, and Roberta Quinlan. In August 1948, the title changed to *Musical Miniatures*.

Harvey Harding passed away in 1958 at the relatively young age of forty-six. Other than hosting *Musical Almanac*, he was featured on Mutual Broadcasting's *Faith in Our Times* radio show for ten years.

## *Broadway Minstrels/ Broadway Jamboree*

Premiered May 10, 1948 on NBC Monday 8:00 pm; ran until July 19, 1948

Cast: Various

Not a lot of details exist about this variety show which had various formats before its run ended. The program began as an all-black show with the gospel group, the Deep River Boys, and tap dancer Derby Wilson. The second show also featured all-black entertainers. Along with the Deep River Boys, jazz vocalist Maxine Sullivan, Tom Fletcher, Theodore Hines, and dancers Carl and Haryette performed.

At the beginning of June, the program's title became *Broadway Jamboree*, with the series presenting both black and white entertainers. The next episodes changed to a hybrid variety and comedy show starring Jack Albertson as a Broadway columnist introducing various acts while attempting to put up with his girlfriend who was seeking a job. Performers on *Broadway Jamboree* included comedian Gus Van and the black quintet, the harmonizing Melodeers.

## *Gabrielle*
Premiered July 13, 1948 on ABC Tuesday and Thursday 7:00 pm; ran until August 12, 1948

Cast: Gabrielle – hostess/singer

Not much is known about this musical program hosted by the French singer with the single name of "Gabrielle." Variously described in show business trade papers as a "French prima donna" or "French/English chanteuse," Ms. Gabrielle, a light soprano whose career was mainly in nightclubs during the 1940s, sang musical numbers in both French and English.

## *Three about Town*
Premiered August 11, 1948 on ABC Wednesday 7:15 pm; ran until October 27, 1948

Cast: Betsi Allison – host/singer
Phyllis Wood - pianist
Bill Harrington - pianist

Advertised as "20 fingers and a voice" or as "two girls and a boy," this show starred vocalist Betsi Allison along with Phyllis Wood and Bill Harrington at the twin pianos. ABC advertised the program thusly, "Aided by two spinet pianos, this talented trio entertains with lively songs and exchanges gay patter about the theatrical world."

## *The Southernaires Quartet*
Premiered September 19, 1948 on ABC Sunday 9:00 pm; ran until November 21, 1948

    Cast: Roy Yeates – lyric tenor
    Lowell Peters – second tenor
    Jay Stone Toney – baritone
    William Edmunson – bass
    Spencer Odom – pianist/arranger

The first network television series to feature people of color as stars of their own show, The Southernaires were a gospel group who also performed other types of music. The group had a lengthy career as radio and concert entertainers before appearing on television. A typical concert presented by The Southernaires would open with spirituals such as "Lord, I Want to be a Christian," followed by traditional songs like "Song of the Volga Boatmen," and then finishing with numbers from well-known composers like Sigmund Romberg.

## *The Ted Steele Show*
Premiered September 29, 1948 on NBC Wednesday and Friday at various times; ran until August 3, 1949

    Cast: Ted Steele – singer/host
    Helen Wood and Michael Rich - dancers
    Nola Day – singer/pianist
    Mardi Bryant – folk singer/guitarist
    Charles Danford - baritone
    The Ted Steele Orchestra
    Producer/director: Ken Redford

Singer/pianist/songwriter Ted Steele had various music programs, both in prime-time and in daytime during the late forties. After a brief stint on NBC in a fifteen-minute series, he moved to DuMont in February 1949 for a thirty-minute show which lasted until July. He then returned to the quarter-hour format on CBS from July to August 1949 evenings at 7:15 pm.

    On a typical half-hour DuMont show, Steele conducted his sixteen-piece orchestra, sang, and introduced stars such as Delora Bueno, who performed Brazilian folk tunes, pop singer Caren Marsh, and comedienne Bibi Osterwald.

On Steele's final show for DuMont on July 12, 1949, he had singer Jerry Wayne substitute for him as host. The show featured Helen Wood and Michael Rich performing a dance to "Lebestraum," the two Marlin Sisters singing "Hurry, Hurry, Hurry," Deanne Munser playing the harp, and clown "Hip" Raymond doing his "one man circus" act.

## *The Earl Wrightson Show*
Premiered November 27, 1948 on ABC Saturday 7:45 pm; ran until February 21, 1952

> Cast: Earl Wrightson – singer/host
> Buddy Weed trio (1948 – 1949)
> Norman Paris Trio and Orchestra (1949-51)

Baritone Earl Wrighston, who specialized in operettas and show tunes, hosted a program of songs starting on ABC, moving to CBS in September 1949 and then back to ABC in August 1951. The series went through a number of title changes from *The Earl Wrightson Show* to *Earl Wrightson at Home* with his move to CBS, and then *At Home* in October 1949, *At Home Show* in September 1950, and finally *Masland at Home Party* in August 1951.

On the premiere of *Earl Wrightson at Home*, the star featured songs from *Carousel* and introduced guest singer Doretta Morrow. The setting for the show was a lush, modern living room reflecting the "at home" theme.

## *Song and Dance*
Premiered December 17, 1948 on NBC Friday 8:00 pm; ran until June 21, 1949

> Cast: Roberta Quinlan – host

*Song and Dance* was a live musical variety series first with singer/pianist Roberta Quinlan as hostess and then in April 1949, Barbara Marshall took over. The team of Ellsworth and Fairchild was featured in dance numbers.

Night club and radio entertainer Roberta Quinlan starred on numerous TV musical shows in the late forties and early fifties. She is best remembered for *The Mohawk Showroom* series described below.

## *Young Broadway*
Premiered December 22, 1948 on NBC Wednesday at 7:30 pm; ran until June 23, 1949

Cast: No regular cast members

Featuring understudies from Broadway shows, this program was initially a live twenty-minute show which allowed NBC to air a ten-minute newsreel after it. The series expanded to thirty minutes in April 1949. Among the entertainers appearing on the show were singers Barbara Marshall and Roberta Quinlan.

## *Chesterfield Super Club*
Premiered December 24, 1948 on NBC Friday 7:00 pm; ran until June 1950

Cast: Perry Como – host and singer
Fontaine Sisters – Bea, Geri, and Marge Rosse
Mitchell Ayers orchestra
Martin Block – announcer
Producer: Doug Rodgers

Popular crooner Perry Como debuted on the quarter-hour *Chesterfield Super Club* on Christmas Eve 1948. After three weeks, the show moved to 11:00 pm, and then in October, 1949, the series became thirty minutes in length and aired on Sunday nights at 8:00.

The initial Christmas Eve show was a simulcast of Como's radio series with the host and guests using scripts and radio microphones. The guests on the first show were the St. Peter's of Alcantra Choir from Port Washington, Long Island. The choir included Perry Como's son Ronnie who sang a duet with his dad.

Less than a year later when the show became a half hour, more guest stars appeared. Como's premiere thirty-minute show on October 16,

1949 with guest Milton Berle was up against Ed Sullivan's *Toast of the Town*. On that show, the Fontaine sisters, dressed in old-fashioned driving dusters and sitting in an old jalopy, sing "Get Out and Get Under," while a grease monkey works underneath the vehicle. The mechanic turns out to be Milton Berle wearing a Texaco overall. Como performs several solo numbers as well as songs with the Fontaine's.

On a November 27, 1949 edition, the guests were singer Patti Page and pianist Victor Borge who gives Como a piano lesson. Como also does a comedy bit based on the hit song at the time, "Mule Train."

After the Chesterfield show ended, Perry Como moved to CBS with a thrice-weekly fifteen- minute series simply called *The Perry Como Show*. In 1955, Mr. Como had a one-hour variety show on NBC on Saturday nights. In 1959, his variety series moved to Wednesdays where it lasted until 1963. After that, Como did periodic variety specials, particularly around Christmas time.

## *Arthur Godfrey and His Friends*

Premiered January 12, 1949 on CBS Wednesday 8:00 pm; ran until June 1957

> Original Cast: Arthur Godfrey – host
> Jeanette Davis - singer
> Bill Lawrence -singer
> The Mariner's Quartet
> Archie Bleyer Orchestra

Radio personality and daytime television star brought his informal manner to prime time in 1949 on this weekly musical variety series – one of two prime-time shows Godfrey hosted on CBS at the same time. The other series was *Arthur Godfrey's Talent Scouts*. Although primarily known as a raconteur and interviewer, Godfrey also sang and played the ukulele. His major hit song was the "Too Fat Polka (She's Too Fat for Me)" in 1947.

His initial variety program was perhaps too easygoing. As *The Billboard* pointed out,

> . . . the show simmers down to one of extraordinary slow pace, leavened by the inimitable Godfrey personality and the various supporting stints. . . . Godfrey himself could aid somewhat by

becoming more mobile himself, or in effecting some further gimmicks. The extent of his activities on opening night was to shed his jacket because of the heat, show photos of his family and stand up for a duet with Miss Davis. During the course of this last, he fondled Miss Davis's string of pearls in a rather interesting manner.[41]

*Arthur Godfrey and His Friends* featured songs from his group of regulars whom he called "little Godfrey's." Everyone on the show knew who the "big Godfrey" was. Sometimes his variety program would feature special episodes with big production numbers.

Over the years, Godfrey did expand his repertory company of singers to include The McGuire Sisters, Marion Marlowe, Carmel Quinn, Julius LaRosa, and Pat Boone. Despite his on-air persona of friendliness and cheerfulness, Godfrey disliked it when any of his regulars seemed to get more attention than he received. He ended up firing his original orchestra leader, Archie Bleyer when Bleyer recorded Godfrey's daytime competition, Don McNeill of *The Breakfast Club*. He also terminated the Mariners, the female singing group The Chordettes, and most notoriously Julius LaRosa whom Godfrey said had lost his "humility." Arthur Godfrey's popularity declined over the years, and after a brief stint as co-host of *Candid Camera* in 1960-61, his TV appearances were limited.

## *Music in Velvet*

Premiered January 16, 1949 on ABC Sunday 9:30 pm; ran until April 17, 1949

> Cast: Johnny Hill – host/singer
> The Velveteers
> Don Lindley Orchestra
> Producer/director: Ed Skotch

Singing and dancing were the highlights of this series with no talking. Credits and song titles were superimposed on camera shots of the orchestra or on the hands of harpists.

Featuring Johnny Hill and the "smooth sounds of The Velveteers," the program began in 1948 on local television in Chicago. On an early show, Hill, a baritone, sang, George Barris displayed his guitar artistry, and the team of Kermit and Gloria performed two numbers – a classical dance and a barefoot Hawaiian number.

ABC brought the series back on July 15, 1951 with a new host, orchestra leader Rex Maupin. This version of the show ran until October 28, 1951.

## *The Skip Farrell Show*
Premiered January 17, 1949 on ABC Monday 9:00 pm; ran until August 28, 1949

>Cast: Skip Farrell – singer/host
>Jack Lester - announcer
>The Honey Dreamers –singing group
>Adele Scott Trio
>Russ Wilt -pianist
>Bill Moss orchestra
>George Barnes Octet – jazz/pop instrumentalists
>Joanelle James - singer

*The Skip Farrell Show* was a music program from Chicago that ABC, in need of inexpensive prime-time programming, picked up for a network run. Charles "Skip" Farrell subsequently became a regular on Tennessee Ernie's Ford's daytime TV show. He died at age forty-three in 1962 from a heart attack.

## *Sing-Co-Pation*
Premiered January 23, 1949 on ABC Sunday 7:45 pm; ran until October 30, 1949

>Cast: Jack Brand – host
>Dolores Marshall
>George Barnes Octet
>Jack Fascinato Trio

This Chicago music program featured singer Dolores Marshall, a soprano. Marshall was billed as the "Harvest Moon Girl" since she had won the annual Chicago Harvest Moon Festival singing competition.

The title of the show changed to *Serenade* in October 1949.

Jack Brand also hosted an infomerical-type show called *Action Autographs*.

## Manhattan Showcase

Premiered February 28, 1949 on CBS Monday, Wednesday, Friday 7:15 pm; ran until June 16, 1949

> Cast: Johnny Downs
> Helen Gallagher
> Tony Mottola Trio
> Producer: Barry Wood

Another early-evening music program featuring young talent, *Manhattan Showcase* occupied various time slots and different days of the week during its three and one-half months on the air. Originally, the show's format consisted of Downs and Gallagher performing an opening number and then they alternated with each doing a solo.

Singer/producer Barry Wood hosted this show when it was called *Places, Please* featuring up-and-coming singers. Helen Gallagher would find more fame playing Maeve Ryan on the ABC daytime drama, *Ryan's Hope*.

Virginia Gorski joined co-host Helen Gallagher in April. Gorski later changed her last name to "Gibson" and played Liza in the motion picture, *Seven Brides for Seven Brothers*. Gorski and Gallagher were both replaced by Evelyn Ward in June right before the series ended.

## Backstage with Barry Wood

Premiered March 1, 1949 on CBS Tuesday 10:00 pm; ran until May 24, 1949

> Cast: Barry Wood – host
> Producer: Barry Wood
> Director: Kingman T. Moore
> Writer: Charles Speer
> Sponsor: Household Finance Corp.

Singer Barry Wood presented young entertainers on this live music show. On the first episode, the dance team of Russell and Aura performed a couple of routines. Blues singer Gigi Durston did a duet with Wood of "My Darling, My Darling" and also performed two solo numbers.

## *Vincent Lopez*
Premiered March 7, 1949 on DuMont Monday, Wednesday, Friday 6:45 pm; ran until June 1950

>Cast: Vincent Lopez – maestro/pianist
>Ray Barr - pianist

Orchestra leader and flamboyant pianist Vincent Lopez began a radio show in the 1920s. He brought his talents to television in the late 1940s on a musical program that had an early evening time slot when it premiered in March 1949 for three nights a week. The show, also known as *Vincent Lopez Speaking*, not only featured music including piano duos with Lopez and Ray Barr but interviews as well. From Lopez's experience on radio, he knew that one piano sounded thin so he decided to make the program ". . . a two-piano show."[42] In May, the series expanded to five nights, and then in July 1949, the show moved to prime-time at 7:30 pm.

Lopez's initial appearance on television was on Ed Sullivan's *The Toast of the Town* with orchestra leader Russ Morgan. "I teamed up with Russ to do 'Twelfth Street Rag.' Ray Block (sic), the musical director of the show conducted while doing a shag and tearing up sheets of music and throwing them into the air. The audience loved it. When we finished, I knew TV was for me."[43] For his first guest on his own program, he invited Russ Morgan to appear.

In addition to the fifteen-minute series, Lopez had a half-hour Saturday evening show beginning in January 1950 on DuMont which ran until July of that year. That program, called *Dinner Date with Vincent Lopez*, included his regular singers, Ann Warren and Lee Russell.

In 1957, Lopez returned to prime-time television with a thirty-minute series on CBS which lasted one month.

## Delora Bueno
Premiered March 10, 1949 on DuMont Thursday 7:00 pm; ran until May 5, 1949

Cast: Delora Bueno – hostess/singer

Singer/pianist Delora Bueno performed songs on her self-titled show that preceded the *Jack Leonard Show*. Bueno billed herself as the "Brazilian from Dubuque" as in Dubuque, Iowa. Her father had come to Iowa to study agriculture, married a woman from the United States, and then returned to Rio De Janeiro when Delora was a young girl. She came back to the States in 1944 appearing in nightclubs and eventually on TV. Bueno sang in eight different languages.

After this series ended, Bueno starred on a themed-variety show called *Flight to Rhythm*. See Chapter 13 for details.

## Jack Leonard
Premiered March 10, 1949 on DuMont Thursday 7:15 pm; ran until May 5, 1949

Cast: Jack Leonard – host and singer
Virginia Oswald
Bob Curtis – pianist

Not to be confused with the rotund comedian Jack E. Leonard, Jack Leonard was one of the most popular vocalists of the 1930s singing with the Tommy Dorsey Orchestra. After he left Tommy Dorsey, he was eventually replaced by Frank Sinatra. Leonard's co-star on his DuMont musical program was Broadway songstress Virginia Oswald.

## The Fred Waring Show
Premiered April 17, 1949 on CBS Sunday 9:00 pm; ran until May 30, 1954

Cast: Fred Waring – host; orchestra leader
The Pennsylvanians – male/female choral group

Fred Waring, born in Tyrone, PA in 1900, formed his first band at the age of seventeen. He was interested in blending instrumental music with vocal harmonies. In 1923, he had his first radio show on a station in Detroit. By 1933, he presided over a CBS radio show sponsored by Old Gold cigarettes. His radio shows were heard on ABC, CBS, and NBC at various times over the next twenty-four years.

In 1949, he began his television program on CBS following Ed Sullivan's *Toast of the Town*. This musical series featured seven soloists and thirty members of The Pennsylvanians choral group. Early shows also had a dance contest. Later iterations of the program had no live studio audience meaning no applause or laughter after performances.

On an October 1950 episode, Waring opens the show conducting his orchestra. The first number performed by The Pennsylvanians is "Big Wide Wonderful World." A production number built around the theme of "Autumn in New York" follows. Various popular songs by members of the Pennsylvanians are performed in groups, duets, and as solo numbers. A salute to minstrel shows is the finale. With the male members of the Pennsylvanians in blackface, Waring describes minstrel shows as "wholesome and entertaining." While wildly inappropriate by today's norms, such displays apparently were deemed "good, clean fun" in the 1950s.

## *The Sonny Kendis Show*

Premiered April 18, 1949 on CBS Monday and Wednesday 7:15 pm; ran until January 6, 1950

    Cast: Sonny Kendis – host/pianist
    Gigi Durston –singer
    Producer: Barry Wood

This live music series started as a twice-a-week show, but by September 1949, CBS began airing it four nights a week. Gigi Durston sang in between the acrobatic piano playing of Kendis. As reviewer Leon Morse described, "His fingers roam across the keys at breakneck speed and he really gives the impression he is doing the impossible at times."[44] Kendis was backed by a bass player and a drummer.

## *Blues by Bargy*
Premiered April 23, 1949 on CBS Saturday 7:45 pm; ran until April 22, 1950

   Cast: Jeanne Bargy – hostess

This music show featured singer/pianist Jeanne Bargy, the daughter of pianist/conductor Roy Bargy. In addition to the Saturday evening program broadcast on the CBS network, Jeanne Bargy also appeared during the work week on WCBS in New York.

   After her TV series ended, Ms. Bargy helped to form the Prince Street Players which specialized in musical versions of children's fairy tales. Bargy composed the music for these presentations.

## *Mohawk Showroom*
Premiered May 2, 1949 NBC Monday through Friday 7:30 pm; ran until November 23, 1951

   Cast: Morton Downey - host
   Carmen Mastren combo
   Roberta Quinlan - hostess
   Harry Clark Trio
   Bob Stanton – announcer
   Sponsor – Mohawk Carpets

Tenor Morton Downey, the father of controversial talk-show host Morton Downey Jr., presided over this program on Mondays, Wednesdays, and Fridays; singer Roberta Quinlan appeared on the Tuesday and Thursday installments. The initial show featured Downey backed by guitarist Carmen Mastren and his group of musicians. Downey sang a variety of songs from popular ballads to novelty numbers. Singer Roberta Quinlan became the sole host of the series in December 1949 when the show was cutback to twice a week – Tuesdays and Thursdays.

   Petite blonde Roberta Quinlan's first hit song was something called "Buffalo Billy." She also recorded the theme from the *Showroom* series – "Especially for You." After the series went off the air, Quinlan spent several years touring and singing with bands. Johnny Carson's *Tonight Show* aired from the same studio as the *Showroom* series. Carson used to joke about walking on Roberta Quinlan's carpets since he moved into Ms. Quinlan's former dressing room. She made a guest appearance on the *Tonight Show* in 1968 to celebrate her and Carson's mutual birthday on October 23. Roberta Quinlan passed away on July 1, 1989.

### *The Cliff Edwards Show*
Premiered May 23, 1949 on CBS Monday/Wednesday/Friday at 7:45 pm; ran until September 19, 1949.

> Cast: Cliff Edwards
> The Tony Mottola Trio
> Edith Parker - singer

This live musical series, previously on the radio, was designed to fill the remainder of the half-hour after the CBS news.

Cliff Edwards, nicknamed "Ukelele Ike" and the voice of Jiminy Cricket in Disney cartoons who introduced "When You Wish upon a Star," hosted the fifteen-minute show with young, brunette singer Ellen Parker and the Tony Mottola trio. As *The New York Times* described Edwards' unique singing style, "It cannot be said that Cliff actually sings a song, being more given to sort of talking his way through a number..."[45]

His way of introducing songs was kind of corny, but then again this was early television. For example, on one show he produced a beat-up king-size cardboard compass and explained that, since the indicator pointed south, it was time to play some "south-of-the-border" music.

Edwards had a special segment during which he asked viewers to send him unusual hats which have a sentimental value. He would then select a hat he had received and tell its story. For instance, on an early show, Edwards put on a jockey cap and told an old race track tale.

### *The Three Flames Show*
Premiered June 13, 1949 on NBC Monday 10:00 pm; ran until August 20, 1949

> Cast: The Three Flames (Tiger Haynes, guitarist; Roy Testamark, pianist; and Bill Pollard, bassist)

One of the first network shows to feature black entertainers as hosts, during its run, the program had guests such as Dizzy Gillespie, Errol Garner, and Dinah Washington. The Three Flames, known for their 1947 recording of the novelty song, "Open the Door, Richard," had a local fifteen-minute daytime show on the NBC station in New York that began in February 1949 and, starting in March, the group starred on a thirty-minute nighttime show on the same station called *The Flame Club*. On an early episode of the local show, the Flames guest stars included vocalist Avon Long, pianist-singer Martha Davis, and trumpeter Hot Lips Page. The Three Flames usually appeared wearing berets on their heads.

## *The Meredith Wilson Show*

Premiered July 31, 1949 on NBC Sunday 8:30 pm; ran until August 21, 1949

> Cast: Meredith Wilson – conductor, musician, monologist
> Norma Zimmer – singer
> Talking People – three men and two women singing group
> Producer/director: Bill Brown
> Writer: Jay Franklin Jones
> Sponsor: General Foods

A half-hour summer replacement music series for *Author Meets the Critics*, on the premiere of *The Meredith Wilson Show*, Wilson repeated a number he had done on his radio show. In an attempt to demystify opera, he introduces four singers in full opera costumes to perform a portion of the quartet from *Rigoletto*. He then has the vocalists sing the material in English and subsequently speak the lines. Saying that in no form can the exact content of an opera be understood, Wilson advises the audience to relax at operas and enjoy the music without hunting for hidden meanings.

His guests on the first show were Alice Pearce, performing some satirical numbers, and Edward Everett Horton, doing an imitation of acting in silent films. The two guests also appeared with Wilson in a sketch where he played the flute.

Later in his career, Meredith Wilson composed the music for *The Music Man* and *The Unsinkable Molly Brown*. Norma Zimmer, the singer on this series, later became the "Champagne Lady" on *The Lawrence Welk Show*.

## *Capitol Capers*

Premiered August 1, 1949 on NBC Monday and Wednesday 7:30 pm; ran until September 7, 1949

Cast: Gene Archer – singer/host
Cliff Instrumental Quartet

*Capitol Capers*, a summer replacement for *Mohawk Showroom*, aired live from NBC's Washington D.C. studios twice a week. Gene Archer's voice has been variously described as both a baritone and a tenor. Mr. Archer spent his entire career with the NBC affiliate in the nation's capital and also worked for the Washington Redskins football team singing the team song, "Hail to the Redskins."

A few days after *Capitol Capers* ended, Archer and company began hosting *Sunday Date* on NBC as described in Chapter 13.

## *Words and Music*

Premiered August 2, 1949 on NBC Tuesday and Thursday at 7:30 pm; ran until September 8, 1949

Cast: Barbara Marshall – singer/host
Jerry Jerome Trio
Producer/director: Duane McKinney

On the first episode of this summer replacement show for *Mohawk Showroom*, Barbara Marshall did most of the quarter hour seated at the piano. Her back-up group, the Jerry Jerome trio, was made up of a clarinetist, an accordion player, and a bass player. The bass player performed a duet with Ms. Marshall.

About Barbara Marshall, the show business trade paper *Variety* in reviewing the August 4, 1949 edition of the program wrote that "She blended ballads, novelty, and show tunes with equal facility and also demonstrated a good TV personality."[46]

*Words and Music* was one of three replacement shows for *Mohawk Showroom* during the summer. The other two were *Capitol Capers* and *Practice Tee*.

## *The Little Revue*
Premiered September 4, 1949 on ABC Sunday 8:30 pm; ran until April 21, 1950

    Cast: Nancy Evans - vocalist
    Dick Larkin
    Bill Sherry - vocalist
    Gloria Van - vocalist
    Billy Johnson
    Nancy Doran and Dick France – dancers
    Bill Weber Marionettes
    Rex Maupin Orchestra
    Producer/ director: Greg Garrison
    Writer: Dan Shuffman

This thirty-minute musical program originated from Chicago and was pure musical entertainment. A review in *The Philadelphia Inquirer* described the show thusly, "It comes from Chicago, where they seem to have mastered the art of presenting smooth, competent programs without a lot of silly chit-chat. This Little Revue has no talking (in) it whatever. A good orchestra offers popular and semi-classical music, there are dancers – ballet and otherwise – and some excellent vocalists."[47]

## *Al Morgan*
Premiered September 5, 1949 on DuMont Monday at 8:30 pm; ran until August 30, 1951

    Cast: Al Morgan - host
    Billy Chandler Trio
    Director: Don Cook

This music show starring singer-pianist Al Morgan first appeared on local Chicago station WGN in April 1949 before being broadcast on DuMont. Basically, Morgan played the piano backed by the Billy Chandler trio and sang for thirty minutes. He occasionally had guest stars or talked with members of the studio audience such as with couples celebrating their wedding anniversary.

    In reviewing an early episode, *Variety* commented that "Morgan knows how to put over a song, his piano gymnastics make lively video fare and he projects good showmanship. But it's too much to expect of any entertainer to effectively sell eight ditties in 30 minutes. . ."[48]

## *Sugar Hill Times*

Premiered September 13, 1949 on CBS at 8:00 pm Tuesday as a one-hour show; ran for a total of five episodes until October 20, 1949.

>  Cast: Willie Bryant – initial host
>  Regulars: The Chocolateers – six female dancers
>  The Jubileers
>  Don Redman orchestra
>  Producer: Barry Wood
>  Director: John Wray

Designed to compete with Milton Berle's *Texaco Star Theatre* on NBC, this musical series had an all-black cast. Originally called *Harlem Jubilee*, CBS found that the title had already been registered, and so it was changed to *Uptown Jubilee* but that name was also rejected because it was similar to an already registered title. The series was finally named *Sugar Hill Times*.

The acts on the first show included comedian Timmy Rogers, the dance team of Colen and Atkins, singer Juanita Hall, singer/musician Louis Armstrong, dancer Jimmy Smith, male dancer Laverne French, and singer Harry Belafonte who performed "Tenderly" and "Alone." Belafonte was so popular on the initial installment that he was signed as a regular on the series. The backdrop for the show was an artist's rendering of Harlem from the air.

The program was reduced from sixty minutes to thirty beginning October 6 when it moved to Thursdays at 8:30 alternating with *Inside U.S.A. with Chevrolet*.


## *Wayne King Show*

Premiered September 29, 1949 on NBC's Midwest Network Thursday at 10:30 pm; ran until June 26, 1952

>  Cast: Wayne King – host and conductor
>  Nancy Evans –female vocalist (left the series in 1951)
>  Harry Hall – male vocalist

The Don Large Chorus
Producer: Ken Craig
Director: Bill Hobin
Writer: Gerry Morrison
Sponsor: Standard Oil of Indiana

Wayne King's big-band orchestra that had been heard on the radio came to television to entertain on this program airing live from Chicago. On the premiere, Wayne King performed his typical compositions, usually waltzes, along with singers Hall and Evans. He opened the show by saying his goal was "to be natural and to please you."[49] The episode ended with the ensemble singing "The Lord's Prayer." As noted in *Variety*, the show included such features as ". . . group dancing, impressionistic camera tricks, and snatches of face-to-face confiding in the viewers. It's a friendly type of program."[50]

An October 27, 1949 installment opened with the chorus singing "24 Hours of Sunshine" with King then priming the audience to enter "the land of dreams." Nancy Evans sings "Come Dance with Me" about dancing with her boyfriend. After a commercial, "the land of dreams" theme continues with King playing "In My Solitude" on his saxophone while Evans looks at a scrapbook photo of her with her beau (Harry Hall). The phone rings, and Nancy and Harry Hall sing "In My Solitude" to each other over the telephone. Next Hall performs a song about the circus. The finale is a big production number of "Frankie and Johnny" with the full chorus and Nancy and Harry as Frankie and Johnny. Frankie shoots Johnnie. Before the jury, she says she didn't realize the gun was loaded. The prosecutor barely gets a chance to make his case before being shot by Frankie. After the number, King says, "Verdict: you be the judge."

## *Cities Service Band of America*

Premiered October 17, 1949 on NBC Monday 9:30 pm; ran until January 9, 1950

Cast: Paul Lavalle – conductor
Ford Bond – announcer
Producer/director: Herbert Swope, Jr.
Sponsor: Cities Service

This simulcast of the NBC radio show featured the forty-eight piece Band of America. An early episode presented the Green and White vocal group - the Cities Service barbershop quartet, and emphasized flexible camera work capturing the musical numbers. On a few episodes, live talent worked several feet behind a miniature stage and cutout scenery with the TV camera shooting at a certain height and distance to give the illusion that the talent was actually on a full-size set.

On an episode the day after Christmas in 1949, a ballet dancer and a group of soldiers performed "Parade of the Wooden Soldiers" accompanied by the band. A flamenco dancer did a Spanish number.

## *Paul Whiteman's Revue*
Premiered November 6, 1949 on ABC Sunday at 7:00 pm; ran until March 30, 1952

> Cast: Paul Whiteman - host and conductor
> Enchanters Quintet - four male singers and one female
> Producers: Tony Stanford, Ward Byron, Richard Eckler
> Director: William H. Brown, Jr.
> Writer: George Faulkner
> Choreographer: Valerie Bettis
> Sponsor: Goodyear Rubber

The fifty-piece Paul Whiteman orchestra was featured on this half-hour musical show. Whiteman had two different shows in prime time during the late forties - this variety program and a talent show called *Teen Time*.

The first episode guest starred Eddie Albert, Allyn McLerie, and Charles Laughton. Albert and McLerie perform "Old Fashioned Walk" from their Broadway musical *Miss Liberty* and actor Charles Laughton does a reading from Thomas Wolfe on the glories of October. Two big production numbers are - "Valencia" and "Harp Fantasy." Junie Keegan from Whitman's other series *Teen Time* also sings.

A July 2, 1950 installment presented a salute to George M. Cohan with Earl Wrightson, Junie Keegan, and guest star Lisa Kirk.

During his heyday in the 1920s and 30s, Paul Whiteman was known as the "King of Jazz" for blending symphonic music with jazz. Although true jazz aficionados would no doubt label Whiteman the "King of Commercial Jazz" given that his music was formally arranged and played by a big band.

## *Strictly for Laughs*

Premiered November 22, 1949 on CBS Tuesday, Wednesday, Friday at 7:00 pm; ran until June 23, 1950

>Cast: The Kirby Stone Quintet
>Director: Leonard Valenta
>Producer: Barry Wood

One might think that a show titled *Strictly for Laughs* would be all comedy, but this series was a live music program with the Kirby Stone Quintet singing compositions with amusing lyrics. Their repertoire consisted of songs like "Come Out of the Hen House, Mister" and "I'll Get Myself a Choo Choo Train (And Go Far, Far Away)." Kirby Stone played the trumpet and often did impressions such as one of Louis Armstrong. Others in the quintet were Art Engler, saxophonist, Michael Gardner, pianist and accordionist, Doc Mandel, bassist, and Eddie Hull on drums.

On April 3, 1950, the series title became *The Kirby Stone Quintet*.

## *Melody, Harmony & Rhythm*

Premiered December 13, 1949 on NBC Tuesday and Thursday 7:30 pm; ran until February 10, 1950

>Cast: Lynne Barrett - singer
>Carol Reed - singer
>Charlie Dobson - singer
>Lorenski and Dula - dancers
>Tony DeSimone Trio

The first network TV show to originate from Philadelphia, this program starred three singers. It was a replacement for the Morton Downey and Roberta Quinlan show.

After *Melody, Harmony & Rhythm* left NBC, singer Lynne Barrett continued to entertain on different musical series on local Philadelphia television in the 50s. She performed on *The Girl Next Door*, *The Couple Next Door* with Charlie Dobson, and on the *Tooner Schooner Party* with Mr. Dobson.

# Classical and Jazz Music Shows 11

EXCEPT FOR OCCASIONAL SPECIALS on PBS, classical and jazz music programs are virtually nonexistent on television today. Such was not the case in the late 40s.

### NBC Television Concert Hall
Premiered August 29, 1948 on NBC Sunday 7:30 pm; ran until September 26, 1948

This five-week fifteen to thirty-minute series presented ballet and classical music. Not much is known about who performed on this program with one exception. Tenor Felix Knight, who had starred as Tom-Tom in Laurel and Hardy's *Babes in Toyland* and was a member of the Metropolitan Opera apparently made several appearances. The final program in the series presented the "First Piano Quartet," a musical group consisting, obviously, of four pianists.

### Eddie Condon's Floor Show
Premiered January 1, 1949 on NBC Saturday 8:30 pm; ran until September, 1949

> Cast:  Eddie Condon – jazz guitarist and orchestra leader
> Joe Bushkin - pianist
> Billy Butterfield - trumpeter
> Sidney Bechet - saxophonist
> Peewee Russell – clarinetist

Jazz guitarist Eddie Condon who starred on his own NBC show.

Eddie Condon and his orchestra played jazz compositions each week and hosted legends from the world of jazz like Louis Armstrong, Ella Fitzgerald, and Woody Herman on this variety show. The first episode featured drummer Gene Krupa as the special guest.

The program was resurrected by CBS in May 1950 and ran until June 1950. Before NBC aired the series, New York stations WPIX and WNBT had broadcast the show locally in New York City.

Condon's first appearance on television was in the early 1940s when CBS' Worthington Minor walked past Town Hall in New York City where Condon's group was performing. He thought that the group would be ideal for TV. As Condon described in his autobiography, "In a few weeks jazz was the hit of television. We were small enough as a group to be covered by one camera; as each man played his solo improvisation he could be featured in a close-up. The fact that we wore no uniforms, that we lounged, smoked, and whispered instructions even while the music was proceeding, gave action and reality to the scene."[51] However, the FCC limited television airtime during World War II, and so Condon's jazz series did not continue.

## *Adventures in Jazz*
Premiered January 28, 1949 on CBS Friday 8:00 pm; ran until June 24, 1949

>Cast: Fred Robbins – host
>Bill Williams – host

*Adventures on Jazz* was a live half-hour show featuring jazz singers and musicians. New York disc jockey Fred Robbins was the regular host with DJ Bill Williams filling in for him when Robbins left the show for a period of time to fulfill other commitments. The program featured jazz greats such as Duke Ellington, Miles Davis, and Ella Fitzgerald.

A March 4, 1949 program hosted by Bill Williams was somewhat unusual in that it presented a quintet made up of music critics playing a rendition of "Exactly Like You." Their performance was judged by the likes of Bobby Sherwood, Will Bradley, and Joe Thomas.


## *Penthouse Sonata*
Premiered June 19, 1949 on ABC Sunday 8:30 pm; ran until July 17, 1949

>Cast: June Browne – singer/hostess
>The Fine Arts Quartet – Leonard Sorkin (violin), George Sopkin (cello), Sheppard Lehnhoff (viola), and Joseph Stepansky (violin)
>Producer/Director: Ed Skotch

Emanating from Chicago, this thirty-minute program presented light classical music. On an early show, soprano June Browne sang "Let My Song Fill Your Heart" and "O Cease Thy Singing, Maiden Faire." *Variety* described the Fine Arts Quartet as four musicians sitting in fixed positions with grim faces playing such numbers as "Nobody Knows De Trouble I've Seen," "Serenade," "Drink to Me Only with Thine Eyes," and "Andantino."[52] The show business publication indicated that the series would be better on radio than on television.

## U.S. Marine Band

Premiered July 9, 1949 on NBC Saturday 8:00 pm; ran until August 20, 1949

Cast: Major William Santelmann – conductor

The first band of a major service branch to appear on a weekly network television program, the U.S. Marine Band presented summer concerts comprised of classical and popular music as well as marches. The Marine Band is America's oldest continuously active professional musical organization. The band also had a long-running radio series.

## *The Voice of Firestone*

Premiered September 5, 1949 on NBC Monday 8:30 pm; ran until June 1959

Cast: Howard Barlow – orchestra leader
Hugh James – announcer

In March 1948, NBC did a special simulcast of *The Voice of Firestone* radio program over its TV network. The radio version had commenced in the late 1920s. Eighteen months after the special simulcast, this thirty-minute program featuring classical and semi-classical music became a fixture on the network's Monday night line-up until June 1954 at which point the program transferred to ABC for a five-year run. ABC brought the show back in 1962 but it lasted for only one season.

On the premiere episode on NBC, soprano Mary Van Kirk was the guest singing numbers ranging from "Swing Low, Sweet Chariot" and Brahms' "Lullaby" to the theme song from *Samson and Delilah*.

*The Voice of Firestone* always had a small, but loyal audience. Over the years, to attempt to increase its ratings, the show did try to incorporate more popular music into its repertoire. For example, on a 1950 program with guest singer/actress Jeanette MacDonald, in addition to the movie star singing songs from her films, the orchestra performed "California Here I Come" and a medley of songs from Walt Disney's *Snow White*.

The Firestone Tire and Rubber Company was one of the earliest sponsors of television shows beginning in 1944. The tire company sponsored a series of short documentary films on NBC under the title of *Televues* in that year. Ranging in length from ten to fifteen minutes, the films covered subjects such as football and dairy farming. In April 1944, NBC began airing the program in Philadelphia and Schenectady, NY as well as on its New York City station, making *Televues* one of the first network series.

## *Chicago Jazz (aka Sessions)*

Premiered November 26, 1949 on NBC Saturday 8:30 pm; ran until December 31, 1949

Cast: The Tailgate Seven
Connie Russell

Featuring the Art Van Damme Quintet and singer Bette Chapel on the premiere, *Chicago Jazz* was yet another fifteen-minute program originating from the Windy City. Jazz accordionist Art Van Damme had a show called *Sessions with Art Van Damme Quintet* on NBC's Chicago affiliate beginning in August 1949. The quintet consisted of a drummer, bassist, guitarist, and vibraphone player in addition to Van Damme. The program aired four times a week from Tuesday through Friday. NBC decided to broadcast the show nationally beginning in late November. The first broadcast took place on a bare set and was all music – no talking. The premiere closed with the group packing up their instruments and Van Damme packing away his accordion.

After the first national broadcast, another jazz group, The Tailgate Seven along with singer Connie Russell took over the program which was renamed *Chicago Jazz*.

ABC-TV's *Barn Dance* with the singing team of Lulu Belle and Scotty and emcee Jack Stillwell in the center.

# Country and Western Music Shows   12

NOW RELEGATED TO CABLE channels like CMT and to occasional prime-time network specials, country and western music was featured on several late 1940s network programs.

## *America Song*
Premiered April 21, 1948 on NBC Wednesday 8:00 pm; ran until April 25, 1949

>Cast: Paul Arnold – host
>Nellie Fisher and Ray Harrison – dancers
>Producer: Fred Coe
>Director: Ira Skutch

*America Song* was a music series consisting of American folk songs and dances. An "s" was added to the word "song" in its title in 1949.

A typical episode had Arnold singing solos such as *Casey Jones* or *Bluetail Fly* accompanying himself on guitar, or the singer performing while Fisher and Harrison danced, or Arnold vocalizing off screen with the camera focused on the two dancers. Songs were performed in front of photo-mural backdrops or simple sets. Fisher and Harrison would act out the folk song stories in dance.

The weekly budget for the show, as with most television programs at the time, was very small. Arnold received $100 a week, Fisher, $125 since she also choreographed the dance numbers, Harrison got $100 weekly, and $120 was used to cover scenery and props.

## Village Barn

Premiered May 17, 1948 on NBC Monday 9:10 pm; ran until May 29, 1950

Cast: Zebe Carver – emcee (1948)
Dick Thomas and Dick Dudley –emcees (1948-49)
Dick Dudley – emcee (1949)
Bob Stanton – emcee (1949)
Ray Forrest and Rosalie Allen – emcees (1949)

Others who appeared on the program:

Romolo De Spirito – also known as "The Road Agent" or "The Masked Singer"
Piute Pete – singer
Fiddler Leroy "Curly" Fox and his wife, singer Ruby "Texas Ruby" Owens
Pappy Howard and His Tumbleweed Gang
Bill Long and His Ranch Girls
The Dixie Boys
Producer/director: Hal Keith

The first country music variety show on network TV originated from the Village Barn nightclub in Greenwich Village, New York City. In addition to country performers, the program also featured square dancing and an audience participation segment where members took part in activities like hobby horse racing, potato sack racing, and kiddie car racing.

## Hayloft Hoedown

Premiered July 10, 1948 on ABC Saturday 9:30 pm; ran until September 18, 1948

Cast: Elmer Newman – host
Pancake Pete Newman
Jack Day – baritone singer
The Murray Sisters - singers Sophie and Julie Bogdonovich who married Pete and Elmer Newman respectively
Jesse Rogers– singer/guitarist

The Stuff Jumpers
Ranch Square Dancers
The Sleepy Hollow Gang – musicians
Producer: Sid Diskin

This TV version of the country and western radio series, which had started on WFIL radio in 1944, was broadcast from Town Hall in Philadelphia. In addition to the regulars listed above, the show had the mountain music of the Bland Brothers, the tap dancing, black-faced team of Smoky and Henry, the novelty Mexicali singing of Peewee Miller, accordionist Monte Rosci. Early guests included singing instrumentalists the Milo Twins and singer Wesley Tuttle.

## *Kobb's Korner*

Premiered September 22, 1948 on CBS Wednesday 8:00 pm; ran until June 15, 1949

>Cast: Trombonist Stan Fritts and His Korn Kobblers (pianist Marty Gold, bassist Charles Koenig, trumpeter Nels Laakso)
>Maw Shufflebottom (Hope Emerson) – owner of a general store in which the show was set
>Josiebelle (Jo Hurt) – Maw's daughter
>Betty Garde (1949)
>Writer: Charles Speer
>Director: Kingman T. Moore
>Producer: Barry Wood

Live from New York, this series featured the Korn Kobblers – musicians, dressed in vintage 1910 clothes, who played, other than their regular instruments, items like whiskey jugs, ash can lids, washboards, whistles, and sirens. The show was set in Shufflebottom's General Store, U.S.A.

On the debut, Hope Emerson sang "When Pa Was Courtin' Ma" and did various comedy bits, Jo Hurt yodeled, and the dance team of Jimmy Allen and Joan Nobles performed. Stan Frits had the role of Ma's husband.

## Saturday Night Jamboree

Premiered December 4, 1948 on NBC Saturday 8:00 pm; ran until July 2, 1949

>Cast: Elton Britt – host and yodeler
>Chubby Chuck Roe – comic
>Sophrony Garen – lead singer
>Ted Grant – violinist
>Eddie Howard – banjoist
>John Havens – guitarist
>Edwin Smith – accordionist
>Gabe Drake – bassist

*Saturday Night Jamboree* aired live from New York City. In addition to the regulars, the program featured two guest stars per episode. Boyd Heath took over hosting this half-hour country music show when yodeler Elton Britt left after three airings.

The program was canceled after seven months apparently because of inability to find a sponsor.


## ABC Barn Dance

Premiered February 21, 1949 on ABC Monday 8:30 pm; ran until November 14, 1949

>Cast: Hal O'Halloran and Jack Stillwell – emcees

This TV version of radio's country and western series, *National Barn Dance*, was telecast from the Eighth Street Theater in Chicago. On the premiere episode, square dancing opened and closed the show with dance caller John Dolce. Announcer Jack Stillwell was the master of ceremonies presenting husband and wife singing duo Lulu Belle and Scotty (Wiseman); the Sage Riders (instrumental quartet); comic Holly Swanson; and yodelers the DeZurick Sisters also known as the Cackle Sisters. Lulu Belle and Scotty Wiseman wrote the classic ballad "Have I Told You Lately that I Love You?"

## *Sunday at Home*
Premiered July 3, 1949 on NBC Sunday 7:15 pm; ran until July 31, 1949

Cast: Obed ("Dad") Pickard – banjo, guitar, fiddle
Leila ("Mom") Pickard – piano and organ
Obed ("Bub") Pickard, Jr. – singer/guitarist
Charlie Pickard – singer/guitarist
Ruth Pickard Colwell – singer/guitarist/fiddle player
Ann Pickard Rhea - singer
Producer/director: Carroll O'Meara

Country radio and recording artists the Pickard family starred on this quarter-hour musical program broadcast from Hollywood and kinescoped for the East coast. On a set resembling an old-fashioned parlor, the family sang songs and reminisced.

The opening program included folk ballads, standards like "Love's Old Sweet Song" sung in a bluegrass style, a medley of Southern favorites, and hymns.

The family got its start on the *Grand Ol' Opry* show broadcast over WSM radio in the 1920s.

## *The Paul Arnold Show*
Premiered October 24, 1949 on CBS Monday, Wednesday, and Friday 7:15 pm; ran until June 23, 1950

Cast: Paul Arnold – host/singer

Singer/guitarist Paul Arnold, who previously starred on *American Song*, performed country and western tunes on this fifteen-minute program that aired live from New York. In January 1950, the series began broadcasting every weeknight.

After his network shows ended, folk singer Arnold had a series of programs on local radio and television during the 1950s through the early 1980s. In 1951, he sang on *Uncle Sam's Songs* airing on New York's WNEW on Sunday evenings. He did a radio show, *Paul Arnold Sings*, on WINS in 1952 and, in 1956, Arnold had a series from Washington DC called *Footlight Theatre with Paul Arnold*. In 1981, he presented a show on KIEV radio titled *Paul Arnold's America*.

Singer Alan Dale who had his own show on the DuMont network in 1948.

# Themed-Variety Shows 13

WHETHER TAKING PLACE in a specific setting and/or with entertainers playing characters instead of themselves or with an ongoing story line, themed-variety shows were numerous in the early days of television. Several such shows were set in fictional nightclubs supposedly to allow viewers to think they were visiting a swanky club without ever leaving home.

## *Disc Magic/Musical Merry-Go-Round*
Premiered July 25, 1947 on NBC Friday 8:00 pm; ran until March 11, 1949

   Cast: Jack Kilty – singer and disc jockey
   Frederic (Fritz) DeWilde – engineer
   Eve Young – singer
   Producer/director: Edwin S. Mills

Initially *Disc Magic* featured musical comedy star Jack Kilty playing popular records with some live performances from singer Eve Young as an aspiring artist wanting to break into the big time. Guest stars also performed. Kilty played what were called "T-Records," short for "television records." When he placed a blank record on the turntable at his desk and put down the tone arm, the picture dissolved to a 16mm "Soundie," which was a two to three minute musical film – the music videos of their day. After the film ended, the TV picture dissolved back to the blank record. Kilty picked up the tone arm, and the program proceeded. Kilty would often carry on a discussion with Fritz DeWilde in the role of Kilty's radio engineer, and with Eve Young. Comic Ben Dova and dancers Mylo and Tamis guest starred on the first show.

In October 1947, the show's title changed to *Musical Merry-Go-Round* and presented live entertainment exclusively with singer Penny Gerard, comedy bits by Fritz DeWilde, and other guest stars.

Fritz DeWilde was the father of actor Brandon DeWilde. Born Eva Nadauld, Eve Young, who sang with the Benny Goodman orchestra, changed her name again to Karen Chandler in 1952. Her biggest hit song as Karen Chandler was "Hold Me, Thrill Me, Kiss Me."

## *Brill's Playroom*

Premiered January 9, 1948 on DuMont Friday 7:00 pm; ran until May 28, 1948

Cast – Hubert Brill – host

One of the most obscure series on DuMont, *Brill's Playroom* probably represented the height of magician Hubert Brill's career. Very few details about the content of the program are available other than it was a thirty-minute family variety show starring Brill along with guest stars.

Coming from a wealthy family, Brill attended private schools and received a law degree from Yale University. However, his love of magic consumed his life. He went to California in 1937 and was anticipating taking the bar exam when he was offered a job supervising the magic sequences in the Mae West film, *Every Day's a Holiday*. He continued to work mostly behind the scenes in movies as a technical adviser as well as appearing in nightclubs with his magic act. Brill also was hired to investigate casinos and individual gamblers to ensure that they were not cheating at cards. Presumably, his television series featured many card tricks as well as other feats of magic.

## *For Your Pleasure/Girl about Town*

*For Your Pleasure* premiered April 15, 1948 on NBC Thursday at 8:00 pm and ran until September, 1948. *Girl about Town* premiered September 8, 1948 on NBC Wednesday at 8:00 pm and ran until June 1949. *For Your Pleasure* resumed in July 1949 for three months.

Cast: Kyle MacDonnell
Norman Paris Trio – pianist, guitarist, and bassist
Jack and Jill – dancers (April to June 1948)

Both *For Your Pleasure* and *Girl about Town* featured Kyle MacDonnell. As producer/director Ira Skutch, who worked at NBC in New York at the time, tells it:

> One night in 1947 we opened the station early. John Royal wanted us to audition Kyle McDonnell because he had just seen her in *Make Mine Manhattan*. She did two songs. We aired it so Royal could watch her at home. Then we went back to test pattern.
> He liked the audition, and he put her on a show called "For Your Pleasure," and she became the first real television star, which didn't really mean much. Basically, she got some local publicity and local column items, and of course recognition among the people who had television sets.[53]

The original *For Your Pleasure* was a live quarter-hour music series set in a nightclub. *The New York Times* raved about Ms. MacDonnell saying that she was the most "videogenic" young lady on television. The paper went on to note, "With both engaging grace and winning casualness she strolls amid the tables set on the studio floor in simulation of a café."[54]

After *For Your Pleasure* ended, NBC reformatted the show to thirty minutes, titled it *Girl about Town,* and changed the setting from a nightclub to the idea that what viewers were watching was a dress rehearsal for a live show that would air later. Kyle MacDonnell remained the host with the Norman Paris Trio, but Johnny Downs was added as co-host. Downs played MacDonnell's press agent and booked her engagements. Singer Earl Wrightson replaced Downs shortly after the series premiered. Fred Coe produced *Girl about Town* with Ira Skutch as director. Its sponsor was Bates Fabrics. Beginning in April 1949, the show's title changed to *Around the Town.*

On the initial episode of *Girl about Town*, MacDonnell discusses with Downs the plans for her show later in the evening and interviews guests - tennis pro Alice Marble and orchestra leader Russ Morgan. Every so often, her director would indicate when she should burst into song. Special film clips of Ms. MacDonnell taken at various places in New York City showed her talking and singing all around the city.

In July 1949, NBC brought back *For Your Pleasure.* The program was now on Saturday at 8:30 pm for thirty minutes. The Norman Paris trio continued as part of the show. Earl Sheldon conducted the orchestra, and the dancers were Mata and Hari. Special guests on the premiere, directed by Richard Goode, included Jackie Gleason doing a monologue about how, as a kid, he became a member of "Soft Drinks Anonymous" after getting the "milk shakes," Mata and Hari (Ruth Mata and Eugene Hari who were billed as "dance satirists"), performing a Hindu dance ballet, Hazel Shermet singing a novelty composition, "Television's Bad for Love," and singer Donald Richards performing a duet with MacDonnell on "She Didn't Say Yes."

## *At Liberty Club*
Premiered June 25, 1948 on NBC Friday 8:00 pm; ran until September 16, 1948

> Cast: Jacqueline Turner – host
> D'Artega and his combo
> Writer: Sy Frolick
> Producers and Directors: Roger Muir, Franklin Heller

Another music show set in a fictional nightclub, this one was presided over by French chanteuse Jacqueline. She didn't use her last name. The title of the show apparently came from the idea that the program featured "at liberty" (unemployed) talent. The concept was that such entertainers gathered at the club to discuss their show business prospects and display their acts. In July 1948, the series moved to Fridays and was shortened from thirty to fifteen minutes.

In an early episode, Jacqueline presented comedienne Sharon DeVries, who provided a comic rendering of an aria from *Romeo and Juliet*, and baritone Gordon Gaines.

## *You're Invited*
Premiered July 1, 1948 on ABC Wednesday 8:00 pm, ran until September 20, 1948

> Cast: Romo Vincent – host and performer
> Producer/director: Ralph Warren

In a house party setting, various entertainers performed on this informal half-hour series. Singer/comic Romo Vincent met viewers at "the front door of his house" and invited them in to see the show. On an early episode, Vincent opens rehearsing "Sometimes I'm Happy." Myrna Galle performs a ballet routine to a Chopin waltz followed by a routine done by the Turner Twins. A ventriloquist entertained with his two dummies, and Galento & Leonardo did a ballroom dance to "Moonlight Sonata."

*You're Invited* was the only television show rotund entertainer Romo Vincent headlined. He spent the later years of his career playing small parts on TV and in the movies. For instance, he appeared as a mailman on *Here's Lucy*, a desk clerk on *Switch*, and a chef on *The Love Boat*.

## *The Alan Dale Record Shop*
Premiered August 10, 1948 on DuMont Tuesday 7:00 pm; ran until September 1948

> Cast: Alan Dale – host/singer
> Janie Ford - singing partner
> All Greiner - pianist
> Director: James Caddigan
> Writer: Sandy Howard

This fifteen-minute series first appeared in May 1948 on the New York DuMont station before being aired nationally. In reviewing an episode shortly after the show premiered on WABD and before it aired over the DuMont network, *Variety* indicated that ". . . Dale impressed as a nice kid with a good voice. His manner and delivery before the cameras were off-handed, but without the ease given such delivery by more experienced performers. Miss Ford, on the other hand, seemed completely at home."[55]

On the early local show, Dale (real name Aldo Sigismundi) lip synched to his own recordings. He was in his early twenties at the time having been a vocalist for Carmen Cavellaro and then for the George Paxton orchestra. Before hosting his own show, the singer had been a regular on the CBS radio show *Sing It Again*.

In his autobiography, Dale reflected on his experience with his first TV show, "The lights were very hot, and I'll never forget the blue lipstick. My set, of course, was a record shop. I was the 'proprietor.' This setting made it a simple matter for guest stars to drop in to see how their respective records were doing, or, if they were not recording artists, just to browse around.

Because of my low budget, I usually pantomimed a synchronization to my recordings."[56]

Dale also recalled that to increase the profile of his series, DuMont dreamed up a "feud" between him and the network's popular wrestling announcer Dennis James. "Dennis came on my show and insulted me, and I appeared from the wrestling arena, during his show, and threw lines at him. He and I received more mail than anyone else on the network that year."[57]

Guests on this program included Morey Amsterdam, Henny Youngman, Jack Carter and Dale's good friend Buddy Hackett. While DuMont ceased airing the show nationwide in September 1948, the program continued locally in New York until March 1949.

In June 1950, CBS gave Dale another chance at his own series. *The Alan Dale Show* aired at 11:00 pm on Fridays until December 1950, when it was slotted in the early evenings five nights a week. The CBS program ran until January 16, 1951. At about the same time, Dale was also a regular on the TV version of *Sing It Again* which ran until June 1951.

Having gained a reputation as difficult to work with, the remainder of Alan Dale's singing career was spent mainly appearing in nightclubs with a few appearances on television and in one film, Columbia's *Don't Knock the Rock* in 1956.

## *The Gay Nineties Revue*
Premiered August 11, 1948 on ABC Wednesday at 8:00 pm; ran until January 14, 1949

> Cast: Joe Howard – host and songwriter ("I Wonder Who's Kissing Her Now?")
> Lulu Bates - singer
> The Florodora Girls
> Ray Bloch Orchestra

Based on the radio show of the same name which ran on CBS from 1939 to 1944, this thirty-minute variety program was set in an 1890's nightclub. Eighty-one-year-old Joe Howard, who had hosted the radio series, dressed in top hat, tails and with a cane, opened an early show singing "Whistle a Song." Next up, jazz singer Lulu Bates performs followed by Honey Murray who, after her tap dance performance, does a cakewalk with Howard. The Townsmen Quartet, wearing straw hats, harmonize followed by opera soprano Genevieve Rowe singing and doing a duet with Howard, "I Don't Like Your Family." The Three Arnaut's - two guys and their sister – a novelty act, play their violins in unusual positions such as on top of each other's heads as well as two of the brothers playing one violin together. The three then do a number without violins dressed in tail feathers chirping as birds (after all this was early TV). The finale included all of the acts singing various songs.

## Club Seven
Premiered August 12, 1948 on ABC Thursday 8:00 pm; ran until March 17, 1949

>Cast: Johnny Thompson – singer/host
>Bobby Byrne Orchestra

Originally called *Thompson's Talent Show*, this program included young singers, dancers, and acrobats performing in a nightclub setting with diners at tables giving the home audience the idea that they were viewing a floor show consisting mainly of vaudeville acts.

One typical episode had singers Ed, Mack, and Lorraine, vocalist Betsy Reilly whose forte was novelty songs, and monologist Lord Buckley. Lord Buckley was a character created by Richard Myrle Buckley that combined an exaggerated aristocratic bearing with rhythmic hipster language. For example, Lord Buckley would say "Hipsters, flipsters, and finger-poppin' daddies: knock me your lobes" instead of "Friends, Romans, countrymen, lend me your ears."

*Club Seven* left the air in March 1949 but returned in September 1950 with singer Tony Bavaar as the host and aired Monday through Friday at 7:00 pm. The show ranged in length from ten to thirty minutes depending on how long the evening news program, which shared its time period, lasted. This version of the series ended in September 1951.

## Crystal Room
Premiered August 15, 1948 on ABC Sunday 8:30 pm; ran until September 12, 1948

>Cast: Maggi McNellis – emcee

Set in an imaginary nightclub, this series featured dinner club acts of the time including comics and singers. Comedian Willie Shore, singer Fifi D'Orsay performing "Oh Johnny," balladeer Earl Wrightson, and disc jockey Art Ford appeared on the premiere. Performers would be sitting at tables like in a nightclub with McNellis interviewing them before they did their act. Actor/writer/producer Carl Reiner made his first television appearance on this show.

## *Places Please!*
Premiered August 16, 1948 on CBS Monday, Wednesday and Friday 7:15 pm; ran until February 25, 1949

>Cast: Barry Wood – host/singer
>Director: Ralph Levy
>Producer: Barry Wood

Young performers from Broadway and nightclubs appeared on this live fifteen-minute music fest to debut their acts on television. The show gave viewers a glimpse of what it was like backstage at a variety show with, for example, cast members limbering up in the background while a vocalist performed a number and while stagehands moved props. Singers like Mary LaRoche and Carlton Carpenter appeared on very early episodes of the program that were broadcast on the local CBS station in New York during July 1948.

Host and producer, Barry Wood started his career as a singer and appeared on radio's *Your Hit Parade*. During World War II, he introduced such songs as "Any Bonds Today?" and "We Did It Before (And We Can Do It Again)." Wood not only hosted musical shows like *Places Please* and *Backstage with Barry Wood* but also produced several series profiled in this book including *Stop Me If You've Heard This One*, *Kobb's Korner*, *Manhattan Showcase*, *Fifty-Fourth Street Revue*, *Sugar Hill Times*, *The Sonny Kendis Show*, and *Strictly for Laughs*. In the 1950s, he produced *Wide Wide World* and *The Bell Telephone Hour*.

## *Fashions on Parade*
Premiered August 20, 1948 on DuMont Friday 8:00 pm; ran until January 7, 1949

Cast: Adelaide Hawley – host/narrator
Producer: Leon Roth, Charles Caplin
Director: Raymond Nelson

*Fashions on Parade* could be described as a variety show built around presentations of the latest in female fashions, or, alternatively, as a fashion show with musical interludes. Either way, the series used "Conover Cover Girl" models to wear current fashions within a story line that included a musical revue with stars from Broadway. For example, one story line concerned the different events associated with a wedding such as a party for bridesmaids in cocktail dresses, the marriage ceremony showing how the attendees were dressed, and the newlywed's hostess gowns. Another episode titled "See America First" was set in different areas of the United States such as Sun Valley, New Orleans, and Hollywood with appropriate fashions displayed.

The fashions were shown as each story line unfolded. Generally, street clothes, sportswear, and cocktail dresses were featured in their own scenes with the grand finale presenting evening gowns.

Adelaide Hawley, who narrated each episode, also picked out the fashions to be worn. Miss Hawley had been a radio commentator on women's issues as well as narrator of MGM's "News of the Day." During each episode, Hawley pointed out fashion trends, accessories for the outfits, prices, and fashion details.

Before and after its run on DuMont, the show aired on local New York stations.

## *Champagne and Orchids*
Premiered September 6, 1948 on DuMont Monday 8:00 pm; ran until January 10, 1949

Cast: Adrienne (Meyerberg) – hostess/ singer
Robert Turner – announcer
David Lippman

Set in a nightclub, Adrienne sang torch songs in English, Spanish, and French during this fifteen-minute show. She usually did at least one number in French like "A Toi Mon Coeur" and would model and describe her gown. Actor Yul Brynner appeared on one show as a guest, and "Gentleman of Song," singer Eric Thorsen, on another.

Adrienne's mother, Margaret Matzenauer was a mezzo-soprano opera star of the Metropolitan Opera; her father Eduardo Ferrari-Fontana was a tenor with the opera. Adrienne herself became famous after appearing in nightclubs across the United States.

## *Captain Billy's Mississippi Music Hall*
Premiered September 17, 1948 on CBS Friday at 8:30 pm; ran until November 26, 1948.

> Cast: Captain Billy Bryant (Ralph Dumke) – emcee
> Betty Brewer –actress
> Johnny Downs – actor, singer, dancer
> Juanita Hall
> George Jason
> Bibi Osterwald
> The Vic Smalley Orchestra
> Writer/Producer: Robert Maxwell
> Producer: Paul Killiam

Originally a local show called *Captain Billy's Show Boat* that had premiered August 16, 1948, this live thirty-minute series was set on a Mississippi show boat. The program had to change its title under threat of court action by Edna Ferber and Oscar Hammerstein II, who claimed exclusive rights to the words "show boat."

The first episode presented a burlesque version of a beleaguered college football team titled "Do or Die for Dear Old Hogwash" with original songs by Melvin Nam Repus. The titles of other shows in the series included "Lillie Lovelorn's Revenge" with Johnny Downs and Virginia Gibson, "The Farmer's Daughter," and "Dora Darling Dilemma."

Ralph Dumke, the host of *Captain Billy's Mississippi Music Hall*, had a long career on episodic television appearing on episodes of *I Love Lucy*, *The George Burns and Gracie Allen Show*, and *The Andy Griffith Show*, among others.

## *Admiral Presents the Five Star Revue - Welcome Aboard*
Premiered October 3, 1948 on NBC Sunday 7:30 pm; ran until February 20, 1949

Cast: Russ Morgan and his Orchestra
Writer/director: Victor McLeod

Orchestra members were dressed in sailor suits for this nautically-themed music variety series. The show opened with a Navy signalman waving flags in time to "Anchors Aweigh." The premiere presentation featured Phil Silvers as the emcee doing, among other things, playing "Stardust" on his clarinet, Dean Martin and Jerry Lewis performing a comedy routine, and the Four Step Brothers dancing.

Vincent Lopez and his band replaced Russ Morgan in November 1948. In December, the title of the program was shortened to *Welcome Aboard* when Admiral no longer sponsored the show.

## *The Dennis James Carnival*

Premiered October 31, 1948 on CBS Sunday 8:30 pm which was its first and last episode

Cast: Dennis James – host
Producer/director: Ralph Levy
Writer: Jay Burton
Sponsor: General Electric

This was the first variety show to be canceled right after its premiere episode. Sportscaster and game show emcee Dennis James, dressed as a carnival barker, hosted this half-hour of novelty acts. The basic premise of the series had James inheriting a carnival left to him by his uncle and struggling to keep it going. Acts on the episode included Leonardo and Zola, fire-eating dancers; knife thrower Victoria Raine; juggler Risko; and magician Dagmar who sawed a girl in half. General Electric canceled the show after its first episode because its executives didn't want to be associated with a program about carnival acts and because of a barrage of protests from Emerson Radio, which sponsored *The Toast of the Town* with Ed Sullivan that followed *Carnival*.[58] The series was replaced by *Riddle Me This*.

## *The Fashion Story*
Premiered November 4, 1948 on ABC Thursday 8:00 pm; ran until March 1949

>Cast: Lucky Marshall (Marilyn Day) – aspiring singer who works as a model
>Julio (Carl Reiner) – fashion photographer
>Head of fashion agency (Dennis Bohan)
>Polly (Pamela O'Neill) – fashion commentator
>Walter Fleicher Trio
>Roger Stearns – pianist
>Producer: John Nasht Associates
>Writer: Rosemary Roth

Somewhat similar to *Fashions on Parade*, *The Fashion Story* was a mixture of fashion show, music, and comedy with an ongoing story line of Lucky Marshall who hoped to, one day, be a success in show business as a singer. She had to contend with her gruff young boss who gave her a hard time. The format provided the Marshall character with many opportunities to display her vocal talent. Many episodes took the form of "rehearsals" for a fashion show which permitted the models to show off various outfits with the description of the material being read off camera. Since the agency had a full-time pianist to play during rehearsals and two male singers – Don Saxon and Hayes Gordon, songs were easily incorporated. Ten manufacturers of men's and women's clothes cooperated in the presentation of the program. Doris Lane, Patsy Davis, Elaine Joyce, and Aina Shields were models on the program.

In one episode, Lucky has gotten a job as a singer at the Penquin Club. Julio and she rehearse a sketch with Lucky singing songs with men's names in the title and Julio acting out the character in the song title. For example, Lucky performs "Danny Boy," and Julio plays "Danny." Models appear for a fashion show put on by Steve Breagan (Hayes Gordon) displaying spring coats and a one-piece travel dress that looks like a suit. In an ongoing story line, Steve is romancing Lucky and gives her a puppy. In response to the gift, Lucky sings "I Didn't Know What Time It Was" followed by "Faraway Places" which introduces a segment on summer fashions and beach wear. At the end of the show, Polly and Julio warn Lucky to take it slow in developing her relationship with Steve. Lucky closes the episode singing "Can't Help Loving That Man of Mine."

Carl Reiner appeared on *Fashion Story* at the same time as he was performing on *Inside USA* which was on CBS immediately following this show. He had to dress in a cab as the taxi took him from *Fashion Story* to the CBS studio for *Inside USA*.

## *The Morey Amsterdam Show*

Premiered December 17, 1948 on CBS Friday 8:30 pm; ran until October 12, 1950

> Cast: Morey Amsterdam – host
> Charlie (Art Carney) – the doorman at the Golden Goose Café
> Lola (Jacqueline Susann) – the cigarette girl at the nightclub
> Johnny Guarnieri Orchestra
> Producer: Irving Mansfield

Comedian Morey Amsterdam hosted a comedy/variety series set in a fictional New York nightclub called "The Golden Goose Cafe." The show first aired on CBS radio beginning on July 10, 1948 and continued to be broadcast on radio until February 15, 1949. The same cast was in both the TV and radio versions but different scripts were used since the shows aired two nights apart.

In a January 1949 review of the program, *The New York Times* remarked that, "Mr. Amsterdam has not been helped very much by his script writers." The paper went on to say that the show "... has been on the routine side and has placed too much of a burden on one person. What his material lacks in substance, Mr. Amsterdam tries to conceal by his flair for mugging but the result too often is awkward." *The Times* did note the work of Art Carney on the series stating that he "has the important gift of knowing when to throw away a line and of keeping his clowning always under control. He should have a bright future in TV," which of course he did particularly as Ed Norton on *The Honeymooners* with Jackie Gleason.[59]

The show moved to the DuMont network on April 21 1949 and was sponsored by DuMont TV sets. Because of intellectual property claims by CBS, the Art Carney character became Newton the waiter and the Jacqueline Susann character became simply Jackie. The nightclub's name changed to the Silver Swan.

Amsterdam and Lou Meltzer were the writers for the DuMont program which Amsterdam produced and David P. Lewis directed.

Don Russell was the announcer. The premiere episode guest starred singer Vic Damone and ballroom dancers Mary Raye and Naldi. Amsterdam opens the show on a faux nightclub set with the orchestra and audience in the background. He sings his signature novelty tune "Yuk-a-Puk' and performs a comedy bit with Carney who does impressions of trees. For example, Art meows like a cat signifying a pussy willow. Jackie exposes her ignorance of baseball in a routine with Morey. Damone sings "So in Love," and Amsterdam does a segment playing his cello and telling jokes.

Morey Amsterdam was a guest on several shows during the early days of television. He later gained fame in the 1960s playing Buddy Sorrell on *The Dick Van Dyke Show*.

Jacqueline Susann, who was married to the producer of *The Morey Amsterdam Show* – Irving Mansfield, later became an author of such books as *Valley of the Dolls*, *The Love Machine*, and *Once Is Not Enough*. Irving Mansfield produced several other TV series in the late 1940s, most notably *Arthur Godfrey's Talent Scouts*, *Stop Me If You've Heard This One*, and *This Is Show Business*.

## Café de Paris
Premiered January 17, 1949 on DuMont Monday, Wednesday, and Friday 7:45 pm, ran until March 4, 1949

    Cast: Sylvie St. Clair – hostess and singer
    Jacques Aubuchon
    Stan Free Trio
    Director: Byron McKinney
    Producer: James Caddigan

*Café de Paris*, a quarter-hour show, was set in a rundown Paris nightclub which St .Clair supposedly had inherited from a relative. Since she had no money to operate the club, St. Clair hired three street musicians, the Stan Free Trio, on a percentage basis and was guaranteed an income from a television contract she signed to air a show from the club for 2000 francs per telecast.

## *School House*
Premiered January 18, 1949 on DuMont Tuesday 9:00 pm; ran until April 19, 1949

>Cast: Kenny Delmar – the teacher
>Writers: Joe Stein and Sidney Resnick

A variety half-hour set within a classroom with the teacher as emcee and the "students" as performers aptly describes this series. Apparently, the concept originated in vaudeville with Gus Edwards' "School Days" routine where a teacher introduced his class of entertainers. In 1948, DuMont had a similar series on its New York station titled *School Days* with Happy Felton as the professor using studio audience members as his students to perform such gags as reading poems they wrote about themselves and volunteering to answer questions by making a barnyard noise.

A typical episode of *School House* presented a cast of "students' who were dancers, jugglers, singers, and comedians. One episode starred comic actor Wally Cox, singer Amy Staley, clarinetist Kenny Bowers, and comedian Arnold Stang. On that installment, Delmar, dressed in a scholarly robe, does a bit as a German professor instructing the class about Richard Wagner with Stang playing Brunhilda from *The Ring of Fire*. Stang also does a routine about the poem, *The Rhyme of the Ancient Mariner*.

## *Hotel Broadway*
Premiered January 20, 1949 on DuMont Thursday at 8:30 pm; ran until March 17, 1949

>Cast: The Striders – bellhops.
>Johnny Desmond – the hotel's night manager
>Producer/director: Harvey Marlowe
>Writer: Bob Rocke

DuMont attempted to replicate the successes of *Toast of the Town* and *Texaco Star Theatre* in a half-hour variety show set in a fictional Broadway hotel. The Striders, a black quartet representing bellhops, introduced each act in song. The group consisted of tenor Eugene Strider, brother, Charles, a baritone, and brother, James, a bass along with Ernest Griffin, a tenor.

The second episode of the series had singer Jerri Blanchard, the dance team of Rose & Rana, and Avon Long, a black singer-dancer. Country and western novelty act, Harry Ranch and his "Kernels of Korn" also performed.

## *Masters of Magic*

Premiered February 16, 1949 on CBS Wednesday 7:45 pm; ran until May 11, 1949

> Cast: Andre Baruch – host
> Producer: Sherman H. Dreyer Productions

An early evening quarter-hour program that was not music, *Masters of Magic*, initially called *Now You See It*, presented various magicians performing their feats of legerdemain. The show was sponsored by the Pioneer Scientific Corporation to sell its "Polaroid Television Filters" which were designed to reduce glare from external light sources on the screen of a television set. Each episode opened with smoke clouding the TV screen out of which the program's title appeared. The host, dressed in a magic costume, would then appear in some type of magical setting such as a Genii's lamp or a sorcerer's crystal ball. Each week would feature a different guest magician who would perform about five of his magic tricks.

## *The Lambs Gambol*

Premiered February 27, 1949 on NBC Sunday 8:30 pm; ran until May 22, 1949

> Cast: No regular cast members
> Johnny McManus Orchestra
> Producer: Herb Leder
> Sponsor: Maxwell House Coffee

Using the resources of New York's all-male Lamb's Club, a theatrical association, different variety and dramatic acts were featured on this program. The Lamb's Club was founded in England in the early 1830s when essayists Charles and Mary Lamb held an open house for writers and actors.

Each year, the Lamb's Club in New York put on a night of entertainment and festivities that became known as the Lamb's Gambol.

Each installment of the TV show opened with a chorus singing:

"We're Lambs – We're Lambs
We're Actors – Singers – Showman
Happy Lambs.
We are here to sing the
Praises of a coffee that's the top
Just try it and you'll find
That it is good to the Last Drop
We're Lambs – We're lambs
Tragedians, Comedians and Hams
We are proud to be the host
To our friends from coast to coast
At the Maxwell House Gambol of the Lambs"

The setting for the series was a facsimile of the Lamb's Club with several males dressed as women to perform female roles. Viewers were told the difference between a "shepherd" – the President of the club and a "collie" – the guy in charge of the show.

On the first episode, Bert Lytell opens the show by presenting many of the most famous members of the group including Gene Tunney, Guy Kibbee, and Otto Kruger. Mac Perrin, Leo Bernache and Jack Wilson, dressed in drag, do a routine with special lyrics to Gilbert and Sullivan music. Comic Bobby Clark performs a scene from the Broadway show *As the Girls Go* playing the husband of the first female president of the United States who has little to do, and so he ends up shaving the White House barber. He later dresses as a manicurist to obtain evidence on a representative from the opposition who wants to get him into a compromising position with the real manicurist in order to embarrass the President, hopefully leading to her resignation. Comedian Jack Tyler does a drunk routine titled "Hitting the Bottle." Females would be featured in future shows as special guest stars.

The second episode of the program has Joan Edwards doing a musical routine dedicated to her uncle Gus Edwards. Otto Kruger performs a "Minuet" sketch. A comedy sketch, "Babes Must Play," features Senator Ed Ford, Jay Jostyn, Ralph Dumke, Jed Prouty, and Jerry Bergen. Joe Verdi does an "Income Tax Expert" skit.

Bert Lytell, who presided over the debut of *The Lambs Gambol*, had a lengthy career in show business initially appearing in silent pictures. In early television, he played the father on *One Man's Family* and hosted the *Philco Television Playhouse* and *Hollywood Screen Test*.

*The Lambs Gambol* ended after General Foods, the maker of Maxwell House Coffee, withdrew its sponsorship.

## *Campus Corner (aka The Quadrangle)*
Premiered March 18, 1949 on CBS Monday and Friday 7:45 pm; ran until April 11, 1949

Cast: Beverly Fite
Producer/director: Ralph Levy

This quarter-hour series featured the vocal talents of Beverly Fite, billed as the "dancing songstress," and other young singers. Set in a college drugstore, the initial episode had a thin story line about a Dean of Women (Claire Granville) loosening up and getting "hep." On the final show, Fite sings "Zing Went the Strings of My Heart." Singer Rudy Whissler performs "Spring Is Near," while Lorna Lynn does "My Baby Just Cares for Me."

Fite was backed by a quartet comprised of tenor Frank Stevens, tenor Burt Taylor, baritone Dean Campbell, and bass Bob Burkhardt. Buzz Davis, who appeared as a student, was the musical director and played piano.

Ms. Fite got her start in show business as a dancer in the original production of *Oklahoma!*. She later appeared on such shows as *School House* and *The Robert Q. Lewis Show*.

## *Rehearsal Call*
Premiered March 20, 1949 on ABC Sunday 9:15 pm; ran until April 24, 1949

Cast: Dee Parker – hostess/singer
Leonard Stanley Trio
Producer: John Pival

The first network show to originate from Detroit, this fifteen-minute songfest was another program that took the viewer behind the scenes of a television variety series showing how a musical production is put together. The crew, including the director and prop men, appeared on the program with singer Dee Parker who previously had performed with the Vaughn Monroe and Jimmy Dorsey orchestras.

## *Benny Rubin Show*
Premiered April 29, 1949 on NBC Friday at 9:00 pm; ran until June 24, 1949

>Cast: Benny Rubin – agent
>Vinnie Monte – nine-year-old office boy who performed Al Jolson impressions
>Mady Sullivan – Benny's secretary
>Charlie Ford – organist
>The Creators – instrumental trio
>The Rex Maupin Orchestra
>Producer: Jerry Rosen
>Director: Larry Schmah, Jr.
>Sponsor: Bonafide Mills

Star Benny Rubin, known for his comedic skill in telling stories using various dialects, played a theatrical agent presenting different acts on this program. On the first episode, the Andrew Twins perform a Spanish dance number, Lou and Lillian Bernard play the harmonicas, and movie actress Edith Fellows sings and participates in a sketch with Jackie Coogan.

On another typical episode, Rubin opens the show talking with his secretary who says that her aunt bought a house of glass but the windows are brick. The family has to stand in front of the windows to change clothes. Benny speaks with Jerry Cooper who was in an auto accident with his Ford car sandwiched between a Plymouth and a Cadillac. He says he now owns a "Plymouthfordalac." Cooper then shows up in person to sing "I'm Just a Prisoner of Love." Also appearing on the show were Benny Baker, doing a comedy routine about "Singing in the Rain" with Rubin spraying him with seltzer, and Thelma Baker, a hillbilly comedienne, singing and accompanying herself with cymbals between her legs. The finale features a square dance number with corny skits and country and western songs. Perhaps the most interesting part of the program was the commercial for Bonny Maid's "enamelized rugs" – rug-sized pieces of linoleum for use in any room.

Benny Rubin had a long show business career. After his NBC show, Rubin starred on *Benny's Place* on WPIX in New York and on an amateur talent contest called *Hold that Curtain* from KLAC in Los Angeles. He may be best remembered for his numerous appearances on Jack Benny's series and specials.

## *Paradise Island*
Premiered April 1949 on twenty-two TV stations; ran for twenty-six weeks

  Cast: Danny O'Neil – host/singer
  Anne Sterling – singer
  Everett Hoagland Orchestra
  Producer: Jerry Fairbanks

This quarter-hour variety series was syndicated to local stations beginning in April 1949. Produced by Jerry Fairbanks Productions and set on a fictional South Sea island, the show was filmed in Mexico City to reduce costs.

On the premiere, O'Neil sings an original song, "Paradise Island" written as the program's theme along with other compositions like "There'll Be Some Changes Made." Sterling vocalizes "Hokus Pokus," and guest Tony Larue plays Brahms "Fifth Hungarian Rhapsody" on the xylophone. Everett Hoagland performs "Cuanto Le Gusto."

The series made frequent use of original songs to minimize the costs for using already published music. In addition to singers, the show included specialty acts like banjo players, pianists, accordionists, mimics, and a variety of dancers.

The successful syndication of this series led producer Fairbanks to consider a syndicated sequel with a Western setting. But that effort never materialized.

## *Flight to Rhythm*
Premiered May 5, 1949 on DuMont Sunday 6:30 pm; ran until September 22, 1949

Cast: Miguelito Vlades – singer and orchestra leader
Delora Bueno – singer

Larry Carr – singer
Nick (Ralph Statley) - bartender
Roberto and Alicia - dancers
Bob Pfeiffer - announcer
Writers: Rhoda Cantor and Larry Menkin
Director: Pat Fay
Producer: Bob Loewi

*Flight to Rhythm*, a serialized musical comedy, was set in a Rio de Janeiro nightclub named Club Rio. A bartender named Nick narrated and hosted each episode which featured the music of different South American countries each week. Miguelito Valdes opened each show singing "Babalu," a song also popularized by actor/musician Desi Arnaz. Singer Larry Carr played an airline pilot who was in love with Delora Bueno.

The series debut focused on the music of Brazil celebrating that country's independence day with Bueno singing the national anthem and Valdes performing a medley of Carmen Miranda tunes. Accompanying herself on guitar, guest star Olga Quelo sings "The Makumba Song" hitting notes that could break crystal. Dancers Roberto and Alicia perform, and Bueno sings "Brazil" and is joined by Valdez in completing the number. Nick performs a song about the popularity of coffee in Brazil which is interrupted by a flower delivery for Bueno from DuMont celebrating the singer being named "good neighbor of the year" for her work on better relations between the Americas. Among the compositions that Bueno and Valdes sing is "Cuban Pete" later made popular by Desi Arnaz.

Another episode highlighted the music of Peru. A segment superimposed an image of Bueno in the lower left of the screen with dancers appearing on the rest of the screen for the number "The Girl Who Came from Peru." Guest Jose Duval performs "Granada," while Valdes and Bueno do a duet in Spanish and then in English to show how translations from the original language are often inadequate. Nick, who is reading a book about mummies, is featured in a dream sequence about actually discovering a Peruvian mummy. This segment is acted out by Roberto and Alicia.

The program aired Sundays at 6:30 pm during the summer but moved to Thursdays at 8:00 pm in August 1949.

## Versa-Tile Varieties
Premiered August 26, 1949 on NBC Friday at 9:00 pm; ran until December 14, 1951

> Cast: George Givot – original host
> Jerry Jerome orchestra
> Writer: Charles Lowe
> Director: Mark Hawley
> Producers: Charlie Basch and Frances Scott
> Sponsor: Bonafide Mills (Anne Francis appeared in Bonny Maid floor coverings commercials)

This series catchphrase was "In TV, it's VT!"since Bonafide Mills made Versa-Tile floor coverings.

On the debut of this thirty-minute variety program set in a nightclub, Three Beaux and a Peep, a vocal ensemble, perform along with juggler Jack Parker on a unicycle. Audrey Palmer does an impressionistic "bat" dance, and the Charles Duo (male and female) entertain with their roller skating act.

After two months, "the Greek ambassador of Good Will," George Givot left and was replaced by comedian Harold Barry as host. On a November 18, 1949 installment, Barry has as his guests Frank Cole Co., the Wallace Brothers, and the Croydens. Guests on an early 1950 program included The Charioteers, Johnny Long and his orchestra, the Carroll sisters, musical novelty duo Fayne and Fosler, and comediennes Kay LeVelle and Netta Parker.

Singer Bob Russell became the host in fall 1950 with the show presenting more new talent instead of already established acts.

The program moved to ABC in September 1951 at 9:30 pm with yet another new host, Lady Iris Mountbatten, the great granddaughter of Queen Victoria, and with a new focus on kids presenting skits and stories. A November 2, 1951 episode with Lady Mountbatten told the story of a young girl from rural America who dreams of Hollywood stardom in an episode titled "From Farm to Fame." In this tale with music and dancing, Mary Worth is the young girl dreaming of being a star. She arrives in Tinsel town to audition for a movie. Mary performs a tap dance routine which the kid director says is "Pretty good. But not good enough for Hollywood." She is then taken under the wing of a kid playing a Latin lover in the movies. Mary goes on to become a hit on Broadway and then star in a movie directed by the same person who originally turned her down. On this note, Iris Mountbatten tells the viewers that *Versa-Tile Varieties* wants to promote similar rags-to-riches achievements and has established a scholarship to do so. During the episode, Ms. Mountbatten introduces various commercials for Versa-Tile including one with two men dressed as medieval fools, "Wear and Tear," who try to damage different kinds of floor tiles. They are successful in leaving black marks from a cigarette on two different brands, but, when the Bonny Maid appears with Versa-Tile, they can't leave even the smallest blemish.

## *Sunday Date*

Premiered September 11, 1949 on NBC Sunday at 7:15 pm; ran until October 9, 1949

>Cast: Gene Archer – host/singer
>Producer: Jack Caldwell
>Director: Jac Heins

A review in the August 31, 1949 issue of *Variety* states that this fifteen-minute music show debuted August 28 on NBC with singer Helen Lee as the hostess.[60] Supposedly, the program was set in a sidewalk café off Central Park featuring young singers and musicians. According to the show business paper, in addition to Helen Lee, who was a former singer with the Jimmy Dorsey and Larry Clinton orchestras, the premiere also featured dancer Shirley Levitt, the four Paulette Sisters, Joe E. Marks doing a rhythm monologue routine, and the Cavalier Trio with Dick Style.

However, *The New York Times* of September 8, 1949 reported that *Sunday Date* starring Gene Archer of *Capitol Capers* fame along with Jeanne Warner and the Cliff Instrumental group would begin on September 11. TV listings in newspapers at the time confirm the premiere date as September 11 and Gene Archer as host of this program. Apparently, Helen Lee hosted this music show for a brief few weeks until Gene Archer took over.

## *Inside U.S.A. with Chevrolet*

Premiered September 29, 1949 on CBS Thursday at 8:30 pm; ran until March 16, 1950

Cast: Peter Lind Hayes
Mary Healy
Mary Wickes
Sheila Bond
Jay Blackton orchestra
Writer: Sam Taylor
Producer: Arthur Schwartz
Director: Sherman Marks

At the time, one of the most expensive shows produced with a weekly budget of $22,000, this program was based on the Broadway musical *Inside U.S.A* and the book with the same title by John Guenther. The every-other-week program focused on the diversity and beauty of America. Peter Lind Hayes played a minstrel guiding viewers to various locales in the United States.

The first episode begins with a simulation of Hayes crossing America in a Chevrolet arriving in various states like Tennessee and California. Hayes along with Lee Goodman and Jim Kirkwood then do a take-off on football coaches wanting to recruit top talent by pretending to be music coaches looking for an all-star trombone player. Other sketches include "The Head of the Family" with guest star Margaret O'Brien, Hayes, and his wife Mary Healy. Singer Marion Colby singing "Tennessee Fish Fry" with Sheila Bond dancing. The finale features the trademark advertising song, "See the U.S.A. in Your Chevrolet." The series aired on a biweekly basis until the beginning of 1950.

The final episode of the program begins with Hayes and his wife talking about their anniversary and singing "That's Love." Next the skit "Forty Winks" features Hayes as an exhausted guest at a Florida hotel being given the Rip Van Winkle Room that had many devices for inducing sleep but which ends up driving Hayes out of the room and onto the golf course. Dancer Sheila Bond performs a number called "The Tale of a Wealthy Widow." Guest star Joan Blondell, as a Mae West-type, appears in a sketch as "Annie Fae West" attempting to drive the new sheriff, Cary Gooper (Hayes) out of town. Mary Healy sings "Green Up Time," and the stars of the show, for a final time, drive off in a Chevrolet.

## Studs' Place

Premiered November 26, 1949 on NBC Saturday 8:45 pm; ran until January 28, 1952

Cast: Studs Terkel – himself
Grace (Beverly Younger) – blonde waitress
Wynn (Win Stracke) – folk-singing handyman who also did some cooking and cleaned up the kitchen
Mr. Lord (Phil Lord)
Mr. Denby (Jonathan Hole)
Chet Roble – jazz pianist

First set at Studs' bar in New York, this quarter-hour series, broadcast from Chicago, presented songs and stories from Studs Terkel and his friends. Terkel played a philosophical bartender with singer Carolyn Gilbert offering vocal selections. After a month on the air, the show became part of a variety/anthology series called *Saturday Square,* on which four or five mini-dramas were presented that all took place in different establishments on the same small square in Chicago. When that series ended, *Studs' Place* returned as a thirty-minute show with Studs as the owner of a Chicago barbecue restaurant.

The premiere presentation on November 26, 1949 features Carolyn Gilbert singing "Blue Moon," "Don't Cry Joe," and "Fools Rush In." Terkel tells stories about gamblers, gives a modern, slang version of the story of *Carmen,* and recites the poem *Winklin', Blinkin', and Nod.* The show was produced by Norman Felton, outlined by Charles Andrews, and directed by Duane Bogle.

A 1950 installment concerned Studs becoming an insufferable snob after attending an opera and his friends disliking the airs he is putting on. He learns a lesson when an opera star, the very British Mr. Seton-Seton, stops by his place for a visit.

Another 1950 episode deals with a father whose wife is expecting their first child. The dad-to-be doesn't want to face the responsibility that fatherhood will bring and is thinking of leaving his wife. He becomes embarrassed when his spouse shows up at Studs' Place, and the regulars throw her an impromptu baby shower. But, the guy is put back on track by Studs and a neighborhood kid pretending to be Studs' son when the two engage in father and son banter about baseball.

The concept of the series was that there would be no scripted dialogue. The story line for each episode was based on a four or five page outline with the cast making up its own lines. Through rehearsals, the actual dialogue would be worked out so that when the episode aired, the cast members pretty much knew what each was going to say. Episodes ended with the credit "Dialogue by the Cast."

Studs Terkel, a life-time liberal activist and voice of working people, is most remembered for his oral history books about World War II (*The Good War*), the Great Depression (*Hard Times*), and tales of working-class Americans (*Working*).

## *Hollywood House*
Premiered December 4, 1949 on ABC Sunday 7:30 pm; ran until March 5, 1950

> Cast: Dick Wesson - bellboy
> Jim Backus –desk clerk
> Gale Robbins
> Billy Worth Trio
> Producer: Joe Bigelow
> Director: George Cahan
> Writers: Joe Bigelow and Ukie Sherin

Another variety series with an underlying theme, the setting for *Hollywood House* was a hotel lobby where entertainers wandered in and performed. The opening theme for the show was "There's a Small Hotel." Dick Wesson played the bellhop at the hotel. Jim Backus joined the series later as the manager. Also performing on later shows were singer Gale Robbins and the Page Cavanaugh Trio. However, early programs in the series featured Alan Mowbrey as the desk clerk, Polly Bergen (then spelled "Burgin") as the singer, and Sara Allgood as the hotel's maid.

A review in the *Long Beach Independent* pointed out, "'Hollywood House' . . . is not so good. The program offers some slapstick in a haphazard sort of way with all the old comedy props or water squirting, head beating, and pratt falls. Chief thing wrong with the show is that it is on TV."[61]

On an early episode, Dick Wesson tries wooing Polly Bergen first by doing impressions of Humphrey Bogart and James Cagney and then by getting advice from Sammy Davis Jr., playing a bellboy from the hotel across the street. Davis does impressions of singers Nat King Cole,

Johnnie Ray, and Vaughn Monroe and then performs a tap dance routine. Later on the show, Mowbrey talks Wesson into impersonating a French entertainer to impress Polly. Wesson sings a romantic song followed by a novelty number of "Frere Jacques" with lyrics from a French restaurant's menu.

Dick Wesson later appeared as a semi-regular on the comedies *The People's Choice* and *The Bob Cummings Show* as well as writing scripts for the latter series and for *The Beverly Hillbillies* and *Petticoat Junction*.

Milton Berle from *Texaco Star Theatre* with guest star Ethel Merman.

# Comedy Variety Series 14

**USUALLY HOSTED BY A STAND-UP** comedian, the shows in this chapter emphasized comedy routines over musical numbers.

## *Texaco Star Theatre*
Premiered June 8, 1948 on NBC Tuesday 8:00 pm; ran until 1953

Cast: Milton Berle – host
Fatso Marco
Sid Stone – announcer
Alan Roth Orchestra

Milton Berle starred on the first episode of this series but didn't become the regular host until September 1948. In the meantime, stars such as Harry Richman, Morey Amsterdam, and Jack Carter performed hosting duties.

On the premiere episode, Berle participates as the "clumsy" member of a tumbling act called the "Moroccans" and tries to understand the double-talking Al Kelly. Pearl Bailey sings "Tired" and "Good Enough for Me," and Senor Wences does his ventriloquist act. Flamenco artists Rosario and Antonio dance to "Capriccio Espagnol" and "Fire Dance." Berle also performs a bit with harmonica player Stan Fisher. Adagio dancers, the Andreas, do a number. The Russ Case Orchestra provided musical backup, and Betty Alexander welcomed the audience.

With Milton Berle as host, *Texaco Star Theatre* was a top-ranked television show in the early days of network television. Berle became known as "Mr. Television." He loved to be the center of attention and, unlike other TV variety hosts like Ed Sullivan, Berle usually participated in the acts of most of his guest stars. He would wear a whistle around his neck in rehearsals and used the device to stop rehearsal several times if he thought something wasn't perfect. "Everybody hated him for it," said writer Jay Burton, "so they had a pool, and they would bet on how many times he would stop the rehearsal. Once, eighty-seven won. Milton stood up and said, 'I had eighty-five.'"[62]

The program always opened with men dressed as service station workers in Texaco uniforms singing:

> "Oh, we're the men of Texaco
> We work from Maine to Mexico
> There's nothing like this Texaco of ours
> Our show tonight is powerful
> We'll wow you with an hourful
> Of howls from a showerful of stars
> We're the merry Texaco Men
> Tonight we may be showmen
> Tomorrow we'll be servicing your cars"

With the quartet ending like this, "And now, ladies and gentlemen – here he is – Mr. Television himself – your Tuesday night _____ – Milton Berle!" The blank was filled in by the quartet with the name of some fictional or historical figure like "Cinderella" or a Roman chariot driver and then Berle would appear in some outlandish costume as that figure to do his opening monologue. His jokes included lines like "Tennis anyone? Well, I've got a new racket." He liked to single out people in the audience with barbs such as "Will you wake up that lady sitting over there?" and read letters supposedly from viewers – "If you're the worst comedian in the world, I'm the Mayor of Cleveland. Signed, the Mayor of Cleveland."

As noted above, Berle liked to become involved in the acts on his show. After a trampoline performance by the Paul and Paulette Trio, Berle, dressed as a theater usher, enters the stage and jumps up on the trampoline, fumbling around, getting up and falling several times. On the same show (January 18, 1949), the comedian does a skit with impressionist Florence Desmond lampooning a Noel Coward play with Berle appearing as Coward. Next, dressed as a Mountie in honor of singer Tony Martin's favorite vocalist Nelson Eddy, Berle and Martin sing a sappy love song together. In the finale, with Carmen Miranda and Tony Martin, Berle appears on stage dressed like Miranda, and the trio sings "Brazil."

A March 22, 1949 installment guest starred actor Keye Luke and singer Ethel Merman. After his opening monologue, Milton Berle introduces three male acrobats known as Los Gottos. Keye Luke and Berle engage in comic banter and do a take-off on how the show would be done in China with Berle and Luke dressed in Oriental costumes as a comedy duo. Next, Ethel Merman performs "I Got Rhythm" as only she could. Subsequently, she and Berle do a duet with the song "Friendship." All during the episode, Milton wipes his brow with a handkerchief apparently affected by the hot lights. After a lengthy comedy bit for Texaco products, black entertainer Tony Hale does a tap dance routine. The finale is a salute to Tin Pan Alley with songwriters Alex Kramer ("Far Away Places"), Charles Tobias ("Don't Sit under the Apple Tree"), Maude Nugent ("Sweet Rosie O'Grady"), and Lew Brown ("The Best Things in Life Are Free"). The show closes with Berle and Merman singing "The Varsity Drag."

A February 28, 1950 episode is another good example of the type of comedy on the show. In a take-off of the movie *Spellbound* called *Smellbound*, about a psychiatrist and his patients, a nurse advises Mr. Hockflaish that after 3965 treatments he is cured. He no longer thinks he is Abraham Lincoln. Mr. Hockflaish turns around, puts on a Napoleon hat and says "I must be off. I don't want to miss the next bus to Waterloo!"

Berle comes in to see the doctor played by Victor Jory. Jory asks him: "What's that scar on your neck?" Berle responds, "Oh that? That's where I had my appendix taken out." Jory replies, "But your appendix should come out of your side – how come they took your appendix out through your neck?" Berle retorts, "I'm so ticklish."[63]

Later in the show, Mr. Berle introduces singer Rudy Vallee as "Mr. Death Vallee." Vallee begins singing, "On the road to Mandalay. Where the flying fishes play," and a dozen fish fall down upon him. He then sings, "Don't know why. There's no sun up in the sky. Stormy weather," and the cast picks up seltzer bottles and sprays him.

After 1953, Texaco dropped sponsorship of the show with Buick picking up the program for a season changing the title to *Buick-Berle Show*. In 1954, the program was simply called *The Milton Berle Show*. That series ended in June 1956 with Berle then guest starring on other shows as well as attempting two comebacks, *Milton Berle Starring in The Kraft Music Hall* from October 1958 to May 1959 and *The Milton Berle Show* on ABC from September 1966 to January 1967.

## Buzzy Wuzzy

Premiered November 10, 1948 on ABC Wednesday 7:30 pm; ran until December 8, 1948

  Cast: Jerry Bergen
  Producer: M-J Productions

This fifteen-minute comedy variety series, sometimes titled *The Jerry Bergen Show*, lasted for a few short weeks. The program featured the comic antics of Jerry Bergen, pint-sized comedian, who specialized in funny pantomimes and routines playing the violin and in double talk. He may be best remembered for his role as Bolo in the Judy Garland/Gene Kelly musical *The Pirate*. *Variety* reported on November 24, 1948 that Bergen was to be replaced by up-and-coming funny lady Imogene Coca. However, apparently the program was canceled before Coca took over.

## The Arrow Show

Premiered November 24, 1948 on NBC Wednesday 8:30 pm; ran until May 19, 1949

  Cast: Phil Silvers - host from November 1948 to March 1949
  Hank Ladd – host from April to May 1949
  Jack Gilford – regular
  Sponsor: Arrow Shirts

On the premiere show hosted by Phil Silvers, the initial skit concerns the show's writers, Larry Marks, Ernie Glucksman, Danny Simon, and Neil "Doc" Simon, being in bondage to Silvers. Another sketch involves Connie Sawyer and young actor Len Hale in a domestic squabble. The Mack Triplets sing some numbers and Herbert Coleman, a young black singer, also performs.

In April 1949, veteran radio comic Hank Ladd took over hosting this series which was then also known as *The Hank Ladd Arrow Show*. On his first show, he does a routine insulting the sound engineers who then cut off his microphone. Ladd also performs a satire of Tennessee Williams' plays. Guest Jackie Gleason satirizes the movie *The Lost Weekend* by doing his routine about a young kid who gets drunk on soft drinks, weaves down Third Avenue in New York, is hit by the DT's and is scared out of his mind by Mickey Mouse. Guest Carol Bruce sings "St. Louis Blues." The series was also known as *Arrow Comedy Theatre*.

## *Alice Pearce Show*
Premiered January 28, 1949 on ABC Friday 9:45 pm; ran until March 4, 1949

    Cast: Alice Pearce – actress/singer/comedienne
    Mark Lawrence – pianist
    Director: John Heaton

Known for playing the original Gladys Kravitz on TV's *Bewitched*, Alice Pearce began her show business career appearing on Broadway in *New Faces of 1943*. This led to the comedienne performing at the Blue Angel nightclub with her accompanist Mark Lawrence who helped to write her material. Pearce would use props such as an old pocketbook for a hat and mangy mink neckpieces in her nightclub performances.

    In 1949, she brought her act to this weekly fifteen-minute TV show. The premiere had Pearce performing many of the satiric comedy routines from her nightclub act including "Wait for the Dial Tone, Nelly" and a new song celebrating network television "I'm in Love with a Coaxial Cable." Mark Lawrence accompanied her on the piano.

## *Jack Carter and Company*
Premiered March 12, 1949 on ABC Saturday 8:30 pm; ran until April 21, 1949

    Cast: Jack Carter – host
    Writers: Mel Diamond, Mark Lawrence, Dick Manny, and Ruth
        Arrons
    Director: Sean Dillon
    Producer: Kenny Lyons for Mildred Fenton Productions

This thirty-minute comedy variety show hosted by comedian Jack Carter featured sketches, monologues, and songs. On the premiere episode, Carter opens with his usual comedy routine, Sonny King sings "Sorrento," and the finale is a skit satirizing operettas.

About the debut, *Variety* gave the show a positive review writing, "This new half-hour vaudeo presentation comes the closest yet to approximating the sparkle and verve of Milton Berle's 'Texaco Star Theatre' and gives comedian Jack Carter his best TV showcaser to date."[64]

In the early days of television, comedian Jack Carter was a very busy entertainer hosting several variety programs. While starring on this ABC series, he also appeared on *American Minstrels of 1949*.

## *The Henry Morgan Show*
Premiered March 28, 1949 on NBC Monday through Friday 7:30 pm; ran until April 15, 1949

Cast: Henry Morgan – host

Probably best-known for appearing as a panelist on many Goodson-Todman game shows, in particular, *I've Got a Secret*, Henry Morgan also had his own radio and television series. His first TV show, *On the Corner*, ran for five weeks on ABC Sundays at 6:30 pm. On the series, Morgan would flip through the pages of *Variety* to find his guests with many of them being little-known singers and novelty acts. During a commercial on the first show, when a young model attempted to demonstrate the features of an Admiral refrigerator, the shield around the refrigerator light came apart leading Morgan to assure viewers that not all of the company's appliances fall apart. Perhaps the ribbing of the sponsor was too much for the firm and that's why the show was canceled after five of a projected thirteen episodes had aired.

Next NBC featured Morgan on both a radio show on Sundays after *The Fred Allen Show* as well as on a five-night-a-week fifteen- minute television program which lasted about a month. A week after the television show premiered, Henry Morgan reduced the number of shows to three a week (Monday, Wednesday, and Friday) citing that the workload was too heavy, with the time for TV production and rehearsals, to have a series on every weeknight.

While the actual format of his thrice-weekly NBC shows is unknown, presumably it was similar to his Sunday radio show which had special guests like Fred Allen and also a cast of regulars – Arnold Stang as his comic foil Gerard, singer Lisa Kirk, and comic actress Patsy Kelly.

An example of Morgan's type of humor is found in a script from his April 10, 1949 radio program where, in his opening monologue, he talks about the circus coming to town, "One of the new attractions this year is a girl doing a tap dance on a high wire. Really, Imagine, even in the circus, they've introduced wire-tapping . . . But I think the act that interested me most was the wild man of Borneo, The way he went around shrieking and tearing his hair and throwing himself on the floor . . . why, I haven't seen anything like that since I lost my last sponsor!"[65]

Morgan did have problems with the network censors on his TV program. For instance, the following was deemed "too suggestive:" "Charlie runs the lighthouse up at Boothbay. I was passing the lighthouse the other day. Charlie was cleaning his wick. Had his wick hanging out the window." The last two sentences were deleted and replaced with "Charlie was at the window waiting for a wreck."[66]

Morgan once said, "What television wants is young, fresh talent – and I 'm gonna stay at it until they find some."[67] After the end of his fifteen-minute TV series, he tried once more with a show of his own. In January, 1951 he came back to NBC with a thirty-minute comedy/variety series called *Henry Morgan's Great Talent Hunt* which started as an offbeat talent contest. By April of that year, the title changed to simply *The Henry Morgan Show*, the talent contest was dropped, and the series became another incarnation of comedy skits and music. It ended at the beginning of June 1951.

## *Cavalcade of Stars*

Premiered June 4, 1949 on DuMont Saturday 9:00 pm; ran until September 26, 1952

    Cast: Jack Carter - host
    Sammy Spear Orchestra
    Don Russell - announcer
    Producer/director: Milton Douglas

In response to big variety shows like *Texaco Star Theatre* and *Toast of the Town*, DuMont put on the *Cavalcade of Stars*, which is probably best-remembered for starring Jackie Gleason beginning in 1950. However, before Gleason, Jack Carter and then Jerry Lester hosted the show.

With Jack Carter as the host, the show blended elements from both the Milton Berle variety series and the Ed Sullivan program. Carter would open a show with a brief comedy monolog and then introduce acts like Sullivan did on *Toast of the Town*. Entertainers ranged from opera singers and ballet stars to dancers, singers, and novelty acts. Like Berle, Jack Carter would appear in at least one comedy sketch with the major guest star on that week's program.

The opening episode had Carter performing his usual comedy monologue and then doing impersonations. After guest star Peter Lorre recites *The Telltale Heart*, he participates in a comedy skit with Carter about a mad doctor. Joan Edwards sings, accompanying herself on the piano, and then does a song about the lot of a wife neglected because her husband watches TV all the time. Carter and Edwards perform a duet of "A You're Adorable." Gene McCarthy and Tommy Farrell present a comedy routine. The three Fontaines do acrobatics and dance, while the Arnauts do their standard bird whistling routine.

About this first episode, producer/director Milton Douglas noted that, "Near the end of the show that first night I sent word back stage that we were running two minutes short. The message got mangled and they thought I was warning that we were going two minutes over. Jack Carter ... and Peter Lorre ... were doing the final sketch when they got the signal to speed up. They breezed through like Whirlaway. We finished *four minutes short!*"[68]

DuMont followed up *Cavalcade of Stars* with a spin-off of sorts called *Cavalcade of Bands* beginning in 1950. That show focused exclusively on music with different big bands each week such as Lawrence Welk, Guy Lombardo, and Duke Ellington. *Cavalcade of Bands* ran until September 1951.

With DuMont's inability to compensate the hosts of *Cavalcade of Stars* with salaries comparable to what other networks could pay them, the series eventually left the air.

### Fireball Fun-For-All
Premiered June 28, 1949 on NBC Tuesday 8:00 pm; ran until October 27, 1949

    Cast: Ole Olsen and Chick Johnson - hosts
    Bill Hayes -singer
    Marty May - actor
    June Johnson (Chick Johnson's daughter)

J.C. Olsen (Ole Olsen's son)
The Buick Belles
Al Goodman Orchestra (June-July)
Charles Sanford Orchestra (July-October)

Hosted by the comedy team of Olsen and Johnson, this variety series was based on their Broadway show *Hellzapoppin'* with fast-paced, slapstick comedy, bad puns, and sight gags using all sorts of gimmicks like things falling from the ceiling, a trap-door used to bring up or drop down comedy acts, exploding pianos, gun shots, etc. Olsen was the straight man; Johnson was at the center of most of the slapstick. He liked to use a revolver to shoot at things. Novelty acts and singers were interspersed among the comedy skits.

Originally a summer replacement for *Texaco Star Theatre*, *Fireball Fun-For-All* returned in fall 1949 at a new time – Thursday 9:00 pm where it lasted for only a few weeks before it was canceled.

A fall episode opens with a marching band, midgets and the performers parading in front of the camera. Olsen and Johnson do a monologue with a variety of sight gags like a man selling oranges for 10 cents apiece, having an accident with a vehicle, and then selling orange juice. Bill Hayes, later to star on *Days of Our Lives*, sings a number about Halloween. The main sketch involves the comedy team running a private detective agency with several quirky cases including looking for jewels and the crooks who stole them in a haunted house. The detective agency's motto was "Don't be swindled by others – come to us." Their secretaries would place letters in envelopes only to then tear up the envelopes because they were replying to anonymous letters. The episode also includes an elaborate production number called "Manhattan Symphony" with singers and dancers, a dog act with canines jumping over one another, and a bicycle acrobatic couple.

## *The Ed Wynn Show*
Premiered October 6, 1949 CBS Thursday 9:00 pm; ran until July 4, 1950

Cast: Ed Wynn
Lud Gluskin orchestra
Producer: Harlan Thompson

Writers: Hal Kanter, Leo Solomon, Seaman Jacobs
Sponsor: Speidel

Vaudeville comedian Ed Wynn, nicknamed "the perfect fool," hosted his own half-hour variety show originating in Hollywood and kinescoped for broadcast to the rest of the country.

On the premiere, Wynn, wearing a small hat and glasses, performs an opening monologue and then introduces guest stars Gertrude Niesen, who does a calypso number, and the acrobatic dance act of Francois and Giselle Szonyi.

Writer Hal Kanter remarked that "Ed was a courtly gentleman of the old school until their backs were turned. Gertrude Niesen was on the first show. He was so courtly to her. Then she got a laugh during rehearsal, and he said to her, 'Please, my dear, don't do that.' Afterwards in his dressing room, he said, 'If that broad tries to f___ me up on the stage that way, tell her I'm going to fart all over her.' He was furious."[69]

On another episode, Wynn jokes that television breaks up homes because he knows of a man who bought a TV set and then never spoke to his wife again since he is always watching television. His wife leaves him, but he doesn't realize it until he sees her on TV wrestling. In sketches, Wynn visits a French café where he meets a cigarette girl who dances the can-can. In the middle of the show, the comedian does a lengthy commercial with a violinist advertising Speidel watch bands. The final sketch is one in a music store where Ed meets Mel Torme who sings "Careless Hands."

A December, 1949 installment had as guests legendary silent film actor Buster Keaton and poker-faced singer Virginia O'Brien. At the beginning of the show, Wynn arrives on a sleigh pulled by four gorgeous women and participates in a sketch set in a hotel about waiting for an elevator. Virginia O'Brien steps off the elevator as a surprise and sings "Only a Bird in a Gilded Cage." Ed Wynn's sketch with Buster Keaton involves no dialogue – each uses cue cards as subtitles to communicate. Set in a grocery store with Ed as the clerk and Buster as the customer, the skit deals with Buster buying some molasses. When asked to pay, Buster indicates that he put his money in the bucket now filled with molasses. Unbeknownst to Keaton, Wynn puts molasses in Buster's hat which he is unable to remove. Keaton then performs a slapstick routine with the sticky liquid.

Later in the 1950s, Ed Wynn starred on his own self-titled situation comedy which lasted one season.

## *The Herb Shriner Show*
Premiered November 7, 1949 on CBS Monday, Tuesday, Thursday, Friday and Saturday 7:55 pm; ran until February 1950

Cast: Herb Shriner
Producer: Robert Mann
Director: Alex Leftwich
Writers: Herb Shriner, Norman Barash, and Carroll Moore

Radio humorist Herb Shriner had a five-minute show most evenings on CBS where he gave folksy monologues about life in his home state of Indiana. The show replaced *Ruthie on the Telephone*. In a review of the program, *The Billboard* indicated that "The comedian sits on a chair and chats about his home town and the people in it. There isn't too much chance to exploit the medium, but given more time Shriner would undoubtedly be entertaining. His comedy is unpretentious and relaxing and he's the kind of guy anybody would invite into his home."[70]

In October 1951, ABC brought Shriner back to nighttime television in a half-hour series that lasted for a single season. A few years later in 1956, CBS featured Shriner on another prime-time program which lasted only half a season.

The stars from the premiere of *Toast of the Town* with Ed Sullivan in 1948. Standing behind Sullivan to the left is Richard Rodgers and Oscar Hammerstein II, to Sullivan's immediate right is Dean Martin, and on the left, with his arms folded, is Jerry Lewis.

# Mixed Comedy, Music & Novelty Variety Shows 15

THE PROGRAMS DESCRIBED in this chapter were true "variety" shows featuring a mixture of musical, comedy, and novelty acts.

## *The World in Your Home*
Premiered December 22, 1944 on NBC Friday 8:45 pm; ran until January 9, 1948

> Cast: No regular cast members
> Producers: John Williams, Paul Alley, and Herbert Graf
> Sponsor: RCA Victor

This weekly fifteen-minute variety-type series featured RCA Victor recording artists, films that Walt Disney made for the Coordinator of Inter-American Affairs, and other types of short films. The show began on the New York NBC station on November 17, 1944 and aired on that network beginning in December. The first network installment presented U.S. Coast Guard Seamen Whitemore and Lowe playing dual pianos performing a Prokofiev prelude and a special arrangement of Strauss waltzes. The episode ended with a Walt Disney film about malaria-carrying mosquitoes.

As *The Billboard* described the opening of this first network presentation, "The show started with WNBT's (now WNBC) new moving station break. It then dissolved to a film of a family sitting around one of the new RCA 18 by 24 receivers on which were the words 'RCA Presents.' Film camera then dollied right into the screen and dissolved to the title *The World in Your Home*. At that point, sound conked out but came back in again with the announcement of artist credits."[71]

## Hour Glass

Premiered May 9, 1946 on NBC Thursday 8:00 pm; ran until March 6, 1947

>Cast: Helen Parrish – emcee
>Eddie Mayehoff – emcee
>Producer: Howard Reilly
>Director: Ed Sobel
>Sponsor: Standard Brands

Considered the first real network variety series, *Hour Glass* presented a mixture of comedy, drama, and music introduced initially by Evelyn Knight. The program opened with a photo of a full hour glass pouring sand and closed with a shot of an empty hour glass.

After a succession of guest hosts, Helen Parrish became the permanent emcee. When she went on maternity leave, comic actor Eddie Mayehoff took over. Guest performers on the series included Edgar Bergen and his dummy Charlie McCarthy, Edward Everett Horton, Joe Besser, and Joey Faye. Although Howard Reilly was originally selected to produce the series, writers Ed Rice and Harry Hermann took over this task with each producing a show every other week. The show eventually had a chorus line of six girls who were hired on a week-to-week basis.

In addition to singer Evelyn Knight lip-synching (because of the Petrillo ban) to recordings of "Grandfather's Clock" and "The Lass with the Delicate Air," the premiere episode of *Hour Glass* included a one-act play "Moonshine" with actors Paul Douglas and James Monks, comedian Joe Besser in a comedy skit about the military called "The Rookie," ballroom dancers, comedian Doodles Weaver with a story about a hungry rabbit, and a film segment about South American dancing. *The Billboard* did not give a glowing review to the debut saying "The production's hourglass was empty before the sand in the actual glass had run out, both literally and talent-wise."[72]

The May 16, 1946 installment had dancer Tommy Wonder; vaudevillian Eddie Hanley; Al Gordon and his dogs; Wally Boag and his balloons; the Skating Carters, a roller skating act; singer Gertrude Niesen; and a one-act play "Meet the Missus" starring Pert Kelton, Anne Thomas, and Jack Albertson.

Other examples of short dramas presented on the series included an August 1, 1946 episode staging "Finger of God" by Percival Wilde about a man who intended to bilk women out of their money but then has a change of heart. The August 15, 1946 show featured a dramatic presentation titled "Western Night" about a badly injured cowboy who eventually dies from his wounds. However, such one act plays were dropped in subsequent episodes due to difficulties in staging and finding suitable talent. [73]

After the series had been on the air for several months, the format changed to a sixty-minute musical featuring Eddie Mayehoff as a civil service worker who dreamed of Walter Mitty-like fantasies. For example, when Eddie's wife sends him out to buy groceries, he performs a monologue about frozen food which ends with a man in a fur parka rushing up to him and saying "Captain Mayehoff, the balloon is ready for take-off." The episode then involves a balloon voyage to the South Pole with Eddie being marooned there with only a talking penguin for a companion.[74]

## *Bristol-Myers Tele-Varieties*

Premiered January 5, 1947 on NBC Sunday 8:15 pm; ran until April 13, 1947

    Cast: Various
    Producer: Wes McKee
    Directors: Ed Sobol and Fred Coe
    Writer: Richard Straus

Bristol-Myers used this fifteen-minute series of short program tryouts to determine which type of show could best sell their Tru-Shay lotion.

The series premiered on December 8, 1946 on WNBT in New York before airing in January on the full NBC network. Three variety acts normally appeared on each installment. On the December 8 program, the acts were Tommy Farrell, Herb Howard, Betty Barto, and Ann Crowley. On the following week's installment, ventriloquist Senor Wences appeared along with impersonator Bob Hawkins, and amateur baton twirler Connie Stevens.

## Show Business, Inc.
Premiered March 20, 1947 on NBC Thursday 8:00 pm; ran until May 4, 1947

    Cast: Helen V. Parrish and John Graham – co-hosts
    Producer: Fred Coe

This experimental one-hour variety series presented a combination of vaudeville acts and film clips. The premiere episode had skaters, The Four Carters, and Gus Van singing *McNamara's Band* and then doing impressions of Bert Williams and Stepin Fetchit. The episode then transitions to a narrated film piece with montages and dream effects about a musician in a haunted Vienna opera house during World War I who subsequently dies at his instrument. Near the end, a narrator does Wagnerian double-talk commenting on a silent film playing on the screen.

## Toast of the Town (aka *The Ed Sullivan Show*)
Premiered June 20, 1948 on CBS Sunday 9:00 pm; ran until June 6, 1971.

    Cast: Ed Sullivan – emcee
    Ray Bloch Orchestra

This long-running variety series presented a smorgasbord of acts ranging from opera singers to rock singers, stand-up comedians to novelty acts, scenes from Broadway shows to dramatic recitations.

    Various titles were considered for the program originally – *Top of the Town*, *Tops in Town*, *Talk of the Town*, and *Toast of the Town* with the latter winning out. The show's theme song went as follows:

    "Here's the 'Toast of the Town'
    The pride and boast of the town!
    The cream of the crops
    From classics to pops
    We have found the tops for you!
    We've looked all aroun'
    Up town and down
    From East Side to West
    To bring you the best

We've pulled out the stops for you!
So now come meet and greet the man
New York's Ed Sullivan
He's the host on the 'Toast of the Town'!"
(Words by Mina Bess Lewis and music by Ray Bloch)

Broadway newspaper columnist Ed Sullivan, who had previously had his own radio show, put on two big shows in Madison Square Garden that were televised. Impressed with Sullivan's showmanship, Worthington Miner, manager of program development for CBS, met with Mr. Sullivan and adman Marlo Lewis to develop a variety program for the network. Miner wanted a "non-performing" emcee with an instinct for spotting talent to host the series which is why Ed Sullivan was chosen. Miner also wanted the show to present the "stars of tomorrow" – not just established talent.[75]

While on-screen personalities that succeeded on early television were performers with a relaxed casual air that viewers could identify with as "friends," Ed Sullivan did not present such a screen persona. Often awkward when introducing his guests, perhaps his long career on television was simply due to the fact that he did not get in the way of the performers. Viewers figured that he acted like they would if they had a weekly live show.

On the first episode, guests included Monica Lewis, sister of producer Marlo Lewis, singing a medley of songs; Kathryn Lee performing a ballet number; pianist Eugene List, playing Chopin's Polonaise; Ruby Goldstein, who was to referee an upcoming fight between Joe Louis and Jersey Joe Walcott; John Kokoman, a fireman from the Bronx who had won a citywide singing contest; the up-and-coming comedy team of Dean Martin and Jerry Lewis, and composers Richard Rodgers and Oscar Hammerstein II. Sullivan interviewed fight referee Ruby Goldstein and Broadway composers Rodgers and Hammerstein. Martin and Lewis performed their stand-up act which *Variety* considered risqué for television.[76]

In response to a review of his show in *The New York Times* which compared his hosting duties with those of Milton Berle, Sullivan replied that he thought the paper misunderstood his position on the program. "They (CBS) wanted a working newspaper man sufficiently versed in show business, to nominate acts that could live up to a 'Toast of the Town' designation. As it is a Sunday show, they wanted a certain measure of dignity and restraint, rather than a vain attempt to work with acrobats, tumblers, etcetera, which Berle does brilliantly."[77]

The title of the series was changed to *The Ed Sullivan Show* on September 18, 1955, and it became the longest-running prime-time variety show in TV history.

## *The Gulf Road Show Starring Bob Smith*
Premiered September 2, 1948 on NBC Thursday 9:00 pm; ran until June 30, 1949

>Cast: Bob Smith – host
>Producer: Rod Erickson
>Writers: Dick Campbell and Edward Kean
>Sponsor: Gulf Oil

Howdy Doody's own "Buffalo" Bob Smith hosted this prime-time variety half hour that experimented with different segments over the series run. The show replaced *You Are an Artist*.

The first episode had Smith leading the studio audience in a community sing-along, engaging in an audience participation stunt by having four females compete in a screaming contest, reminiscing at the piano about the year 1922 while showing some newsreel clips from that year, playing accordion with the Enoch Light orchestra, having band leaders Fred Waring, Vincent Lopez, and Blue Barron perform with him in a "kitchenware" band, and doing commercials for Gulf Oil. Segments changed in later shows with Smith interviewing persons of note like the author of *Sorry, Wrong Number* and then showing clips from the Barbara Stanwyck film, doing other features on new inventions, books, and movies, holding talent contests and musical quizzes. Howdy Doody appeared on the Christmas show singing "All I Want for Christmas Is My Two Front Teeth."

## *The Bigelow Show*
Premiered October 14, 1948 on NBC Thursday 9:30 pm; ran until December 28, 1949

>Cast: Paul Winchell and his dummy Jerry Mahoney
>Joseph Dunninger - mentalist
>Dan Seymour – announcer

Producer: Frank Telford
Director: Craig Allen
Sponsor: Bigelow-Sanford Carpets

This variety show featured the unusual combination of ventriloquist Paul Winchell and mentalist Dunninger. Dunninger did a mind-reading act and had a standing offer of $10,000 to anyone who could prove that he used an accomplice.

On the opening show, Dunninger reads the mind of guest star Billy Rose who jotted down his thoughts sitting in another room with a concrete wall between him and the mentalist. Other segments included Peg Marshall and the four Holidays performing a novelty tune and Paul Winchell doing a comedy routine with his dummy Jerry Mahoney presumably bumbling through some attempts at magic to out-do Dunninger.

Dunniger performed many of his mentalist feats with the studio audience. For example, he would ask audience members to think of a name, place, number, or thing, and he would then select a person and identify their name, birth date, or title of a book they were thinking of.

The series switched networks to CBS in October 1949 before being canceled in December of that year. On an October 19, 1949, after Dunninger completes a mind-reading act with members of the studio audience, Paul Winchell and Jerry Mahoney do a minstrel number in blackface, and then guests Billie Burke and cartoonist Bob Dunn try to stump Dunninger.

## *American Minstrels of 1949*

Premiered January 13, 1949 on ABC Thursday at 8:00 pm; ran until March 17, 1949

Cast: Jack Carter – emcee
Pick Malone and Pat Padgett – black-face comics
Mary Small - singer
Jimmy Burrell - singer
Estelle Sloan – dancer
Producer: Ed Wolf
Director: Fred Carr
Writer: Billy K. Wells

Old and new acts appeared on this one-hour variety show – a combination of minstrel entertainment and vaudeville. The series alternate title was *Pick and Pat*. Apparently some Americans loved the extreme racial stereotyping of that act.

In addition to singers Mary Small and Jimmy Burrell and dancer Estelle Sloan, the first show had the comedy team of Smith and Dale doing their bank robbery skit, the Calgary Brothers, and Nelson's Cats. On other episodes, black-face comedians Pick and Pat sang Stephen Foster tunes, guest star Rudy Vallee performed "Darktown Strutters Ball," and Jean Carroll sang "Blue Skies." Between the musical numbers, the entertainers performed comedy routines including pies in the face, seltzer bottles, and bad puns.

### *Vaudeo Varieties*
Premiered January 14, 1949 on ABC Friday 8:00 pm; ran until April 15, 1949

Cast: Eddie Hubbard – emcee

From Chicago, this program, hosted by Eddie Hubbard, presented five different acts each week. The show, which featured vaudeville, radio, and nightclub performers, first aired locally on Chicago television station, WENR. Hubbard was a singer, disc jockey, and ukulele player. The singing Lind Brothers were the featured guests on his second show.

### *Window on the World*
Premiered January 27, 1949 on DuMont Thursday 9:00 pm; ran until April 14, 1949

Cast: No regular cast members
Merle Kendrick orchestra

Given the small budgets for DuMont shows, this variety program attempted to give an illusion of singers and comics performing from far off locales by dressing the set to appear exotic and using stock footage of foreign cities. An off-screen narrator described each location for viewers.

For example, on a March 25, 1949 airing, the episode starts with images from Acapulco including scenes of boat rides, a market, and horses. Dancer Estelle Sloan performs an energetic number to the accompaniment of Mexican music in front of a painted background of a café. After the Mexican dance, Sloan does an Irish jig. The next part of the show features women in different outlandish fashions including a large rectangular hat and striped gowns that looked like barber poles. Performers Monroe and Grant appear doing back flips and other acrobatics on the trampoline. After a commercial for DuMont television sets featuring Mr. and Mrs. Hall and their babysitter Betty commenting about DuMont products, Ellen Doja, an opera singer, does two operatic pieces. The next segment is footage of people carrying baskets on their heads in a marketplace. The final act is the vaudeville team of Smith and Dale with Joe Smith playing the president of the Eskimo National Savings Bank and Charlie Dale as a difficult new client who wants to open an account with $7 in quarters. A robber bursts into the bank. Smith asks him to shoot holes in his jacket so he can prove he was robbed. Dale wants him to shoot through his hat so he can impress his wife. When the thief tries to do that, he realizes that he is out of bullets. Smith and Dale rush in and apprehend him.

The show's narrator ends the episode by saying "There's always fun and excitement in your Window on the World."

## *Admiral Broadway Revue*

Premiered January 28, 1949 on NBC and DuMont Friday 8:00 pm; ran until June 3, 1949

> Cast: Sid Caesar
> Imogene Coca
> Mary McCarty
> Marge and Gower Champion
> Producer/director: Max Liebman
> Writers: Mel Tolkin, Lucille Kallen, Ray Carter
> Choreographer: James Starbuck

A theatrical production consisting of brief, loosely connected skits, songs, and dances – this definition fits *Broadway Revue* precisely. Every week Admiral sponsored a cast of talented comedians, singers, and dancers who put on a show usually around a central theme. *Friday Night Frolics* was the original title for the program.

Each episode opened with a group of men and women dressed as admirals singing "The top of the evening to you. It's time for Admiral Broadway Revue." For the first show to go on, TV cameras had to be brought to the studio from Ebbets Field in Brooklyn where they had been used to broadcast a Dodger's baseball game.[78]

The central theme for the second show, which aired on February 4, 1949, was "show business." Sid Caesar appears in a skit as a Russian singer and musician serenading a couple in a tavern who do not want to be entertained, but his character will not take "no" for an answer. Bobby Van sings "It's a Good Day from Morning to Night" impersonating Cary Grant, James Cagney, Jimmy Stewart, Walter Brennan, and Peter Lorre and topping off the number with a tap dance routine. "Non-entities in the News," a regular segment on the show, featured Imogene Coca as scientist Madame Mercury working on a secret formula, Mary McCarty as Esmeralda Kumquat the "Pie Queen of 1949" showing how she made pie crust with unusual ingredients, and Sid Caesar as Dr. Argus Delapidus summarizing events at the United Nations in British, French, and Russian dialects. Next Coca appears as a torch singer in a comedy take-off singing about her love for "Jim." Mary McCarty, as a silent film star, performs a number about her time in the movies. Following that, Marge and Gower Champion are seen rehearsing in a studio that is supposed to be soundproof but isn't. The musical interruptions inspire their dance routines. Before the finale, Sid Caesar does a monologue previewing a gangster film with all the appropriate sound effects. The closing number has a circus theme with clowns, acrobats, tightrope walkers, a snake charmer, and a strongman.

The overall subject of the February 11, 1949 installment was "That's News" featuring an "events of the day" production number with Gower and Marge Champion. "Non-entities in the News" focuses on the most unimportant people of the time with Imogene Coca as a huntress who shoots a moose, Mary McCarty as the winner of an ice cream freezing contest who is still chilled to the bone, and Sid Caesar as a feral boy raised by animals commenting on living in America. Next Bobby Van does an impression of a kid playing his favorite tunes on a jukebox as a pantomime dance. James Starbuck and Imogene Coca present an elaborate take-off on classical ballet, and Mary McCarty sings about her customers at the Tango Palace Dance Hall where she works for ten cents a dance.

After that, Imogene Coca performs a monologue as a trombonist in an all-female band. Marge and Gower Champion then portray newspaper reporters who dance about falling in love with one another. Sid Caesar does an extended monologue about a war film featuring air force pilots and imitating the sound effects of a plane starting and taking off and engaging in a dogfight with German pilots. The finale concerns a penthouse murder reported in the newspapers about a love triangle involving a wife, her lover, and her husband and the subsequent trial performed as an interpretative dance.

This program was the first pairing of Sid Caesar and Imogene Coca who went on to star in *Your Show of Shows*. Apparently, Mary McCarty was hired as the comedienne for *Admiral Broadway Revue* because the ad agency wasn't sure Coca could do comedy.

*Admiral Broadway Revue* was the first series to be aired on two networks – NBC and DuMont, at the same time. Admiral discontinued its sponsorship of the series in June 1949 supposedly because it could not keep up with the demand for its TV sets.

## *Show Business, Inc* (aka *Danton Walker's Broadway Scrapbook* and *Broadway Spotlight*)

Premiered March 10, 1949 on NBC Wednesday 8:00 pm; ran until September 4, 1949.

> Cast: Broadway columnist Damon Walker – emcee until June 12, 1949
> Richard Kollmar, radio personality – emcee from June 12, 1949 to September 4, 1949
> Producer: Martin Jones
> Director: Ralph Nelson

Recreating theatrical highlights from prior years with those singers, comedians, and actors that had made the original scenes memorable was the concept of this program.

The opening show had comedian Bert Wheeler recreating a story he told in the "Follies of 1924," actress Florence Reed performing the sleepwalking scene from *Macbeth*, and actress Peggy Wood reminiscing about her role in *Bitter Sweet* and introducing Martha Wright to sing "I'll See You Again."

In May 1949 when the series title changed to *Broadway Scrapbook*, an episode included guests Cedric Hardwicke and Sarah Churchill performing a sketch satirizing the American conception of England's tea-drinking custom, Buddy Baer, ex-fighter turned singer, doing a number, Tilly Losch imitating an exotic hand dancer, and Harry Savoy performing a comedy routine.

The following month, Broadway actor and radio personality Richard Kollmar took over hosting duties because of a change in the program's format that required the emcee to act in some of the sketches. With Kollmar as emcee, the show became a standard variety program with the host introducing various acts. However, he would participate in at least one skit on the show. For example on a June 19, 1949 installment, Kollmar does a vaudeville sketch with comic Joey Faye called "Floogle Street" about a guy asking for directions to that street and encountering crazy people who misinterpret what he is requesting.

## *Front Row Center*

Premiered March 25, 1949 on DuMont Friday 9:00 pm; ran until April 9, 1950

Cast: No regular cast members
Director: Milton Douglas
Sponsor: Whelan Drug Stores

Entertainers from Broadway and nightclubs were featured on this typical variety series with no regular host.

Comedian Frank Fontaine emceed the first installment doing impersonations and stand-up comedy. Actress Marilyn Maxwell, making her TV debut, sings "Powder Your Face with Sunshine" and "Why Doesn't It Happen to Me." The Dunhills, a tap dancing group, perform a number, and the black male quartet, the Striders sing "Sheik of Araby." The final act is pianist Maurice Rocco performing three tunes.

In June 1949 the series expanded from thirty minutes to one hour for the remainder of its run.

## *Garroway at Large*
Premiered April 16, 1949 on NBC Saturday 10:00 pm, ran until June 1951

Original Cast: Dave Garroway – host
Jack Haskell - singer
Cliff Norton - comedian
Bette Chapel - singer
Carolyn Gilbert - singer
Connie Russell - singer
Songsmiths Quartet
Joseph Gallicchio orchestra

Telecast live from Chicago but with no studio audience, Dave Garroway, who would become the first host of NBC's *Today* show, presented an easy going half hour of entertainment. Like Arthur Godfrey and Perry Como, Garroway sought informality on the series such as in one early episode talking about camera angles as the show opened and introducing guests as they supposedly were first arriving at the studio. On the premiere, Carolyn Gilbert sings "The Black Coffee Blues." After she finished, Garroway comes onto the set and gives her a bottle of milk.

In addition to his regular cast, a May 1949 show presented the Four Step Brothers, a dance group, trumpeter Louis Armstrong, and the Art Van Damme Quintet. On a March 12, 1950 installment written by Charles Andrews and directed by Bill Hobin, Connie Russell sings "Cinderella," Cliff Norton does a comedy routine as an orchestra rehearsal conductor, Garroway comments on the new set designs, Margaret Gibson and Charles Tate perform a dance number, and the finale is a Western number.

As writer Jeff Kisselof described, "The unique conceit of 'Garroway at Large' was to include the viewing audience in the show's wink at show business. When a group of dancers ended their routine by diving into a swimming pool, Garroway suddenly appeared on camera and hopped in too. He then called in the overhead camera, so the viewers could see a pile of mattresses and an abashed group of hoofers huddling under the wooden set."[79]

After going off the air in 1951, the series returned to NBC for one season in October 1953 with a cast of new regulars including Skitch Henderson's orchestra.

## *Fifty-Fourth Street Revue*

Premiered May 5, 1949 on CBS Thursday 8:00 pm; ran until March 25, 1950

>    Cast: Jack Sterling – original host
>    Harry Soanik Orchestra
>    Executive Producer: Barry Wood
>    Director: Ralph Levy

This live one-hour music and comedy series had several different hosts beginning with Jack Sterling who was replaced by Al Bernie. Bernie, who was being considered by CBS for his own sitcom, left the show, and Billy Vine took over. Vine, in turn, was replaced by Joey Faye.

Regular performers on the series also continually changed. They included Russell Arms, Marilyn Day, Mort Marshall, John Butler, Carl Reiner, Pat Bright, Cliff Edwards, Wynn Murray, Joe Silver, Joan Diener, the dance team of Bob Fosse and Mary Jane Miles, Virginia Gorski, Annabell Lyons, and Bambi Linn. Each show consisted of three original comedy sketches and four or five original musical numbers. As *The New York Times* indicated, "The weakest spot, as it so often is in revues, has been the sketches, which for the most part have been very labored."[80]

The debut starred Cliff Edwards, Carol Bruce, Fosse and Miles, and Count Reno. In October when Al Bernie became the host, the show moved to Fridays at 9:00 pm appearing every other week, sharing its time slot with *Theater Hour*.

Reminiscing about the series, writer Max Wilk recalled, "Every day we were fixing problems. We used to do what I would call, 'wall writing.' We would be backstage, and the comic would say, 'We need two lines here,' or the producer would say, 'We're under three minutes,' so you would take a piece of paper and put it on the wall, and we would write the stuff and hand it to him to do, and he would say, 'Okay, I'll do that.'"[81]

The last host of the *Fifty-Fourth Street Revue*, Joey Faye, brought his own brand of comedy to the show. On one installment he did a comedy lecture about Brooklyn and performed a burlesque operation in a surgical ward. Faye went on to host a half-hour adaptation of the show called *Joey Faye Frolics* with much of the talent from the *Revue*. Faye's show premiered April 5, 1950. It aired only one more episode on April 12 before it was canceled.

## This Is Show Business
Premiered July 15, 1949 on CBS Friday 9:00 pm; ran until March 1954

   Cast: Clifton Fadiman – emcee
   Bern Bennett - announcer
   George S. Kaufman, Faye Emerson, and Abe Burrows – panel on
      first show
   Producer: Irving Mansfield

Various acts performed and then were able to ask a panel of show business veterans about their act or other "problems" they were having with the panel members trying, often with mixed results, to be funny in providing advice. The show, initially titled *This Is Broadway*, was simulcast on CBS radio. The radio program started on May 18, 1949.

The first television episode included Nancy Andrews, a singing comedienne, harmonica player Stan Fisher, singer Maxine Sullivan, opera singer Lawrence Davidson, comedian Eddie Garr, and child actress Patty Hahn. What their issues were for the panel to discuss is unknown. However, on an October 1949 installment, singer Ginnie Powell tells the panel (Kaufman, Burrows, and guest panelist Billie Burke), that her problem was the inability to speak in public although she had no problem singing in public. Guest Lew Parker asks the panel what he should do now after completing a successful run in England, while Duke Ellington wanted the panel's advice on how to increase nightclub employment for bands.

On a January 29, 1950 airing, the guests were Cab Calloway, broaching the issue of a non-cooperation policy among musicians unions making it difficult for American orchestras to play outside the United States; singer Yvonne Adair, asking the panel what color her hair should be; and comedian Red Buttons, wondering if he should change his first name.

The program was later resurrected by NBC during summer 1956.

## Let There Be Stars
Premiered September 21, 1949 on the West coast and October 16, 1949 on the East coast on ABC, Wednesday 8:00 pm out West and Sunday 9:00 pm in the East; ran until November 27, 1949.

   Cast: No regular cast
   Producers: Leighton Brill and William Trinz

Director: Richard J. Goggin
Writer: Nat Linden

This big-budgeted variety hour consisted mostly of new, young talent. The initial stanza featured talent that had tried out for a Rodgers and Hammerstein road production of "Kiss Me, Kate."

The following acts performed on the first show: singer June Harvey, comedy actress Patti Brill doing takeoffs on four actresses auditioning for a show, Warde Donovan and Carolyn Tanner performing a duet, "A Day in the Park," dancers Roland Dupree and Kay Tapscott, Dolores Starr doing a "hoop ballet," Michael Edwards and Bonnie Murray saluting early musicals narrated by Thayer Roberts, Charles Lind and Gayle Sherwood singing "I Want to See More of You," and the comedy team of Tommy Noonan and Peter Marshall performing a routine about an inquiring reporter. Much later in his career, Peter Marshall hosted the game show *Hollywood Squares* for a number of years.

The show used something called "Teleparencies," a projected background that moved and faded in and out.

## *A Couple of Joes*

Premiered October 27, 1949 on ABC Thursday 11:15 pm; moved to prime time in December 1949 Wednesday 8:00 pm; ran until July 12, 1950

> Cast: Joe Rosenfield – co-host
> Joe Bushkin – co-host, singer and pianist
> Joan Barton – singer (September to February)
> Warren Hull (December to March)
> Beryl Richards (March to July)
> Pat Harrington (March to May)
> Allyn Edwards (March to July)
> J.J. Morgan – a basset hound
> Mike Reilly Orchestra (1949)
> Milton DeLugg Orchestra (1949)
> Bobby Sherwood Orchestra (1950)

The show, a mixture of music, stunts, and giveaways, started on the New York ABC station in August 1949 and included stunts such as a scavenger hunt in which viewers were asked to bring to the studio items like a burned-out light bulb and a moustache cup for "A Couple of Joes Museum" and a contest where viewers tried to stump the cast by phoning in songs. If none of the cast could sing or play the song, the viewer received a prize. Another segment involved Joe Rosenfield calling back those that phoned in song titles and quizzing them.

The breakout star of this program was Morgan, the basset hound whose deadpan reactions to the different acts won the hearts of viewers.

Maestro Paul Whiteman with three-and-a-half-year-old singer Andrea McLaughlin from *TV Teen Club*.

# Talent Shows 16

**THE SERIES PROFILED** in this chapter paved the way for subsequent talent shows like *American Idol*, *America's Got Talent*, and *The Voice*.

## Doorway to Fame
Premiered May 2, 1947 on DuMont Friday 7:30 pm; ran until March, 1948

    Cast: Johnny Olson – host
    Joe Bolton - announcer
    Ned Harvey Orchestra
    Producers/Directors: Lou Dahlman and George Scheck

Supposedly tens of thousands of New York City residents auditioned for this early talent show, but none ever became stars. Each week a special guest star appeared. Art Ford, a New York radio personality, was the initial host of this series when it premiered in May 1947. Johnny Olson took over as emcee in mid-December of that year. The series ended in March 1948, but a year later, the show returned to DuMont and ran until July 11, 1949.

On a March 30, 1949 episode, the performances included Gwen Oberon singing a medley of gypsy songs, the Norbett puppets, acrobatic dancer Vicki Shear, Tom Arden singing "Night and Day," Cook and Brown, African-American dancers, doing a novelty dance, and Paul Draylin, otherwise known as the "cigarette man," entertaining with a magic act involving lighted cigarettes. However, he was cut-off in the middle of his act as time ran out.

Some accounts state that when *Doorway to Fame* returned to television in 1949, the format changed to that of a weekly anthology series with dramatic presentations performed by actors done in front of a black backdrop while another camera focused on miniature sets with the two images then blended together to look like the actors were performing on an elaborate set.[82] While this description makes sense taking into account DuMont's innovations in order to produce TV shows cheaply, no information could be found in the show business periodicals, *Variety* and *The Billboard* to verify this change in format.

Later in his career, Johnny Olson was the principal announcer for many Goodson-Todman game shows, most notably *The Match Game* with Gene Rayburn and *The Price Is Right* with Bob Barker.

## *The Original Amateur Hour*
Premiered January 18, 1948 on DuMont Sunday 7:00 pm; ran sporadically in prime time on various networks until September 26, 1960

Cast: Ted Mack – host
Dennis James – announcer

The granddaddy of all talent contests, *The Original Amateur Hour* began on New York radio station WHN with "Major" Edward Bowes in 1934. The show eventually aired on NBC, CBS, and then ABC radio until Bowes' death in 1946. After the Major's death, Ted Mack hosted the series, which, after its prime-time TV network run, played on Sunday afternoons from 1960 to 1970.

In October 1949, the series began airing on NBC-TV until 1954. A year later it was picked up by ABC and then went back to NBC in 1957 only to land at CBS in 1959 before it returned to ABC in 1960.

Ted Bergmann who worked at DuMont in the early days of television explained why the series left that network:

> We had "The Amateur Hour" on a network of about twenty-six stations until NBC decided they wanted it. They went out and put pressure on the NBC stations that were carrying us by saying, "hey, we have a show we want you to carry at seven o'clock on Sunday," which was when we had "The Amateur Hour." "If you want to maintain your affiliation agreement with us, you'll clear it," so we'd lose them. Then NBC went to the ad agency, Lennen & Newell, and said, "Hey, why are you keeping 'The Amateur Hour' on DuMont? You're gonna lose all your stations. Bring it to NBC."[83]

The catch phrase on the show as it pertained to who may win the talent contest was "The Wheel of Fortune spins. Around, around she goes, and where she stops, nobody knows." The radio version of the program produced more performers who went onto a successful show business career than did the television version. Ventriloquist Paul Winchell, actor/singer James Shigeta, comedian Jack Carter, opera star Robert Merrill, and most notably Frank Sinatra were but a few of the entertainers who launched their careers on *Major Bowes Amateur Hour*. By contrast, few notable performers, other than Gladys Knight and Ann Margret, got their start on the televised *Original Amateur Hour*.

## *Hollywood Screen Test*

Premiered April 15, 1948 on ABC Thursday 8:00 pm; ran until May 18, 1953

Cast: Bert Lytell – host
Neil Hamilton – assistant
Robert Quarry – assistant (1949)

Young actors and actresses paired with already established stars in original dramatic and comedy vignettes as well as in scenes from novels and plays to see who got their "big break" was the premise of this series set on an imitation Hollywood soundstage. The host served as the "director" for the actors. Usually three actor hopefuls were screen tested on each episode paired with the same veteran star. The host interviewed the young hopefuls and the established actor before they performed.

Bert Lytell left the show in 1948 and his assistant Neil Hamilton took over host duties.

A typical episode from 1949 guest starred John Carradine. In one scene, the actor portrays a Broadway producer with Sonia Sorel, Carradine's wife at the time, impersonating a famous British actress in order to meet the famous producer. In the second scene in the episode, Robert Quarry plays a disturbed young man who believes he has a grievance with his good friend played by Carradine. Between the two scenes, host Neil Hamilton talks with Patricia Schneider, director of radio and television promotions for Eagle Lion Films.

Later in his career, Neil Hamilton played Commissioner Gordon on the *Batman* TV series. Hurd Hatfield hosted the series during the 1950-51 television season.

## *Arthur Godfrey's Talent Scouts*
Premiered December 6, 1948 on CBS Monday 8:30 pm; ran until July 21, 1958

   Cast: Arthur Godfrey – host
   George Bryan – announcer (later Tony Marvin)
   Archie Bleyer Orchestra
   Producer: Irving Mansfield
   Sponsor: Lipton Tea and Lipton Soups

One of the longest running talent shows, this half-hour program was a fixture on Monday nights for almost ten years. Talent scouts would show off young talent, and an audience applause meter would determine the winner. For a number of years, the program was simulcast on radio.

Before each act performed, Godfrey would interview the talent scout who had discovered the entertainer. Ordinarily, friends or family of the entertainer or someone who had seen them perform acted as the talent scout. The winners of each week's contest would then appear on Godfrey's daytime show, and some of them ended up as regulars on Arthur Godfrey's weekly variety show on Wednesday nights.

While decrying the fact that the initial show featured mostly singers, *New York Times* critic Jack Gould raved about Godfrey's hosting duties writing:

> If memory serves, it was Fred Allen who described Mr. Godfrey as the Huckleberry Finn of radio. That definition is doubly apt in video. With tousled hair, with a twinkle in his eye that fairly leaps at the camera and with a sublime sense of detachment from all the proceedings about him, Mr. Godfrey appears as an impish little boy enjoying a lark. Yet thanks to a truly uncanny sense of timing and a wonderful and literate disdain for radio's usually pontifical ways, he at the same time instinctively provides an adult and satirical commentary on people and events. It is a capital combination![84]

An early example of a show from 1952 featured talented newcomers singer Ralph Randall, singers the McGuire Sisters, harpist Eugene Bianco, and African-American singer Vera Little. The McGuire Sisters were the audience favorite and later became regulars on Godfrey's variety series. Other performers who appeared on *Talent Scouts* included Edie Adams, Pat Boone, Diahann Carroll, and Don Knotts.

## *The Jacques Fray Music Room*
Premiered February 19, 1949 on ABC Saturday 8:00 pm; ran until October 16, 1949

>Cast: Jacques Fray
>Charles Stark - emcee (February to July)
>Conrad Thibault - emcee and singer (August to October)
>John Gart - organist

Aspiring young classically-trained singers, dancers, and musicians appeared before a panel of judges who evaluated their talent and selected a winner on this series. In between acts, pianist Jacques Fray would play concert and show tunes. On a March 1949 installment, talent ranged from Ruth Freeman, a flutist, to Harriet Talbot and Dean Crane dancing to *Slaughter on Tenth Avenue*, to lyric soprano Angeline Collins.

On the first installment with baritone Conrad Thibault as the permanent emcee, the program's title changed to simply *Music Room*. Ann Ayars, who sang an aria from *La Boheme*, became a regular weekly guest. Other performers were violinist Fredell Lack, who did a piece by composer Bedrich Smetana, and the dance teams of Nicoli, Paul, and Sari and Powell and Walker, who performed classical dances. Fray continued as a regular, but the change in format appeared to emphasize classical variety over talent competition.

## *Paul Whiteman's TV Teen Club*
Premiered April 2, 1949 on ABC Saturday 9:00 pm; ran until March 28, 1954

>Cast: Paul Whiteman - host
>Margo Whiteman - Paul's daughter and co-host (1949 - 1950)
>Nancy Lewis - co-host (1950 - 1953)
>Junie Keegan - singer
>Andrea McLaughlin - singer

Edmund "Skipper" Dawes
Stan Klet – accordionist
Director: Herb Horton
Producer: Jack Steck

This teen talent show, originating from Philadelphia, presented singers, dancers, and musicians with winners receiving professional coaching and returning to the show to compete against the next episode's winner. An audience applause meter determined the ultimate winner who could walk away with appliances or even a new car.

The show started as a way to curb delinquency among juveniles with Whiteman urging teens to build their own teen-age group which could receive an official charter from the maestro. The talent ranged in age from thirteen to nineteen with about ten acts featured each week during the one-hour show. The top three winners from each show were given Benrus wrist watches courtesy of the sponsor. To open and close the program, groups of teenagers competed in a dance contest to also win watches.

Singer Bobby Rydell was one of the talented teens to appear on the show as were singers Diahann Carroll and Leslie Uggams.

## *Talent Jackpot*
Premiered July 19, 1949 on DuMont Tuesday at 9:00 pm; ran until August 23, 1949

Cast: Vinton Freedley – emcee
Bud Collyer – assistant
Producer: Ed Wolf
Directors: Jack Rubin and Bob Loewi

Professional acts performed and were evaluated by the studio audience on this talent show, which previously had been on radio. On the debut of the television show, five acts were presented with $250 allotted for each. An applause meter determined the amount earned by each act. If the meter rated an act as $100, the remaining $150 went into the jackpot which was given to the ultimate winner along with his or her own winnings. Acts included dancers Larry Howard and Irene Rey as well as Verne Hutchinson, a black singer, who won the jackpot. If a contestant won three weeks in a row, he or she was given a one-week theater contract in addition to the jackpot.

Host of the series, Vinton Freedley was a long-time Broadway producer with his partner Alex Aaron. The two built the Alvin Theater (now the Neil Simon Theater). "Alvin" was constructed from the first two letters of Aaron's first name and the first three letters of Freedley's first name.

From left to right, Kukla, Burr Tillstrom, Fran Allison, and Ollie in a 1954 photograph.

# Children's Shows 17

CHILDREN'S SHOWS ON PRIME-TIME network TV? Unheard of today but such was not the case in the 1940s. While one of the most popular early kids' shows – *Howdy Doody*, which began in 1947, did not air during prime time, several others did as profiled below.

## *Small Fry Club*
Premiered March 11, 1947 on DuMont Tuesday 7:00 pm; ran until June 15, 1951

Cast: Bob Emery – host

Starting out as *Movies for Small Fry*, this children's series showed cartoons and films for young kids with narration by Bob Emery (aka Emory). Later, the program expanded to five nights a week with membership cards in a club being offered. Letters from kids were read on air with their photos shown by the host, "Big Brother" Bob. The show also had lessons on good behavior and sketches by actors playing different kinds of animals.

Examples of cartoons aired on the series were "This Is Spring" showing gnomes working underground sending warmth to plant roots and cartoons involving a Cinderella mouse, a circus, and one about kittens. The show also featured "preachers" – "I do, I don't" vignettes which club members sent in like "Always wear rubbers when it rains, wet feet will give you a cold." Birthday greetings were presented by "Alec Electron," a DuMont trademark.

Before *Small Fry Club*, Emery had developed *Triple B Ranch* on radio for Buffalo Bob Smith who went on to host *Howdy Doody*.

## Birthday Party

Premiered May 15, 1947 on DuMont Thursday 7:30 pm; ran until June 23, 1949

> Cast: Bill Slater (1947) - Uncle Bill
> Grace Gioe (1948) - Aunt Grace
> Ted Brown – King Cole (1949)
> Director: Lou Dahlman
> Producer: Bob Loewi
> Creators: Dave Albert and Lou Dahlman

As the title implies, a designated child would receive a birthday party with cake and ice cream, while other kids would entertain, usually sing or dance. Viewers submitted names of children having birthdays which were read on the air.

*The Televiser* reviewed the June 19 and 26, 1947 episodes of this series commenting that the tall emcee seemed to tower like a giant over the children and that, when he talked with the child performers, he seemed to forget that they were not adults. "The frightened children however, answered with long twitching silences – causing much discomfiture to every one." Furthermore, because each child performed in front of two rows of children in the audience, "The children in the back could be seen fidgeting in their chairs, talking to one another, handling small objects, and in general distracting the viewer from what was going on. The worst part was seeing the emcee in the background looking very bored."[85]

"Aunt Grace" who took over hosting in 1948 was born Grace Catherine Gioe in Brooklyn and graduated from Marymount College in Tarrytown, NY. In addition to hosting the series, she also auditioned the kids who appeared on the show.

## The Roar of the Rails

Premiered October 26, 1948 on CBS Tuesday 7:00 pm; ran until December 12, 1949

> Cast: Ray Morgan – announcer
> Writer: Robert Bogardus
> Producer: Raymond E. Nelson
> Sponsor: A. C. Gilbert Company

This quarter-hour series had two runs - the first from October 1948 to December 14, 1948 and the second from October 24, 1949 to December 1949. Each run coincided with the holiday buying season. *Roar of the Rails* was set in the city of Branford, Connecticut in the household of the James family where the grandfather related stories of actual railroad adventures to his grandson Bill James, Jr. Sometimes Billy's father or sister Mary would also appear on an episode. While the grandfather told his story, American Flyer trains, made by the A. C. Gilbert Company operating on landscaped layouts, would illustrate the event.

The opening show told the story of Death Valley Scottie and his world-record speed trial between Los Angeles and Chicago in 1905 in a private train of the Santa Fe Railway. A November 7, 1949 episode dealt with the Johnstown, PA flood of 1889. The city of Johnstown was shown being deluged after a dam broke. A train races into the town ahead of the flood, but a wall of water wrecks the train. More trains later brought relief to city residents. The following week's episode, called the "Moose Burdick Story," related the tale of a retired railroad engineer who saves a town. Moose Burdick smells smoke coming from a box car filled with explosives. He runs the train safely out of town before jumping from the locomotive just before the explosion. Showing train cars exploding was a favorite device of the series writers.[86]

## *Tales of the Red Caboose*
Premiered October 22, 1948 on ABC Friday 7:30 pm; ran until January 14, 1949

> Cast: Dan Magee – narrator
> Writers: Howard Davis, Steve Baun
> Director: Nat Fowler
> Producer: J. E. Hanson
> Sponsor: Lionel Corp.

Not to be out-done by the A.C. Gilbert Company, Lionel also sponsored a program featuring toy trains racing over set courses against miniature backgrounds with a narrator spinning yarns about the trains.

Among other stories, the first stanza presented a race between a steam and an electric locomotive.

## Child's World
Premiered November 1, 1948 on ABC Tuesday 7:30 pm; ran until April 27, 1949

    Cast: Helen Parkhurst – hostess

Kids aged eight to twelve talked about issues of concern to them and their parents on this fifteen-minute show. Topics discussed on the program included jealousy, prejudice, and school. Educator Helen Parkhurst led each discussion group that consisted of five or six boys and girls. She met with the children for the first time only five minutes before the show aired.

    Ms. Parkhurst was the founder of the Dalton School in New York and the Dalton Plan – a student-directed learning approach to education where students are permitted to interact and work closely with each other and with subject-centered teachers.

## Adventures of Oky Doky
Premiered November 4, 1948 on DuMont Thursday 7:00 pm; ran until May 26, 1949

    Cast: Wendy Barrie
    Burt Hilber
    Pat Barnard
    Mellodaires
    Dayton Allen – voice of Oky Doky
    Raye Copland – creator of Oky Doky
    Producer/director: Frank Bunetta
    Writer: Ben Zavin

This kid's show featured a large (thirty inches tall) mustachioed puppet as a cowboy at a fictional dude ranch where kids came to play games, act in skits, and see Oky Doky's adventures. Each installment involved songs and "tall tales" by Buck. The stories were left open ended so they could continue on the next episode. The tales normally had Oky Doky getting into some type of trouble, but, by taking his "magic milk" pills, he got the strength to defeat the bad guys like the Gull Bronson Gang.

    In early 1949 the series length was reduced to fifteen minutes, and then in March, the program aired twice a week- Tuesdays and Thursdays at 6:45. Its name changed to *Oky Doky Ranch*.

## Kukla, Fran & Ollie
Premiered November 29, 1948 on NBC Monday through Friday 7:00 pm; ran until June 1952

Cast: Fran Allison – hostess
Burr Tillstrom – puppeteer
Jack Fascinato – musical director

From Chicago, this classic children's show introduced the "Kuklapolitan Players" created by Burr Tillstrom. Kukla, which means "doll" in Russian, was the bulb-nosed one with a perpetually worried expression. Oliver J. Dragon, with one tooth, was the carefree, extroverted dragon. Other puppets on the show included Fletcher Rabbit, the mailman; Ophelia Oglepuss, an ex-opera star; Beulah Witch, who flew around on a jet-propelled broomstick; Cecil Bill, the stage manager, Colonel Crackle, the Southern gentleman emcee of the company, and Mercedes, a little girl.

Fran Allison stood in front of a raised puppet stage and talked with them in an ad lib discussion. Tillstrom and Allison, along with the producer and director, would meet before each show to decide on the plot for the day.

Director John Peyser recalls that, while working as a demonstrator of television in 1939 for RCA, he and co-worker Bill Patterson booked Burr Tillstrom to perform at the RCA Exhibit at the World's Fair. "Bill Patterson was from Chicago and had seen Burr working in a Chicago department store at Christmas, doing hand puppets. Ollie was born at a party one night where we were all pretty drunk. Burr sat on the floor cross-legged, sewed Ollie and tried out his voice."[87]

The program first aired locally in Chicago beginning on October 13, 1947 under the title of *Junior Jamboree*, but when it began on NBC, the title was officially changed. The late afternoon *Junior Jamboree* series was apparently somewhat different in format from the soon-to-be network version of *Kukla, Fran, and Ollie*. The original show included interviews with sports and entertainment celebrities as well as dramatic bits and information about hobbies. The Chicago Board of Education Radio Council provided top public school students to appear on the show, which was sponsored by RCA Victor.

On a December 5, 1949 segment of *Kukla, Fran, and Ollie*, Ollie and Kukla wanted to thank the new TV stations airing their show on NBC. Ollie wants to write a special song saluting the stations; while other characters sing their own compositions. Madame Oglepuss is designated the official hostess for the salute, sings a song welcoming the new stations, and names several of them. Fletcher Rabbit tells viewers where to write to get the Kuklapolitan newspaper and then performs his own ditty. Beulah the Witch also sings a welcoming number. Next Kukla and Ollie attempt to show viewers how a TV camera works and do a commercial for RCA Victor record players and records for kids. Colonel Crackle presents a salute to TV stations in the South followed by Ollie saluting Midwest stations. The finale features Ollie singing his own composition "Oh Hail, Television" with assistance from Fran.

Sometimes the series put on its own version of fairy tales. A December 28, 1949 show featured Kukla, Fran, and Ollie's version of "Hansel and Gretel" with a lot of role changes. Beulah the Witch, Madame Oglepuss, and Fran argue among themselves over who should play Gretel with each deciding none of them wants the role. Beulah also doesn't want to be typecast as the witch in the story. Ollie plays Hansel and Gretel's father; Fran plays their mother. Kukla appears as Hansel, and Ollie ends up with the role of Gretel. However, Fran takes over as Gretel and Ollie becomes Hansel when Kukla decides he hasn't had time to rehearse a song in the play. After the song, Kukla returns as Gretel with Fran as the witch.

Hugh Downs, who later hosted the game show *Concentration* as well as the *Today* show, was the announcer on *Kukla, Fran, and Ollie*. He replaced a previous announcer who was terminated when he was found backstage trying on the Ollie puppet. Tillstrom was very protective of his creations.

After its prime-time run on NBC ended, the series moved to ABC in September 1954 where it remained until August 1957. The show also appeared on NBC from September 1961 to June 1962 in a weekday five-minute series as well as on PBS from 1969 to 1971 and in syndication during the 1975-76 season.

## *Mr. I Magination*

Premiered May 29, 1949 on CBS Sunday 7:00 pm; ran until September 1949 in prime time.

    Cast: Paul Tripp
    Ruth Enders (Mrs. Paul Tripp)
    Ted Tiller
    Joe Silver

Producers: Worthington Miner with Norman and Irving Pincus
Writer: Paul Tripp
Music: Ray Carter

Each episode of this children's program began with host/singer Paul Tripp, dressed as a train engineer, transporting kids to "Imaginationland" on a wonder-train. Kid viewers were encouraged to send in letters describing something that they wished for, and Tripp would transform the wishes into small plays.

Tripp would begin each program with the following song,

> "Meet Me, Mr. I Magination
> The Man with the magic reputation
> Did I hear you wish to go
> Where you think you cannot go?
> Just ask me, Mr. I Magination
> Can do whatever you
> Would never dream that you could do
> I'm Quite a treasure
> So it's a pleasure
> To introduce to you
> Just guess who
> Mr. I Magination
> The Man with the magic reputation"

The series began in April 1949 on local New York television. On the first episode, Tripp introduces one young boy, who wants to be in the big leagues, to baseball player Rabbit Maranville, who gives the boy some batting instructions. A young girl, who would like to know how people in foreign countries live, has a simulated trip to Mexico to see a traditional hat dance. The final stop of the train always involved a small play about a historical figure with a youngster acting as that personage. On the first show, a boy played Christopher Columbus discovering America.

The 1949 Christmas show concerned the time the holiday almost didn't happen. Paul Tripp travels back in time finding a downtrodden Santa Claus who says that a nasty millionaire, Phineas Prune has purchased the North Pole and is charging him exorbitant rent which is due on Christmas Eve. Prune threatens to take all the toys if Santa doesn't come up with the rent. Mr. I Magination tries to convince Prune to permit Christmas to happen, but Prune says he hates children, having never been one himself. Santa eventually runs into a young boy named Peter who, upon hearing of Santa's troubles, gathers all the kids in the neighborhood to chip in money to help Santa pay the rent. Mr. I Magination lends Santa his train, since Prune has chased away the reindeer, and stops Prune from lighting fires in fireplaces as Santa climbs down chimneys to deliver gifts. Mr. I gives a gift to Mr. Prune, showing him a postcard that Prune wrote to Santa when he was six, proving that Prune indeed was a child. Prune likes the gift of a sailboat and has a change of heart about Christmas.

In a 1950s episode, Mr. I transports a young girl named Jimsey back to 1919 to witness the suffragette movement. They go to Washington D.C. to lobby senators to allow women to vote. Walter Matthau appears as one of two senators against the movement. Jimsey convinces women to go on strike against their husbands to protest their lack of voting rights. The senators, dressed as women, infiltrate the movement to attempt to persuade women to resume their household duties, but the two senators change their minds when Mr. I and Jimsey show photos of them dressed in female attire and threaten to send the photos to the press.

After its prime time run, the series continued until April 1952 on early Sunday evenings.

## Judy Splinters

Premiered June 13, 1949 on NBC Monday through Friday 7:00 pm; ran until August 5, 1949

> Cast: Shirley Dinsdale
> Dorthea Mitchell - pianist
> Producer/director: Norman Felton

Ventriloquist Shirley Dinsdale hosted this fifteen-minute children's show as a summer replacement for *Kukla, Fran, and Ollie*. Her large, pigtailed dummy was called Judy Splinters.

Dinsdale's show originally aired on KTLA, a local TV station in Los Angeles, where she performed with her dummy doing interviews with children. Her NBC series, which originated from Chicago, was different in that it had a story line for each episode which initially concerned Judy Splinter's reactions to her new city.

After its prime-time run, the show aired in New York in the late afternoon until June 30, 1950. The local New York programs dealt with topics like Judy developing her singing voice and going to a music school for lessons, Judy visiting a Swiss watchmaker to buy a new clock with the watchmaker showing her all the clocks and watches in his store and telling her how the Swiss became interested in watch making, and Shirley wanting to inspire Judy to think about what she wanted to be when she grew up.

Dinsdale was the recipient of the first Emmy award as Outstanding TV Personality. Later in life, she became a cardiopulmonary therapist.

## *Captain Video and His Video Rangers*
Premiered June 27, 1949 on DuMont Monday through Friday at 7:00 pm; ran until April 1, 1955

> Cast: Captain Video (Richard Coogan, 1949-1950; Al Hodge 1951- 1955)
> The Ranger (Don Hastings)
> Dr. Pauli (Bran Mossen, 1949; Hal Conklin)
> Producer/creator: James Caddigan
> Writers: Lawrence Menkin and M.C. Brock

"Fighting for law and order, Captain Video operates from a mountain retreat, with secret agents at all points of the globe! Possessing scientific secrets and secret weapons, Captain Video asks no quarter (consideration), and gives none to the forces of evil." That is how each episode of the long-running children's series opened.

Episodes were divided into specific segments with the initial scene showing the Captain's nemesis, usually evil Dr. Pauli, planning to commit some dastardly act against Captain Video and/or another planet. The next scene would show the Captain either unaware of what his nemesis was doing or else trying to thwart the evil plan. Either a commercial or public service announcement would then appear followed by a movie clip from an old Western showing what the Captain's agents were doing. Alternating live scenes with old move clips and inserting commercials would continue for the balance of an episode.

A July 28, 1949 installment where Captain Video is in an interplanetary struggle with his adversary Dr. Pauli is an example of an early episode. Pauli is attempting to cause a total eclipse of the sun by creating radar reflections on the moon so that he can rule the world. While this saga was underway, every few minutes, Captain Video called upon the Video Ranger to tune in scenes from an old Western movie. The hero in those movies was one of the Captain's "secret agents" ignoring, of course, the difference in the time periods. Apparently, the old move clips allowed the actors on the show to change costumes and for the crew to change sets since the series initially was performed live.

Another 1949 episode had the Captain trying to bring moderate reforms to a defeated planet. However, the head of the planet believes that the Captain is coming to visit in order to subjugate its inhabitants. Again the episode cuts to scenes from a Western where one of Captain Video's special agents – a U.S. Marshall – is accused of murder by a crooked sheriff and his posse. Meanwhile, Dr. Pauli is causing problems using his interplanetary transmitter to broadcast to the outer limits. The Captain persists on traveling to the defeated planet even though its head is setting a trap for him.

On episodes with no commercials, public service messages to kids emphasized topics like protecting freedom and fighting discrimination.

*Captain Video* was DuMont's longest-running program. Some of the actors who later became famous that appeared on the series included Ernest Borgnine, Jack Lemmon, and Walter Mathau.

## *Science Circus*

Premiered July 4, 1949 on ABC Monday 8:30 pm; ran until September 12, 1949

Cast: Bob Brown – host

From Chicago, an absent-minded scientist presented experiments before a studio audience on this program. After the series ended, Mr. Brown authored a newspaper column, "Science for You" as well as three books called *Science Circus* about experiments that kids could do at home

For example, one experiment involved making a "knife and fork chimes," by tying a knife, fork, and spoon on a string so that they did not touch one another. The ends of the string were held up to the ears and, as the head was moved, the silver pieces clanged together sounding like chimes. The string conducted the sounds to the ears making them louder and mellower.

Another experiment nowadays may be considered a little dangerous for children. It involved making a cheesecloth bag, putting flour into it, and shaking the bag over a candle flame to show that flour will burn in sudden, sparkling flames. Flour will not burn unless the particles are separated so that oxygen in the air reaches every one. Brown does point out that while the small explosions in this experiment are harmless, children should always be careful around fire.[88]

## *Going Places with Uncle George*
Syndicated to local stations between 1949 to 1955

Cast: Uncle George (Dick Elliott) – host/narrator
Producer: Jerry Fairbanks

Jerry Fairbanks was a master of syndicated programming for local TV stations. One of his early syndication efforts was *Going Places with Uncle George*, a program about unusual people, places, and things aimed at juvenile viewers. Each episode was only ten minutes in length but with commercials, TV stations could fill fifteen minutes of airtime. While many stations aired this series outside of prime time, usually between 5:00 and 6:59 pm, several others did broadcast the show in prime time between 7:00 and 8:00 pm often coupled with Fairbanks' *Paradise Island*.

The show was advertised as "A fascinating adventure-education program with 'Uncle George' taking his audience into the world of sports . . . fantasy . . . curious pursuits . . . strange people."

Sitting in a rocking chair and smoking a pipe, friendly, gray-haired Uncle George would narrate stories about various subjects. For example, on one episode, he relates the tale of "The Master Cat," otherwise known as "Puss 'n Boots." George begins narrating the story and showing illustrations from the book. The remainder of the episode, with Uncle George's voiceover, uses animated puppets to dramatize the tale.

Among his many roles as a character actor, Dick Elliott, who played Uncle George, is best remembered for his role as Mayor Pike on early episodes of *The Andy Griffith Show*.

Jack Gregson, emcee of *Auction Aire*.

# Game Shows  18

GAME SHOWS HAVE BEEN a very popular program genre on network television ever since the beginning of the medium. While most prime-time game shows today offer contestants big money prizes, such was not the case in TV's early days. Moreover, some early game shows featured only celebrities or "TV personalities" playing games for the amusement of the viewing audience with no ordinary people as contestants.

*Face to Face*
Premiered June 9, 1946 on NBC Sunday 8:00 pm; ran until January 26, 1947

    Cast: Eddie Dunn -emcee
    Bob Dunn - artist
    "Sugar"- female who helped with the show's commercials
    Producer: Paul De Fur
    Sponsor: Tender Leaf Tea (Standard Brands)

On this very early game show, cartoonist Bob Dunn drew caricatures of unseen persons based on verbal clues, and then the sketch was compared to the real person when that individual entered the studio. Drawings of three guest participants were featured on each show. In addition, the program had a quiz segment involving identifying a celebrity based on different clues. Bob Dunn also drew lead-ins to the commercials hawking Tender Leaf ice tea, such as the drawing of a kitchen sink gadget with one faucet dispensing ice cubes and the other tea. Packages of tea were given to the three participants on each show. At the end of the program, the Dunn's signed off saying "I'm Bob. . . and I'm Eddie. . . and we're Dunn."

Cartoonist Bob Dunn was best known for the comic strips *Little Iodine* and *They'll Do It Every Time*.

## *Cash and Carry*
Premiered June 20, 1946 on DuMont Thursday 9:00 pm; ran until July 1, 1947

Cast: Dennis James – emcee
Producer: Charles Stark
Sponsor: Libby's

Set in a grocery store with Dennis James playing the part of the store manager, contestants on this program answered questions attached to cans of Libby products for cash prizes ranging from $5 to $15. The game show also included studio stunts and viewer call-ins to guess what was in a barrel. Examples of stunts included a woman swimming in a large bathtub trying to catch live fish and a male contestant allowing his bald head to be used to demonstrate how to paint faces.

This was the first of many game shows hosted by Dennis James. In addition to starring on his own prime-time variety show (see *Dennis James Carnival*), Mr. James emceed shows into the late 1970s. Some of the series he hosted were *People Will Talk*, *PDQ*, *Name That Tune*, and the syndicated nighttime *Price Is Right*.

## *Play the Game* (aka *Let's Play the Game*)
Premiered September 24, 1946 on DuMont Tuesday 8:00 pm; ran until December 17, 1946

Cast: Dr. Harvey Zorbaugh – host/creator
Producers: Harvey Marlowe, Edward Sobol, Richard Goggin

Celebrities played charades on this half-hour show – probably the only game show in the history of television moderated by a professor of sociology from New York University. A panel of six celebrities pantomimed song, book, and poem titles as well as quotations from books. Viewers were asked to call in their guesses to the charades to win a $5 prize.

The show began in 1941 on the New York NBC station, and, after its prime-time run, it was seen locally in New York City on the ABC station until 1948. Hosts of the ABC show were Irene Wicker and Joe O'Brien.

## *Juvenile Jury*
Premiered April 3, 1947 on NBC Thursday 8:00 pm; ran until July 1947

Cast: Jack Barry – host/creator

*Juvenile Jury* featured five children, ranging in age from three to twelve, who were given problems sent in by viewers and asked to come up with solutions. The show started on radio in 1946.

After the 1947 NBC-TV series ended, the network brought the program back for summer runs in 1951, 1952, and 1953. On one 1953 program, the problems presented to the panel of five included what should a mother do with her five-year-old son who wants to be a vet and so puts bandages on the neighborhood pets and do you think it easier to be a mother or a father? Concerning the problem of the young future veterinarian, a little girl on the panel indicated that her mother had previously told her that this would be a topic on the show. Host Jack Barry strongly responded that none of the juvenile jury members were ever informed of the problems in advance. Barry's reply was somewhat ironic given that he was implicated in the quiz show rigging scandal of the late 1950s where contestants on *Twenty One*, a game show he produced and hosted, were given the answers to questions in advance to heighten the drama on the program.

Viewers who submitted the questions for the juvenile jury's consideration received various prizes. In addition, young kids were introduced who presented the panel with their own problems like a three-year-old girl who wanted her dad to buy a new car even though he didn't want to.

CBS aired *Juvenile Jury* during summer 1954. It remained as a Sunday afternoon show until spring 1955 and was resurrected once more in syndication during 1970-71.

## *Party Line*
Premiered June 8, 1947 on NBC Sunday 8:30 pm; ran until August 31, 1947

Cast: Bert Parks – emcee
Mimi Walters – assistant
Director: Ed Sobel
Producer: John Reed King
Sponsor: Bristol-Myers

On this quiz show, viewers were encouraged to send in their name and phone number in order to be selected to answer a question posed by Bert Parks. Subjects of questions included pronunciation, names, songs, and plays. If the person called was watching the show and could answer the question, then he or she would win $5 and a box of Bristol-Myers products. The questions were sometimes illustrated with a demonstration or film clip.

Bert Parks emceed several game shows during the 1940s, 50s, and 60s but is probably most remembered for his long stint as the host of the Miss America Pageant from 1955 to 1979.

## *Charade Quiz*
Premiered December 4, 1947 on DuMont Thursday 8:30 pm; ran until June 23, 1949

> Cast: Bill Slater – emcee
> Mina Bess Lewis, radio producer Herb Polesie, radio actor Bob
>     Sheppard, Jackson Beck – panelists
> Producers: Victor Keppler and Gertrude Catcher

Viewers would send in subjects to be acted out as charades. A repertory company of actors, including a very young Buddy Hackett, would perform the pantomimes. The viewer, whose suggested charade was chosen, won $10. The panel had ninety seconds to guess the subject of the charade. If the panel was stumped, the viewer would win $15.

On the first show, the panel consisted of three members – Lewis, Polesie, and Sheppard. A guest panelist on an early show was none other than actress Lucille Ball. At the dawn of early television, the DuMont studios had no air conditioning and the lights for the cameras generated temperatures above 130 degrees. Supposedly, after being in the studio for a few minutes, Lucy remarked, "This is ridiculous! Haven't these TV clowns ever heard of motion picture studios? Why don't they visit one and see how things are done! This isn't show business ... this is madness! Never again! You can take my part of television and feed it to the birds."[89] A few years later, Ms. Ball apparently changed her mind about being on television.

## *Americana*

Premiered December 8, 1947 on NBC Monday at 8:10 pm; ran until July 4, 1949

> Cast: John Mason Brown (1947-48) –emcee
> Deems Taylor (1948) – emcee for two episodes- January 21 and 28, 1948
> Ben Grauer (1948-49)
> Vivian Ferrer (1949) – co-host with Grauer
> Creator: Martin Stone
> Writer: Jerome Coopersmith
> Producers: Martin Stone and Gordon Duff

"Your program about your country" was the opening slogan for this show. Contestants answered viewer-submitted questions about American history. A panel of four or five adults, known as the "Board of Experts," was involved with the initial shows but that changed to a panel of five high school students in 1948. On June 6, 1949, another format modification had three students playing against three celebrities in a Q and A on American history. Three actors would perform short skits acting out the question after which the contestants would attempt to answer. One such actor was the folk singer Oscar Brand.

On the first show, the panel included Millicent Fenwick, then part of the editorial staff of *Vogue* and later a Congresswoman from New York, Bennett Cerf, publisher and long-time panelist on *What's My Line?*, Lewis Gannett, book critic of *The New York Herald Tribune*, and eleven-year-old Linda Nissen. In the initial segment, three items from colonial days were presented to the panel to guess what they were. They turned out to be a foot warmer, a candle mold, and a sugar-loaf cutter. In another segment, John Mason Brown performed a series of charades for the panel to guess the title of a play, book, or poem. The answers were *A Streetcar Named Desire*, "John Brown's Body," and *Farewell to Arms*. Viewers who sent in a question that stumped the panel won a series of prizes including a set of encyclopedias, luggage, and $50 worth of books of their own choice. However, the viewer had to identify the baby picture of a prominent American to win everything.

## *Stop Me If You've Heard This One*
Premiered March 4, 1948 on NBC Friday 8:30 pm; ran until April 22, 1949

>Cast: Roger Bower -emcee
>Cal Tinney, Lew Lehr, Morey Amsterdam, Benny Rubin, George Givot – panelists
>Creator: Cal Tinney
>Producers: Irving Mansfield, Barry Wood, Larry Schwab

On this comedy game show, based on the original radio series which had begun in 1939 and ran until 1940, the emcee would read jokes sent in by viewers to a panel of three comedians. If one of the panelists recognized the joke, he would say "stop" and finish the joke himself. If the comedian gave a wrong ending, the viewer won a prize.

A radio version of the series was brought back on September 13, 1947, about six months before the TV show debuted. The panel on this radio version, hosted by Roger Bower, was made up of Morey Amsterdam, Lew Lehr, and Cal Tinney. Tinny indicated that the idea for the program came to him while in bed. "I scribbled a note about it on a nearby pad. The next morning I told the idea to my wife. She said it was no good. So I knew then I had a good idea."[90]

On November 11, 1948, actor and radio personality Leon Janney replaced Roger Bower as the emcee. After a lengthy career in broadcasting, Bower became a member of the American Foreign Service Corps.

## *Try and Do It*
Premiered July 4, 1948 on NBC Sunday 8:30 pm; ran until September 3, 1948

>Cast: Jack Bright – emcee
>Eloise McElhone – assistant
>Ken Roberts - announcer
>Thomas Leander Jones' Brass Band
>Producer/director: Herb Leder
>Sponsor: Maxwell House Coffee

Picnic grounds were the setting for *Try and Do It* with an orchestra stationed in a village bandstand. This thirty-minute audience participation show involved contestants performing various stunts to win merchandise.

On the first episode, stunts included having a woman put on a male contestant's bowtie, a guy exchanging shoes and socks from one foot to the other within a minute, several men in a ring putting on their neighbor's hat at given signals, and contestants trying to whistle through a mouthful of crackers.

*The New York Times* panned the show, saying "... it consists of a succession of studio participants attempting dull stunts, with the survivors being escorted to a prize booth for their appropriate rewards. As master of ceremonies, Jack Bright is absolutely simpering in his feigned sweetness and awkward enthusiasm."[91]

Eloise McElhone joined the show beginning with the August 8 installment. She later became a panelist on *Think Fast* and had her own TV talk show in the early 1950s.

## *Winner Take All*

Premiered July 8, 1948 on CBS Thursday 9:30 pm; ran until January 1949.

Cast: Bud Collyer – emcee
Roxanne Arlen – assistant
Bern Bennett - announcer
Producer: Gil Fates

Based on the radio show of the same name, *Winner Take All* involved two contestants answering questions. Each correct answer was worth a point; three points won the game. In addition to winning prizes, the champion went on to compete in another round against a new competitor. Later in the series run, mixed in with oral questions were illustrated ones. For example, contestants had to guess when a balloon would burst and what note a Swiss bell ringer played.

From January 1949 to April 1950, the show continued on the local New York station before returning to prime time on the network. After its final nighttime episode on October 3, 1950, the game show aired on daytime TV first on CBS and then on NBC until April 1952.

The radio version of *Winner Take All* was the first game show legendary producers Mark Goodson and Bill Todman ever sold.

## Tele-a-Pun
Premiered July 9, 1948 on NBC Saturday 8:30 pm; ran until August 1948

    Cast: Johnny Bradford – emcee
    Ray Michael – announcer
    Producers: Boyce DeGaw, Vance Halleck

Broadcast from WNBW (now WRC) in Washington DC, this game show featured contestants from the audience acting out puns through charades. The puns represented famous sayings or people, titles, or places. If the contestant's performance won the audiences' approval, he or she received a prize. If the performance was not approved by the studio audience, the player was brought before the court for "errant punsters" and charged with punning in public places. He or she was defended by "Attorney for the Defense," Ray Michael. Host Johnny Bradford acted as the judge. If the judge dropped the case, the contestant received a consolation prize. A "Tele-a-Pun of the Week" was acted out progressively during the show, and at the end, the completed pun was offered to viewers for solution.

    Host Johnny Bradford was, at the time, better known for his singing talent than for his hosting duties.

## Movieland Quiz
Premiered August 15, 1948 on ABC Tuesday 7:30 pm; ran until November 9, 1948

    Cast: Arthur Q. Bryan – emcee
    Patricia Bright – receptionist and cashier
    Producer: Lester Lewis
    Director: Ralph Warren

With a set depicting the front of a motion picture theater, this show began on Philadelphia's local ABC affiliate in July, 1948 before being aired on the network. For a cash prize, contestants from the studio audience had to identify stars of movies based on photos from the film. Home viewers were asked to identify movies from still photos that were displayed and mail in a letter stating which of the films they would like to see revived

and why. The winning home viewer would receive $25 plus the amount from contestants who missed questions.
Arthur Q. Bryan was later replaced as emcee by Ralph Dumke.

## *That Reminds Me*
Premiered August 13, 1948 on ABC Friday 8:30 pm; ran until October 1, 1948

Cast: Walter Kiernan – emcee
Former New Jersey Governor Harold Hoffman and his daughter, Tex O'Rourke and his secretary, and radio actor Jim Harkins and his wife, Marian – panelists
Producer: Cal Tinney

Home viewers sent in stories which emcee Walter Kiernan related to the panelists, and then each male panel member had to come up with a story which reminded them of the tale told by Kiernan. However, before they could spin their yarn, their female counterpart told the audience what story they thought their male counterpart was going to relate. If the female guessed correctly, then the viewer who sent in the original yarn didn't win. But if the female counterpart guessed incorrectly, then the viewer won money.
The show began on the ABC station in Philadelphia in May 1948 before premiering on the ABC network.

## *Quizzing the News*
Premiered August 16, 1948 on ABC Monday 7:30 pm; ran until March 5, 1949

Cast: Allen Prescott – emcee
Albee Treider - cartoonist
Producer: Bob Brenner
Director: Bob Doyle
Writer: Milt Subotsky

On *Quizzing the News*, a celebrity panel tried to answer questions about current events based on cartoon clues as hints. Guest panelists on the debut included Ray Josephs, Arthur Q. Bryan, Milton Caniff, and Mary Hunter. If the first hint didn't result in a correct answer, another cartoon was drawn, up to the limit of three. Also, viewers could send in a photograph with the face disguised to make identification difficult. A viewer who sent in a photo that was chosen received an automatic washer.

## *Break the Bank*
Premiered October 22, 1948 on ABC Friday 9:00 pm; ran until January 15, 1957

    Cast: Bert Parks – host
    Bud Collyer – co-host
    Janice Gilbert – paid out cash winnings to contestants
    The Song Spinners
    Peter Van Steeden Orchestra
    Writer: Joseph Kane
    Producer: Ed Wolf Associates

*Break the Bank* picked contestants from the studio audience who were asked questions of increasing monetary value on a single topic. Winners could then get a chance to "break the bank" by correctly answering a question worth at least $1000. The radio version of the program began in 1945.

Categories for questions were subjects like "Neighbors," "Men in the White House," and "William Shakespeare." Each category consisted of eight questions worth in progression $10, $20, $50, $100, $200, $300, $500, and the last question to break the bank was $1000 or more depending on if a prior contestant never broke the bank. Sample jackpot questions included: What is the last line of "A Visit from St. Nicholas" ("Happy Christmas to all, and to all a good-night!"); where is Lake Maracaibo located? (Venezuela); and the native state of only one of our presidents was South Carolina, close to the North Carolina border. Which president was that? (Andrew Jackson).

The producer Ed Wolf, who created the show, got the title from a man who presented a quiz show idea to him. Wolf didn't like the concept which ended with a contestant using a hammer to smash a piggy bank, but he liked the title "Break the Bank."

## Picture This
Premiered November 17, 1948 on NBC Wednesday 8:20 pm; ran until February 9, 1949

>Cast: Wendy Barrie – hostess
>Sponsor: Vick Chemical Co.

Early television had several shows built around identifying photos or drawings. Such formats were ideal for the visual medium of TV. *Picture This*, a ten-minute program, was something like a game show involving a guest cartoonist drawing a sketch to fit an idea or caption sent in by a viewer. The cartoons were then autographed and sent to the viewer who suggested the subject.

## The Eyes Have It
Premiered November 20, 1948 on NBC Saturday 8:00 pm; ran until January 27, 1949

>Cast: Ralph McNair – emcee and producer

Coming from NBC's affiliate in Washington D.C., a panel of three political celebrities had to identify a famous person or a place from photos altered in different ways, such as extreme close-ups, unusual angles, or a portion of a photo which gradually widened to reveal more of the picture if the panel didn't identify the subject initially.

After January 1949, the program continued on NBC on Sunday afternoons for another six months.

## Who Said That?
Premiered December 9, 1948 on NBC Monday at 10:00 pm; ran until July 26, 1955.

>Cast: Robert Trout – emcee
>Four Panelists – various celebrities and newsmen including John Cameron Swayze, H.V. Kaltenborn, and Henry Morgan

Created and edited by Fred Friendly, later of CBS news, this program had a panel of four celebrities trying to identify who said a particular newsworthy quotation. If a panel member could not correctly identify "who said that," he or she had to deposit money into a fish bowl. The bowl full of cash would be awarded to a home viewer who sent in the quote or else to a charity.  The premiere show had as panelists – George Allen, H.V. Kaltenborn, Elsa Maxwell, and John Cameron Swayze.

This game show started on NBC radio on July 2, 1948 and ran until August 22, 1950. In January 1949, the TV version moved to Sundays at 10:30 pm and in April to Saturdays at 9:00.  According to an item in *The New York Times*, the panelists were encouraged to remove their shoes before the television program aired because sound engineers discovered that the microphones for the panel were picking up noises from the panelists kicking the table as they crossed and uncrossed their legs.[92]

A September 24, 1949 installment of the show had Bennett Cerf, Leonard Bernstein, and H. Allen Smith as the, presumably, shoeless panelists. The soundtrack from the TV version was used for the radio series during 1950.

Robert Trout left the show in 1951 and was replaced by Walter Kiernan. Kiernan departed in July1954 and John Daly took over hosting duties when, in February 1955, the series moved to ABC.

In a March, 1953 episode hosted by Walter Kiernan, the panelists were journalist Frank Conniff, music critic Deems Taylor, TV personality Dagmar, and newsman H.V. Kaltenborn.  The charity the panelists contributed to was Easter Seals. Quotations came from Rosalind Russell, Fred Allen, Adali Stevenson, Winston Churchill, and Frank Sinatra. The panelist who gave the most correct answers was Dagmar who mentioned that she was lobbying Congress to pass a special tax break for entertainers to allow them to pay their income taxes over their life time instead of paying them only when they were earning big money.

## *Draw Me a Laugh*
Premiered January 15, 1949 on ABC Saturday at 8:30 pm; ran until February 5, 1949

    Cast: Walter Hurley and Patricia Bright – emcees
    Mel Casson – cartoonist of the *Sparky* and *Jeff Crockett* strips
    Jay Irving – cartoonist of *Pottsy* about a New York cop
    Oscar Brand – folksinger

Producer: Milton E. Krents
Director: Howard Cordery

Professional cartoonists drew cartoons from ideas sent in by viewers. One cartoonist was given the description of the cartoon to be drawn but not the caption; another cartoonist was provided with the caption but not the description. An audience panel of four decided which of the two drawings was the funnier.

In the first round of the initial episode, the viewer's cartoon idea was a deep sea diver flirting with a mermaid whose boss goes underwater to say "Johnson, you're fired!" Casson executed the drawing in two minutes. The other cartoonist who had the caption but not the idea showed a foreman on a skyscraper construction job shouting to a riveter falling off the skyscraper past him, "Johnson, you're fired!' The latter won the round. In other elements of the show, Jay Irving was blindfolded and told to draw one of his cartoon characters. Casson was given a scribble and had to make a cartoon out of it. The cartoonists also had to caricature a man based on Jay Irving's verbal description. During the program, Oscar Brand created several ad lib songs describing the cartoons and the prizes.

## *Stump the Authors*

Premiered January 15, 1949 on ABC Saturday 9:00 pm; ran until April 2, 1949

Cast: Sidney Breeze – host/editor
Angel Casey – co-host
Louis Zara, Dorothy Day, Jack Payne – storytellers

From Chicago and featuring some of the city's radio personalities, this series challenged three storytellers to relate a tale based on different objects given to them. Unlike the radio version of the show which made use of a studio audience in deciding which objects should be used to construct a story, the TV version eliminated the audience and was set in a faux living room. The panelists moved about the set picking objects from a bag or box and developed impromptu stories based upon unrelated items such as a nightstick and a pair of glasses. The "authors" did not see the objects until they got them on air.

Each storyteller had thirty seconds to think up a tale based on the objects he or she obtained. They then had four minutes to relate the story. On an early episode, Jack Payne came up with a humorous football tale based on a string of hot dogs, Lou Zara related a mystery involving a skull, a gun, and a bunch of bananas, and Dorothy Day had a romantic story inspired by a pair of baby shoes and a telephone.

## *Riddle Me This*

Premiered January 23, 1949 on CBS Sunday 8:30 pm; ran until September 21, 1952

    Cast: Conrad Nagel – emcee
    John Daly, Ilka Chase – regular panelists
    Bill Hamilton - announcer
    Producer: United World Films and World Video (Martin Ritt,
        Richard Lewine)

This game show not only had several titles during its run but its format also evolved over time. It began locally in New York City in November 1948 under the title *The Eyes Have It* with newsman Douglas Edwards as the host. The initial panel included actress Janet Blair, Paul Gallico, Dale Carnegie, and Charles MacArthur who attempted to answer questions based on excerpts from newsreels over the preceding twenty years.

When it was discovered that NBC's Washington station already had aired a show with this name, the title was changed to *Stop, Look and Listen* with Paul Gallico becoming the emcee. But then it was found that a corporation bearing that name existed to produce films for television, and so the title was changed again to *Riddle Me This* in December 1948. A month later, the series went national on CBS with actor Conrad Nagel as host.

*Riddle Me This* involved four guest experts including celebrities broken into two teams to answer questions, perform demonstrations, or do skits which served as a basis for questions. For example, the teams may have been called upon to design a hat or guess the name of a movie or book from brief film clips presented as clues to the answer.

In March 1949, the series moved to ABC with another new title *Goodrich Celebrity Time*. In April 1950, *Goodrich Celebrity Time* was picked up again by CBS with the format of the series changing from a quiz show to panelists simply presenting skits and performances. The April 2, 1950 version of the series had guests Phil Silvers, Joan McCracken, Joey Faye. and Lenore Lonergan join regular panelists Ilka Chase and John Daly in one of those story lines predicated on the idea that viewers were actually watching an ad lib dress rehearsal for an upcoming show and not the show itself. Robert Q. Lewis and Bert Lahr appeared in cameos as stagehands commenting on the show.

On the episode, Joey Faye talks with host Conrad Nagel about the pending appearance of Phil Silvers saying he knows Silvers well but, when Phil Silvers shows up, he pretends he doesn't know Faye thinking he may be Frank Faye. Ilka Chase is knitting, while John Daly holds her yarn. Daly suggests that Faye make up a quiz based on a routine where people ask him directions to a famous street. Ilka, Joan, and Lenore ask Joey "Can you tell me how to get to _____?" and whisper in his ear the name of the street. Silvers and Daly supposedly ad lib answers based on Faye's directions. Lenore Lonergan attempts to sing a duet with Daly who is more interested in working on a crossword puzzle. Faye and Silvers then have a quiz for Conrad Nagel where Nagel tries to guess which famous "Harry" the two are describing. The episode was written by Bill Jacobson and Larry Markes, directed by Alan Dinehart, and produced by Daniel Mann.

In mid-1952, the panel was dropped altogether, and the series became a musical variety show until it ended in September of that year.

## *Quiz Kids*
Premiered March 1, 1949 on NBC Tuesday 8:00 pm; ran until October 26, 1951

Cast: Joe Kelly – emcee
Cy Harris – announcer
Creators: Lou Cowan and Walter Wade

The *Quiz Kids* featured youngsters who had expert knowledge in various fields. Four or five kids made up a panel answering questions, most of which were submitted by viewers. If a viewer stumped the panel, he or she would receive a prize. Questions ranged from literature to science to sports and math. The kids raised their hands if they knew the answer to a question. The juveniles could remain on the show until age sixteen provided they gave correct answers. The program had started on radio in 1940.

Joe Kelly, the host, dressed in cap and gown with a school bell, read the questions. Occasionally there were guest quizmasters like Milton Berle. Sometimes the format varied with, for instance, a panel of kids competing against a panel of professors to see which team answered most questions correctly.

The show left the air in October, 1951 but returned nine months later during summer 1952. It then became a CBS show during 1953 and was brought back to that network in 1956 for a short run with Clifton Fadiman as the host.

## Think Fast
Premiered March 26, 1949 on ABC Saturday 8:30 pm; ran until October 8, 1950

Cast: Dr. Mason Grove – moderator
Actor Leon Janney, composer David Broekman, and TV personality Eloise McElhone – panelists

This panel show featured three regular panelists and two guests who sat around a large table with each trying to outtalk the others on topics initiated by the moderator. In 1950, Gypsy Rose Lee became the host replacing Dr. Grove who went on to become president of Rutgers University in New Jersey.

## Sparring Partners
Premiered April 8, 1949 on ABC Friday at 9:30 pm, ran until May 6, 1949

Cast: Walter Kiernan – emcee
Producer/director: Sean Dillon

A team of three men competed with a team of three women on this program based on topics in the news.

On the first episode, three cover girl models competed against a team of three magazine cover artists. As *Variety* summed up in a review, "Set is a simulated boxing ring to carry out the title theme, it was the action of the participants in trying to play cute as boxers that corned up the program. Very little rehearsal is needed on an ad lib show such as this but director Sean Dillon should have warned Kiernan where the cameras were. Too often he spoke with his back directly to the lenses and other times he crossed up the participants by blocking them."[93]

## *Ladies Be Seated*
Premiered April 22, 1949 on ABC Friday 8:30 pm; ran until June 10, 1949

>Cast: Tom Moore – emcee
>Phil Patton – assistant
>Producers: Moore and Patton
>Director: Greg Garrison

*Ladies Be Seated*, which started on Chicago radio in 1943 as *Ed East and Polly*, involved contestants participating in a variety of quizzes and stunts for prizes.

On the premiere, host Tom Moore opened with a quiz involving three women from the audience attempting to guess the identity of a historical figure. Next a man and a woman were blindfolded with football helmets on trying to get an apple on a string. Three women then participated in a quiz using noisemakers to indicate the right answer. Two husbands raced against the clock to put on women's clothes. The final stunt was a Granny Be-Bop contest featuring three grandmothers singing and dancing.

One continuing segment on the program was "Whoa Tommy," where a contestant had the chance of winning a bagful of prizes.

## *Bon Voyage* (aka *Treasure Quest*)
Premiered April 24, 1949 on ABC Sunday 9:30 pm; ran until September 2, 1949

>Cast: John Weigel – emcee
>Jack Lester – announcer
>Producer: Alan Fishburn

On this quiz show from Chicago, four contestants, divided into two teams, had to identify countries, cities, industries, and faraway places in general based on photos and other clues. The contestant with the most correct answers received an all-expense paid trip to the place of his or her choice. Beginning with the third show, the title became *Treasure Quest*.

John Weigel, a Chicago-area personality, also was an announcer for the *Lawrence Welk Show* when it started on local television in Los Angeles.

## *Blind Date*

Premiered May 5, 1949 on ABC Thursday 7:30 pm; ran until September 1951

> Cast: Arlene Francis – emcee
> Walter Herlihy – announcer
> Producer: Bernard L. Schubert
> Director: Fred Carr

The first dating game show, *Blind Date*, had six men, three from each of two different colleges, compete for dates with three models. Originally, on the radio version of the program that had begun in 1943, all the male contestants were from the military. On the TV edition, the male contestants could only win anonymously through a telephone conversation with the girls broadcast on a split screen. The females choose the guys with the "best line" to win a date at New York's Stork Club with all expenses paid. Guys from Columbia and Yale participated on the first TV episode.

The series, labeled "America's Most Romantic Program," later varied the format somewhat. For example, a 1950 episode had a "father's night" with fathers attempting to convince a girl to date their sons as well as a father attempting to select a date for his daughter.

Jack Gould in *The New York Times* stated that the major drawback of the program was its forced and contrived nature. "Both the boys and the girls sound as if they had been painstakingly rehearsed."[94]

After the series ended on ABC, NBC picked up the show beginning in June 1952 for two months. In May 1953, DuMont aired the show with actor Melvyn Douglas as host from May until June 1953 when Jan Murray took over. The DuMont series was initially titled *Your Big Moment*.

## Stop the Music
Premiered May 5, 1949 on ABC Thursday 8:00 pm, initially ran until April 1952 but was revived in the mid-fifties.

>Cast: Bert Parks – emcee
>Estelle Loring, Jimmy Blaine, and Betty Ann Grove - the original singers
>Harry Sosnick Orchestra
>Producers: Louis G. Cowan and Mark Goodson

On this combination variety and game show hosted by Bert Parks, based on the radio show of the same name, singers, musicians, dancers, acrobats, and even a cartoonist would supply clues to a song's identity with contestants guessing its title. For example, Bert Parks would blow soap bubbles while the orchestra played "I'm Forever Blowing Bubbles" as a clue to the title of that composition. Betty Ann Grove would sing "Bird in a Gilded Cage" while suspended in a cage wearing feathery adornments to make it easy for contestants to identify the song title. A scene of dancing girls in a harem setting would be a clue to "Scheherazade."

Home viewers could send in official entry blanks with their names and phone numbers to be given a chance at the game with operators calling a lucky viewer to "stop the music" and name the tune. A "mystery melody" segment each week could result in a substantial jackpot for anyone being able to recognize the song's title.

## Hold It, Please
Premiered May 8, 1949 on CBS Sunday 7:00 pm; ran until May 22, 1949

>Cast: Gil Fates – emcee
>Bill McGraw, Mort Marshall, Cloris Leachman - panelists
>Producer/director: Frances Buss

The opening of this program showed a telephone switchboard and an operator played by a young Eva Marie Saint saying "Hold it, please." Contestants sought to answer questions posed by the panel of regulars who danced, sang, and/or acted to illustrate the questions. The contestant who won the regular round could then go for a $1000 jackpot question. Any winner of the jackpot would stay on the show as assistant emcee until a new jackpot winner replaced him or her. As assistant emcee, the contestant could answer any questions missed by a regular contestant and thus win prizes for those answers. Initially, CBS made phone calls to viewers from a list of television set owners. Later, the show directed calls to viewers who wrote in.

Emcee Gil Fates subsequently became a producer for many Goodson-Todman game shows like *What's My Line?* and *To Tell the Truth*.

## *It Pays to Be Ignorant*
Premiered June 6, 1949 on CBS Monday 8:30 pm; ran until September 1949

> Cast: Tom Howard – emcee
> Lulu McConnell, Harry McNaughton, George Shelton – panelists
> Townsmen Quartet
> Producer: Tom Howard
> Creator: Bob Howell
> Writer: Ruth Howard
> Director: Hugh Rogers

*It Pays to Be Ignorant* involved simple questions asked to a panel of comics who responded with outrageous answers. The show had started in 1942 on radio with Tom Howard as host and panelists George Shelton, Harry McNaughton, and Ann Thomas, the latter gave way to Lulu McConnell. The studio audience pulled questions out of a dunce cap. If the panel member failed to answer the question but the audience member could, then he or she would win a prize.

The CBS run filled in for *Arthur Godfrey's Talent Scouts* during the summer. Ruth Howard, who wrote the "Who's buried in Grant's tomb"-type of questions for the show, was Tom Howard's daughter. Howard's son, Tom Jr., arranged the music for the Townsmen Quartet.

NBC resurrected the series in July 1951 and then a syndicated version appeared during the 1973-74 season.

## Fun and Fortune

Premiered April 14, 1949 on ABC Thursday 8:00 pm; appears to have also aired June 6 Monday 9:00 pm and June 18 Saturday 8:30 pm

>Cast: Jack Lescoulie – emcee
>Director: Michael Diskin
>Producer: Mildred Fenton

Although some sources list this game show, the television version of the radio program *Detect and Collect*, as airing only a single episode on June 6, 1949, *Fun and Fortune* seems to have aired at least three times on ABC as a try-out series in search of a sponsor.

Contestants attempted to identify an item hidden behind a curtain based on up to four clues given to them. If the contestant guessed correctly on the first clue, he or she would win $50. The prize money decreased with each successive clue that was needed. One of the "items" on the show was actor Kirk Douglas. The contestant who guessed correctly won a screen test with him.

## Fun for the Money

Premiered June 17, 1949 on ABC Friday 9:30 pm; ran until December 9, 1949

>Cast: Johnny Olson – emcee
>Producer: James Saphier
>Director: Ed Skotch
>Writers: Bob Cunningham, Frank Wait, Frank Barton, Jack Payne

Broadcast live from Chicago, this game show pitted teams of men against female teams performing nine rounds of stunts or answering questions. The contestants were dressed in baseball uniforms and each round of stunts or quizzes was called an inning. On the premiere show, a tricycle race constituted the first inning followed by a pie-eating contest, and then an inning made up of questions. Members of the winning team received $25 each and the losers $5. Individual contestants with the highest score got $100, $50, and $25 in that order, and the top winner had a chance to answer a jackpot question worth $300.

## Cut!/Spin the Picture
Premiered June 18, 1949 on DuMont Saturday 8:00 pm; ran until February 4, 1950

> Cast: Carl Caruso – emcee
> Kathi Norris
> Gordon Dillworth
> Shaye Cogan
> Bob and Eddie Dunn
> Jerry Shad's Quartet
> Alan Scott Trio
> Producers: Jerry Layton and Wilbur Stark
> Director: David Lowe

*Cut!* started out as an hour-long show where entertainers presented sketches, songs, and other bits as clues to the name of a famous person, place, or thing. The other bits included a cartoonist posing a puzzle to be solved. The host would then phone a viewer who had already mailed in his or her name and ask if he or she could identify the person, etc. If the home viewer answered correctly, then that person would be given the opportunity to win a jackpot by identifying the mystery celebrity whose photo was quickly flashed on the screen. Intermittently, the Alan Scott Trio or later Jerry Shad's Quartet would perform.

On June 25, 1949, the show's name was changed to *Spin the Picture* with Eddie Dunn becoming the host. In January 1950 the length of the program was reduced to thirty minutes.


## Majority Rules
Premiered September 2, 1949 on ABC Friday 8:00 pm; ran until July 30, 1950

> Cast: Ed Prentiss – original emcee
> Tom Moore – replaced Ed Prentiss as host
> Announcer: Jack Lester
> Producer/director: Anthony Rizzo

Originating from Chicago, three contestants were asked "yes" or "no" questions on this show. If a majority of the contestants gave the correct answer, they won cash. If the majority responded incorrectly, the viewer who sent in the question won $10. If all three contestants were incorrect, the viewer won an amount contained in a treasure chest.

On the first episode, three female professionals – a doctor, lawyer and merchant made up the panel who were asked question by emcee Prentiss and guests.

Mike (then known as Myron) Wallace became the host on May 21, 1950 until July of that year. Of course, Mr. Wallace was best known for his reports for the CBS newsmagazine *60 Minutes*.

## *Auction-Aire*
Premiered September 30, 1949 on ABC Friday 9:00 pm; ran until June 23, 1950

>Cast: Jack Gregson –emcee
>Charlotte "Rebel" Randall – model assistant
>Kenny Williams, Glenn Riggs – announcers
>Executive Producers: Paul Masterson, John Reddy and Ralph Nelson
>Director: Eddie Nugent
>Sponsor: The Libby Company

On *Auction-Aire*, both the studio audience and home viewers bid for merchandise with food labels from Libby products. Home viewers called their bids into their local station which, in turn, relayed them to the New York Ritz Theater from where the program originated. For example, a refrigerator could be had for 225 Libby food labels. The highest-winning home viewer bidder as well as the highest bidding studio contestant received the merchandise. The winning home viewer had to produce the labels within two hours after the end of the telecast when a local representative stopped by the winner's home. In another segment of the show, viewers could win prizes by determining how many numbers the auctioneer said in his chant of bids.

In a November 1949 review of the show, critic John Crosby remarked,

>On your screen all you get is a succession of pictures of telephone girls with head-phones chattering: "Yes, madam. Just a moment please." Occupying the center of the stage as chief auctioneer is a character named Jack Gregson whose style, if

you can dignify it by that word, approaches that of a barker selling sightseeing bus trips to New Jersey. . . . About the only other thing you have to look at is a girl, one of the hired hands on the show, leering at a prize refrigerator as if it were Clark Gable.[95]

Gregson later hosted the 1951 series *Your Pet Parade* about caring for household pets.

### *Pantomime Quiz Time* (aka *Stump the Stars*)
Premiered October 4, 1949 in New York City while airing in Los Angeles since 1947; initially ran until September 1950

>Cast: Mike Stokey - host
>Producers: Mike Stokey and Bernie Ebert

Taking place on a living room set, this game involved two celebrity teams of four members each trying to guess phrases, quotes, song titles, etc. through pantomime. The series initially debuted in Los Angeles in 1947 and then was picked up by Chevrolet dealers and shown in New York City on WCBS beginning in October 1949. Subsequently the CBS network broadcast the program during the summers of 1950 and 1951. Thereafter, NBC ran the series in early 1952 before it reverted to CBS for summer runs in 1952 and 1953. The series eventually aired on all four networks during the 1950s. Its final airing was on CBS from September 1962 to September 1963 under the title *Stump the Stars* with Pat Harrington as the initial host before being replaced by Mike Stokey.

On an early 1950 episode, the regular panel included Vincent Price, Frank DeVol, Hans Conried, and Adele Jergens up against the guest panel of Marilyn Maxwell, Walter Brennan, Howard Da Silva and Ella Raines. A member of each team was given the chance to communicate, through pantomime, phrases submitted by viewers like "It must be jelly because jam doesn't shake like that," and "Of all the felt I ever felt felt like that felt felt." Each team was given two minutes to guess a phrase. The team that took the least amount of time to guess all their phrases won.

## Twenty Questions

Premiered November 26, 1949 on NBC Saturday 8:00 pm; ran until May 3, 1955

    Cast: Bill Slater – host
    Fred Van De Venter, Florence Rinard Van De Venter, Herb Polesie, and Johnnie McPhee – panelists
    Producers: Roger Bower and Gary Stevens

The TV version of a radio series and old parlor game had viewers send in subjects to be answered by a panel of four regulars and one celebrity by asking up to twenty questions to identify the subject. The panel was told by the moderator if the subject was "animal, vegetable, and/or mineral." Viewers who submitted a chosen subject received a small prize. If the viewer stumped the panel, he or she won a bigger prize.

The show, created by newsman Fred Van Deventer, began on radio in 1946 and featured him, his wife, children, and producer Herb Polesie as panelists.

After a brief run on NBC, the series switched to ABC in March 1950 where it ran until June 1951. Beginning in July of that year, *Twenty Questions* moved to DuMont until May 1954 and then moved back to ABC to end its run. In 1953, Johnnie McPhee was replaced on the panel by Dickie Harrison who, in turn, was replaced by Bobby McGuire (the Van Deventer's son) in 1954. Also, Bill Slater left the show in 1952 to be replaced by Jay Jackson.

## Kay Kyser's Kollege of Musical Knowledge

Premiered December 1, 1949 on NBC Thursday 9:00 pm; ran until December 1950

    Cast: Kay Kyser –emcee
    Regulars: Ish Kabbible (Merwyn A. Bogue)
    Liza Palmer
    Sue Bennett
    Mike Douglas (later host of his own talk show)
    Honey Dreamers
    Dr. Roy K. Marshall – announcer
    Ben Grauer – announcer

Diane Sinclair
Ken Spaulding
Carl Hoff – orchestra director
Director: Earl Ebi
Writers: Bob Quigley and Larry Marks
Producer: Peter Lafferty

Bandleader Kay Kyser, dressed in cap and gown, quizzed contestants about music and other items on this series with the cast performing various musical numbers. Three bearded jurors designated the winners among the participants. Assisting Kyser with the questions was comedian Ish Kabbible. Announcer Ben Grauer was the "Dean of Public Speaking." The idea for the show grew out of an engagement Kay Kyser had during the 1930s at Chicago's Blackhawk restaurant starting as a community sing along and amateur night. Chicago's radio station first broadcast the show beginning on February 1, 1938.

On the first television show, six contestants were chosen to respond to questions submitted by people from across America. Musical clues to the answers were provided with each contestant given three questions related to a central topic. For example, singer Sue Bennett imitated three different singers which the contestant had to identify. Ben Grauer showed different businesses he had worked in during his career and the contestant had to guess the correct occupations. The quiz part of the show was interspersed with musical numbers and jokes from Ish Kabbible like demonstrating his Blizinterit. "What's a Blizinterit?" asked Kyser. Ish responds, ". . . no noise comes out of it unless someone blows-into-it!" The top winning contestants were given a brain buster question to correctly name a song played by the orchestra. The winner of the brain buster would receive a $50 Savings Bond. The runner-up would get a $25 bond; and each of the other contestants would receive $10 each.

# Informational Series

**ENTIRE CABLE CHANNELS** including the Science Channel and the History Channel are currently devoted to programs that seek to educate viewers on topics of special interest. In the past, many such programs aired on prime-time network television and usually covered subjects related to science or the arts.

Informational programs were some of the earliest shows to be broadcast on network television. Several series were simply composed of films that had been made by the government, corporations, educational entities, or other organizations as an inexpensive way to fill airtime. For example, even before ABC had a TV network of its own, the company began airing a series of films in late 1946 under the title *Video Reports to America* that had been produced by outside organizations such as the Automobile Manufacturers Association. These presentations aired over the DuMont affiliate in New York and stations in Washington, Schenectady, Philadelphia, and Chicago. Titles of films in the series included "New Cars," "Housing in the U.S.," "The American Merchant Marine," and "Public Health."

## *Serving through Science*

Premiered June 18, 1946 on DuMont Tuesday 9:00 pm; ran until May 27, 1947

Cast: Dr. Miller McClintock – guest host
Producer: Charles J. Durban
Sponsor: United States Rubber Company

Films from the Department of Agriculture, the Museum of Natural History, and other sources demonstrated 4-H Club activities, food freezing, and nature studies on *Serving through Science*. A series of six short films from the *Encyclopedia Britannica* were aired during the program's run with discussions following starting on August 27, 1946. Dr. Miller McClintock served as guest host.

Perhaps not surprisingly, musical performances were later added to the program to make it more entertaining for viewers.

## *Geographically Speaking*
Premiered October 27, 1946 on NBC Sunday 8:15 pm, ran until December 1, 1946

> Cast: Zetta Wells – hostess and narrator
> Producer: Wesley McKee

This fifteen-minute travelogue program began on NBC's New York station on June 9, 1946 before being aired by the network. Narrated by Zetta Wells, the wife of explorer Carveth Wells, a typical episode took viewers to places like Singapore, Australia, India, and Mexico. Sponsored by Bristol-Myers, the series ended when Mrs. Wells ran out of film of her many trips abroad. She sought to go on other world-wide excursions to replenish her film library, but the series never returned.

According to producer/director Ira Skutch, Mrs. Wells would bring her pet myna bird, no doubt obtained on one of her travel adventures, to the set who would talk with her.[96]

## *Television Screen Magazine*
Premiered November 17, 1946 on NBC Sunday 8:00 pm; ran until July 23, 1949

> Cast: Bill Berns
> Producer/director: Ira Skutch

One of the first magazine-style television programs, this series featured ordinary people talking about their hobbies and other subjects. The first show presented the New York Police Athletic League Chorus. One weekly feature was "Stories about Stamps," with stamp collector Walter Law, an NBC employee, showing different stamps and discussing stamp collecting. Bill Berns had a regular segment titled "While Berns Roams."

The following item from *The Cincinnati Enquirer* illustrates the type of guest that appeared on the series, "Billy Scott, Cincinnati's 'Miniature Opera' impresario, has been asked to take his puppets and stage settings to New York for an appearance on NBC's 'Television Screen Magazine.' The 16-year-old Southgate, Ky., youth who has designed sets for many operas will appear on the television program March 26."[97]

A June 8, 1948 program featured a segment about how to play tennis with tennis stars Bobby Riggs and Sarah Palfrey Cooke, an appearance from Howdy Doody, and a harp solo,

As the show evolved over time, more formal styles and emcees were added starting with George Putnam, Alan Scott, John K. M. McCaffrey, Millicent Fenwick, Bob Stanton, and Ray Forrest.

## *Eye Witness*

Premiered November 6, 1947 on NBC; aired at various times during November and December; in January aired Thursday 8:00 pm; ran until April 1948

    Cast: Ben Grauer – host
    Producer/director/writer: Garry Simpson

A behind-the scenes introduction to the new medium of television, this program aired live with film segments and actor dramatizations. Topics included how a TV set works and how a television studio operates. One 1948 episode chronicled, through dramatizations, the development of television technology including the transmission of images and their reception on home TV sets.

## *The Nature of Things*

Premiered February 5, 1948 on NBC Thursday 9:45 pm; ran until September 1950

    Cast: Dr. Roy K. Marshall – host/producer

Dr. Marshall, director of the Fels Planetarium, presented various scientific topics on this quarter-hour program that aired live from Philadelphia. Following his theory that "science can be fun," Marshall was able to explain to the average viewer scientific phenomena like factors governing air pressure and what meteors are. One show broadcast in April 1948 concerned the workings of a seismograph, including a history of the instrument from ancient China to models used in the nineteenth century to those used in the late 1940s; a discussion of how to decipher the readings on a seismograph; and an explanation of the areas of the world most prone to earthquakes. Other episodes dealt with physics, astronomy, and the weather.

After September 1950, the series aired during the summers of 1951 and 1952 and, thereafter, it appeared on Saturday and Sunday afternoons until 1954.

## *Author Meets the Critics*

Premiered April 4, 1948 on NBC Sunday 8:00 pm; initial run lasted until September 1950

Cast: John K. M. McCaffery
Writer: Jerry Coopersmith
Director: Hal Gerson
Producer: Martin Stone

The premise of the show, which had originated on radio in 1946 with Barry Gray as the moderator, had an author appearing with two critics of his or her recent work. Producer Martin Stone had been asked to do a book review program on the radio in New York and thought a face-to-face encounter between authors and critics would be more interesting. On the television series, one critic liked the book; another did not.

Before being aired by the network, the series had been on the local New York station WNBT as early as July 1947. For television, the producers opened up the format to include authors of ideas such as fashion design, movies, and sculpting as well as writers. For instance, an April 24, 1949 edition of the series presented actors David Wayne and Lillian Gish performing scenes from the motion picture, *Portrait of Jennie*.

*Author Meets the Critics* went from NBC to ABC on October 3, 1949. An ABC episode, written by Jerry Coopersmith and directed by Hal Gerson, featured Max Lerner and his collection of columns published as *Actions and*

John K. M. McCaffrey, host of *Author Meets the Critics*.

*Passions* that dealt with social problems of the day. The critics were J. Raymond Walsh who liked the work, and Godfrey P. Schmidt who didn't.

In 1951, the series was resurrected on NBC and in 1952 appeared on DuMont with Faye Emerson as the moderator. Later in 1952, author and TV personality Virgilia Peterson hosted the program. One February 1953 installment was devoted to Al Capp and his *The World of Li'l Abner* with famous author James Michener claiming that Mr. Capp, through his characters, was very funny. Book critic Edith Walton detested Li'l Abner and all the characters that were part of the comic strip. *Author Meets the Critics* ended in October 1954.

## *What's It Worth*
Premiered May 21, 1948 on CBS Friday 9:00 pm; ran until March 1949

Cast: Gil Fates – host/producer
Sigmund Rothschild – appraiser

Sigmund Rothschild appraised items on this program, highlighting their history and estimating what they were worth. Similar to *Antiques Roadshow*, people on the series showed their objects, explained the circumstances connected with the purchase or ownership of the item, and tried to guess the value. Rothschild then gave his estimate. The guest whose estimate was closest to Rothschild's, received $5. Items appraised on an early show included a set of daggers, an egret's feather, jewelry, and paintings.

Supposedly, one item that Rothschild wanted to present on the show was a human head, shrunken by New Zealand aborigines, but his advisers counseled against such a presentation.

In 1952, Rothschild appeared as the appraiser on a DuMont show similar to *What's It Worth* titled *Trash or Treasure*. He later wrote the book, *A Beginner's Guide to Antiques and Collectibles*.

## *Critic at Large*
Premiered August 18, 1948 on ABC Wednesday 7:30 pm; ran until April 20, 1949

Cast: John Mason Brown – host
Walter Herlihy – announcer

Producer: Ralph Warren

John Mason Brown chatted with guests involved in the various arts about current issues facing the art world on this thirty-minute series. Discussions took place in an informal living room setting about books, film, theater, radio, modern art, fashion, and newspapers. On the premiere show, the topic concerned the state of drama criticism with guests producer/director Brock Pemberton, press agent Richard Maney, playwright Marc Connelly, and playwright/journalist Russell Maloney.

A December 1948 program asked the question – Do Movies Honestly Portray American Life? Participants during the series run included author James Michener, producer Billy Rose, and publisher Bennett Cerf.

The program's announcer Walter Herlihy was the brother of announcer and emcee Ed Herlihy.

## *Teenage Book Club*

Premiered August 27, 1948 on ABC Friday 7:30 pm; ran until October 29, 1948

Cast: Margaret C. Scoggin - host

Moderated by Margaret C. Scoggin, the superintendent of Work with Young People for the New York Public Library, this program involved a group of teenagers reviewing a new book each week. Guests on the series included Betty Betz, author of *Your Manners Are Showing*, Harry Haenigsen who did the comic strip *Penny*, poet Louis Untermeyer, Carl Glick, writer of such works as *Shake Hands with the Dragon* and *Mickey, The Horse that Volunteered*, John Campbell, editor of *Astounding Science Fiction*, Gareth Garreau, who wrote about his experiences as a bat boy for the New York Giants, and journalist Ed Wallace.

## *Princess Sagaphi*

Premiered September 6, 1948 on NBC Monday 8:00 pm; ran until January 7, 1949

Cast: Princess Annette Sagaphi

This fifteen-minute travelogue featured films of exotic Far East locales narrated by Princess Sagaphi who, supposedly, was an expert on that region of the world. Other than appearing on this series, nothing much else is known about Annette Sagaphi.

## *I'd Like to See*
Premiered November 5, 1948 on NBC Friday 9:00 pm; ran until March 29, 1949

    Cast: Ray Morgan – host
    Kuda Bux – the man with the X-ray eyes

Viewers sent in suggestions about unusual things they would like to see such as nostalgic pictures from the past or current matters of interest. These were then presented using film and live demonstrations. According to Brooks and Marsh, the premiere episode featured scenes of the United Nations building, an Edgar Bergen – Charlie McCarthy routine, and film clips of U.S. Presidents.[98] Another episode showed how to carve a turkey and classic film shots of the Dempsey-Firpo fight.

    Kuda Bux, a Pakistani mystic and magician, began appearing on the show in January 1949 until it ended its run in March.

## *Paris Cavalcade of Fashions*
Premiered November 11, 1948 on NBC Thursday 7:15 pm; ran until January 20, 1949

    Cast: Faye Emerson – narrator
    Producer: World Wide Video

Each episode of this fashion series showed films of Paris models wearing the latest designs for women. Faye Emerson, who was married to President Roosevelt's son Elliott at the time, narrated the footage. She left the show in December 1948 and was replaced by actress Julie Gibson.

    Lack of a sponsor led to the program's demise after three months.

## Yesterday's Newsreel
Premiered in syndication December, 1948 at different times on various TV stations; ran for 139 episodes

>Cast: No regular cast
>Producer: Frederick W. Ziv

For some nostalgia, for others a history lesson, this quarter-hour series repackaged theatrical newsreels and sold them to local stations. The first episode featured clips from 1928 about the Presidential election, the Bryd expedition, the Olympics, and Johnny Weismuller's swimming record.

Other episodes reviewed such events as Lindbergh's flight across the Atlantic Ocean, the abdication of Edward VIII in Britain, the assassination of Alexander I of Yugoslavia, and the surrender of Germany at the end of World War I.

*Yesterday's Newsreel* was the first series offered by Ziv for syndication. Probably the most popular series that company put into syndication was Lloyd Bridges' *Sea Hunt*.

## The Johns Hopkins Science Review
Premiered December 31, 1948 on CBS Friday 9:00 pm; ran until May 1949

>Cast: Lynn Poole (1948-49) – host
>Robert Cochrane (1949)

Using films and discussions, this program covered such subjects as cancer, transistors, X-rays, and snails presented by faculty at Johns Hopkins University as well as by other experts. The series sought to explain to viewers the nature and importance of the different research projects conducted at the university.

After leaving CBS, the program aired on the DuMont network in prime time from October 1950 to September 1954 and then on that network Sunday afternoons until March 1955. A January 7, 1952 episode titled "A Visit to Our Studios" hosted by Lynn Poole provided a technical discussion of how the series was produced including the operations of the master control room at Baltimore station WAAM, the personnel in the studio control room with the director Paul Kane, and what the producer, set designer, cameramen and boom microphone operator as well as the episode narrators do. This installment then showed behind the scenes of an episode about glass blowing.

About two years after leaving DuMont, ABC picked up the program with a new title, *Johns Hopkins File 7*, for Sunday afternoons. That version ran until September 1960.

## *Television Close-ups*
Premiered in syndication in late 1948 and aired on local stations at various times; syndicated through the mid-fifties

Cast: Van Des Autels – narrator
Producer: Jerry Fairbanks Productions

This series of twenty-six five-minute mini-documentaries was made for NBC and aired on TV stations across the country. The programs were generally about historical subjects. The episodes were shot without sound and later narration by Van Des Autels was added. While several TV outlets showed this program at 6:55 pm, others did air the series in prime time.

## *Photographic Horizons*
Premiered January 12, 1949 on DuMont Monday 8:00 pm; ran until March 7, 1949

Cast: Joe Costa - host
Peggy Corday

Professional photographers described their techniques for taking photos on this program. The host, Joe Costa was president of the National Press Photographers Association and supervisor of the magazine section of the *New York Daily Mirror*. Peggy Corday was his model.

The series began on the New York DuMont affiliate in December 1947. On a November 10, 1948 episode aired locally in New York, Costa discussed the Truman/Dewey election upset and showed some recent photos from the Presidential campaign. He then announced the winner of the "Video Snapshot" where home viewers took a picture from their TV screen and sent it in to the show. The next segment of the show involved a demonstration of the process of xereography with Costa talking with Joseph C. Wilson, president of the Haloid Company of Rochester, NY. The Haloid Company later adopted the name of the process it created calling itself Xerox.

## What Do You Think?
Premiered January 17, 1949 on ABC Monday 8:30 pm; ran until February 14, 1949

Cast: Robert Hutchins
Linn Williams

Robert Maynard Hutchins, President and then Chancellor of the University of Chicago, may be most remembered for eliminating the football program at that school. However, he was also deeply involved in an educational movement using the "great books" of Western civilization as an educational tool to produce responsible citizens. A TV program based on the Great Books began on Chicago's WENR-TV in late 1948 with Hutchins as a chief participant.

Produced by the Great Books Foundation Forum, this discussion program was picked up by ABC in January 1949. On the next to last episode (February 7, 1949), Charles Percy, then the twenty-nine-year old head of Bell & Howell and later to become a U.S. Senator from Illinois, appeared with newspaper writer Lloyd Wendt to discuss the topic, "Should You Be Good or Clever?"

## And Everything Nice
Premiered March 15, 1949 on DuMont 7:00 pm Tuesday; ran until January 2, 1950

Cast: Maxine Barratt – hostess
Producer/director: Bob Loewi
Assistant producer: Barnaby Smith

The thirty-minute show, *And Everything Nice*, presented fashions, style tips, and entertainment for women including ideas for fashion and makeup for each season of the year and the latest Paris and New York styles. The program moved to Mondays at 8:30 pm in July 1949 and then to 9:00 pm on the same day in September 1949. In reviewing the show in its 9:00 pm time slot, *Variety* commented that the use of a talking mannequin to assist Maxine Barratt in discussing fashions ". . . was corny enough to be embarrassing." The publication went on to say, "Miss Barratt, a one-time dancer, looked sufficiently videogenic but she talked too much. Models were pretty and the styles they showed looked okay but their work still resolved itself into mere posing and posturing."[99]

## *Action Autographs*

Premiered April 24, 1949 on ABC Sunday 10:00 pm; ran until January 8, 1950

> Cast: Jack Brand – host (April to June)
> Ed Prentiss – host (September to January)
> Director: Tony Rizzo
> Producers: Jack Brand, Marge Bishop
> Sponsor: Bell & Howell

Similar to today's infomercials, the intent of this fifteen-minute show was to interest viewers in using Bell & Howell cameras by showing what can be done with film.

The first episode took viewers on a four-month hunt for gold beginning off the Mexican coast with guest, actor Eddie Albert and singer Burl Ives. Later the film showed Albert in the mountains looking for gold and then back at his dressing room at the end of the episode.

Guests on other installments included actors Scott Brady and Buster Crabbe, travel expert Burton Holmes, and race car driver Wilbur Shaw.

## *Crusade in Europe*

Premiered May 5, 1949 on ABC Thursday 9:00 pm; ran until October 27, 1949

> Cast: Westbrook Van Voorhis – main narrator
> Producer: Richard de Rochemont for March of Time Productions in association with Twentieth Century Fox

Editor: Arthur Tourtellot
Sponsor: Time and Life

This half-hour documentary series using combat footage from the U.S. Army, Navy, and Coast Guard as well as from the British War Office and Ministry of Information was based on Dwight D. Eisenhower's book about the Allied campaign in Europe during World War II. The initial installment titled "Prelude to War" told of events that preceded World War II including the Nazi invasions of Austria, Czechoslovakia, and Poland, British Prime Minister Neville Chamberlain's declaration of war against Germany, Germany's invasion of France, and the United States unconcern about the war in Europe.

The story was told over twenty-six episodes with Maurice Joyce reading quotes from Eisenhower's book. The final episode, "Review" summarized the preceding installments highlighting America's entrance into the war after the Japanese attacked Pearl Harbor, the D-Day invasion of Nazi-occupied France, the Battle of the Bulge where Germany struck back against the Allies, and the Nazi surrender.

## *Theatre of the Mind*
Premiered July 14, 1949 on NBC Thursday 9:30 pm; ran until September 15, 1949

Cast: Dr. Houston Peterson of Rutgers University- moderator
Producer/writer: Ann Marlowe

*Theatre of the Mind* focused on helping people with emotional problems by dramatizing a problem such as alcoholism, inferiority complexes, or growing older and then having a panel of psychiatrists discuss how the issue could be resolved. Questions from the studio audience were also answered.

On the first show, the problem dealt with was a domineering mother. The mother in question justified her possessiveness because her husband had deserted her and all she had left was her son who would like to marry. But the mother's interference got in the way of the son's planned life on his own. The panel discussing the problem after the dramatization included Claire Savage Littledale, editor of *Parents' Magazine*, Dr. Edward Strecher, and Dr. Marina Farnum, co-author of *Women – The Lost Sex.*

## *The Amazing Polgar*
Premiered September 16, 1949 on CBS Friday 7:45 pm; ran until October 21, 1949

    Cast: Dr. Franz Polgar – professional hypnotist
    Cy Harrice - announcer
    Producer: Chuck Lewin
    Director: David Rich

Franz Polgar demonstrated the effects of hypnosis on people on this ten-minute show. On the premiere episode, he hypnotized his six studio participants before the program started so as not to affect home viewers. In one demonstration, the good doctor, who had PhD's in psychology and in economics, convinced a subject that his right hand could feel no pain. The man did not react when his finger was placed over a burning match, but did react when the other hand was touched. In another example, Polgar told his subjects that they would feel the seats of their chairs burn when he touched his tie. The subjects leaped to their feet when he later placed his fingers on his tie.

## *Burton Holmes Travelogues*
Premiered October 2, 1949 in syndication at various time in different cities; ran until December 25, 1949

    Cast: Burton Holmes
    Thayer Soule
    Sponsor: Santa Fe Railway

This series of fifteen-minute travelogues, hosted and narrated by world traveler Burton Holmes, focused on various tourist sites in the southwest of the United States. The initial episode concerned the Grand Canyon featuring a four mile trek by mule with, naturally, a commercial from Santa Fe Railways encouraging viewers to write in for the railroad's Grand Canyon travel folder. *The Billboard* described Holmes TV debut thusly,

> Flashily attired in white tie and tails, the distinguished, snowy-haired lecturer was visibly nervous as he opened the program with a quaver-voiced introduction for *his younger* co-narrator

Thayer Soule, also in white tie. The boys indulged in some pointless horseplay about which one of them was going to wear a sombrero, then launched the heavy-handed film narration. The latter featured such moth eaten gags as "Did I hear a rip?" in reference to a lady's struggle to mount a mule, and Holmes's self-conscious tag for the stanza – "Love that mule."[100]

Titles of other episodes included the "Land of Enchantment," "Southwestern Wonderland," "Land of Pueblos," "Navajo & Hopi Land," "Carlsbad Caverns," "Phoenix – City of the Sun," "City of the Angels," "Palm Springs," "San Francisco," and "Yosemite."

## *Portrait of America*

Premiered December 8, 1949 on NBC Thursday 8:00 pm; ran until December 29, 1949

    Cast: Norman Barry – host
    Director: Reinald Werrenrath Jr.

This thirty-minute documentary series profiled typical American families in Chicago to depict the ideal that "family is the foundation of democracy." Each week, the program visited a different Chicago home to show a family's typical evening activities. During each episode, film inserts were used to reveal members of the family engaged in activities outside the home. Large and small, prominent and unknown family units were presented.

## *Kiernan's Kaleidoscope*

Premiered in syndication 1949; aired at various times on local stations

    Cast: John Kiernan – host/narrator

This quarter-hour show narrated by sports columnist John Kiernan, the man who did radio's *Information Please*, presented films about nature and science. The initial episode, "Can Animals Think?" included experiments with various types of animals like dogs, chickens, and monkeys demonstrating their ability to learn. Included was a segment where a guinea pig was taught to read. What the pig read is unknown.

Dione Lucas host of *To the Queen's Taste*.

# Instructional Programs 20

**GRANTED THAT THE LINE** between "informational" programs and "instructional" ones is somewhat blurred, but the series profiled in this chapter are essentially "how-to" shows that attempt to demonstrate how to make something or how to solve a problem. Informational series presented in Chapter 19 were ones that simply wanted to present viewers with facts on different topics.

### *I Love to Eat*
Premiered August 30, 1946 on NBC Friday 8:15 pm; ran until May 18, 1947

>Cast: James Beard – host/chef
>Producer: Wesley McKee
>Sponsor: Borden's Cheese

Chef James Beard showed viewers how to prepare his unique dishes like plum pudding with hard sauce and brandy. The first part of each show presented how to cook a dish with the recipe flashed on the TV screen so that viewers could copy it. The second part of the episode was given over to showing the finished product and eating it. According to Ira Skutch, "As soon as the show ended, the entire crew converged on the set to snatch food and devour it on the spot."[101]

Beard's initial cooking demonstrations were on an NBC daytime magazine series called *Radio City Matinee* in spring 1946 that aired on WNBT in New York. Repairs to NBC's transmitters led to the series airing some episodes in the evenings. Along with Mr. Beard's cooking segments, the show included features on fashion tips, home redecorating, shopping, and other home-related items. The prime-time presentations of *Radio City Matinee* were eventually titled *For You and Yours*, and, when that series ended, Beard's *I Love to Eat* premiered as its own series.

Sponsored for most of its run by Borden, commercials for the company's products were incorporated into each installment as was the case with most live shows during the early days of TV. As noted in an article about *I Love to Eat*, Mr. Beard frequently interrupted his cooking demonstrations with skits plugging Borden dairy products. ". . . Beard interacts with an animated puppet, goes to a fortune teller, introduces a little girl to a giant, invites a song-and-dance team into his kitchen (and gets caught up singing with them), hosts a food-themed game show, and surveys the latest in fashion," all as part of promoting his sponsor's products."[102]

James Beard, the quintessential American epicure, wrote twenty different cookbooks beginning with *Hors D'oeuvre and Canapes* in 1940.

## *You Are an Artist*
Premiered November 1, 1946 on NBC Friday 8:15 pm; ran until January 17, 1950

Cast: Jon Gnagy

On this fifteen-minute instructional series Jon Gnagy started a charcoal drawing at the beginning of each episode and then showed step-by-step how to execute it. A month after the premiere of *You Are an Artist*, Gulf Oil decided to sponsor the show. The series would then open with Gnagy drawing the word "Gulf" and circling it, followed by a slide stating "The Gulf Oil Company and Your Gulf Dealer Presents *You Are an Artist*."

*Television Magazine* described the Christmas 1946 episode thusly ". . . the artist with simple stroke and instructive chatter created a scene with all the accoutrements of the holiday. A tree was there, gifts were there, holly was there – but above all the artist's hand was there . . . and it was definitely in the way through most of his creative instruction."[103]

On virtually every episode, Gnagy had a segment showing a painting from the New York Museum of Modern Art. Two armed guards stood in the TV studio to protect the valuable art work.

After *You Are an Artist*, Jon Gnagy starred on a similar show titled *Learn to Draw* that was syndicated from 1950 to 1955. In addition to showing people how to draw pictures beginning with simple shapes like circles, straight lines, and triangles, Gnagy used the program to sell his *Learn to Draw* hobby kits.

## *Let's Rhumba*
Premiered November 15, 1946 on NBC Friday 8:15 pm; ran until January 17, 1947

    Cast: D'Avalos – Host
    Director: Howard Conley

The title says it all. This was a quarter-hour dance instruction show presented by Hispanic dancer D'Avalos, the first Latino to have his own network show. Each episode featured D'Avalos and his female partner going through some of the basic rhumba steps as he patiently explained to viewers the movements of the dance. The "Ranchero" was the featured dance.

## *Dancing on Air*
Premiered February 2, 1947 on NBC Sunday 8:00 pm; ran until March 2, 1947

    Cast: Ed Sims – emcee
    Radcliffe Hall – emcee
    Various Fred Astaire dancers
    Producer: Stan Quinn
    Director: Ernie Colling
    Sponsor: Standard Brands

Instructors from the Fred Astaire Studios presented a quarter-hour dance instruction series. On a typical episode, teachers featured a particular dance and then showed the audience how it was done. Between numbers, there were some comedy bits and an interview with a weekly guest star.

    *Variety* reviewed the third episode of the series broadcast on February 16 and stated that the show was delayed forty minutes when New York City's NBC station's transmitter failed and a camera went dead. The malfunctioning camera meant that viewers couldn't see the dancers feet "... rendering practically worthless any attempts to teach the rhumba."[104]

## In the Kelvinator Kitchen

Premiered May 7, 1947 on NBC Wednesday 8:30 pm; ran until June 30, 1948

Cast: Alma Kitchell - host
Ray Forrest – announcer
Director: Howard Cordery
Sponsor – Nash-Kelvinator

Cooking with Kelvinator appliances was the focus of this fifteen-minute instructional series. Alma Kitchell first started out as a singer on radio and then had her own radio talk show on ABC titled *Woman's Exchange* before hosting this TV show.

On the debut episode of *In the Kelvinator Kitchen,* also known simply as *In the Kitchen,* Kitchell prepared a plank steak. At the time, ad agencies were experimenting with shows in prime time hoping that the experience would give them sufficient knowledge to take advantage of the time when there would be a large enough daytime TV audience to support such programs.

After the *Kelvinator Kitchen* series ended, Kitchell retired from radio and TV work. She died in 1996 at the age of 103.

## The Wife Saver

Premiered May 22, 1947 on NBC Thursday 8:30 pm, ran until June 26, 1947

Cast: Allen Prescott – host

*The Wife Saver* presented helpful hints for homemakers in a humorous style. Host Allen Prescott began the radio version of *The Wife Saver* on the Blue Network (precursor to ABC) in 1932 and subsequently the program aired at various times on ABC and NBC. At the start of his career in radio, Prescott commented on various news items and then went on to give household hints, many of which were sent to him by listeners. He obtained other such hints by talking to home economics experts, reading books on cooking and home making, and doing his own household experiments.

On television, Prescott would show how to work various kitchen gadgets and give viewers advice on solving household problems like keeping drawers from sticking.

After *The Wife Saver* left network television, Prescott took the show to WFIL-TV in Philadelphia on weekday mornings beginning in 1953.

## *To the Queen's Taste* (aka *Dione Lucas' Cooking School*)
Premiered May 3, 1948 on CBS Monday 8:05 pm; ran until December 29, 1949

Cast: Dione Lucas – host and chef
Producer/director: Paul Byron

Long before *The French Chef* with Julia Child, *To the Queen's Taste* started on the local CBS station in New York with Mrs. Dione Lucas, the first female graduate of the L'Ecole de Corden Bleu in Paris. She owned the Corden Bleu restaurant in New York City from where the show originated. Lucas prepared everything from pot pies to soufflés to strudel.

In October 1949, the cooking show moved from Mondays to Thursdays nights at 7:00 pm where it remained until it was canceled in December. The series was replaced on the CBS schedule by two fifteen-minute musical programs – *Strictly for Laughs* and *The Paul Arnold Show*.

## *At Home and How*
Premiered January 1, 1949 on ABC Saturday 8:00 pm; ran until April 20, 1949

Cast: Louise Winslow – host
Carl Eastman – sidekick

This early "how-to" show was aimed at homemakers providing them with the newest and best ways of handling their tasks. Broadcast on ABC's Eastern network, the program presented demonstrations like how to cover a footstool, making a meal out of turkey leftovers, sewing an evening gown from remnants, and making jewelry from sealing wax.

Hostess Louise Winslow, the Martha Stewart of her day, had a degree in home economics and had been a captain in the Women's Army Corps. Carl Eastman, nicknamed "Shorty" on the show, provided comedy relief and was the taster for Winslow's dishes and critic of her furniture repairs and jewelry creations.

The series, originally seen on Saturdays for a few weeks, moved to Wednesdays at 8:00 pm against *Arthur Godfrey and His Friends* on January 19 for the balance of its run.

## Dr. Fix-Um
Premiered May 3, 1949 on ABC Tuesday 9:30 pm; ran until August 6, 1950

Cast: Arthur Youngquist – host
Ed Prentiss – Youngquist's assistant

Broadcast from Chicago, the program gave helpful household hints showing how to repair broken gadgets and solve other household problems. Examples of Youngquist's hints included how to make a fireplace fan from wall paper strips and how to repair dilapidated walls. On a May 1949 episode, viewers were shown how to remove paint spots from shoes, install a towel hook, paint screens, make weather forecasters out of pine cones, and remove a broken bulb from a lamp socket.

Youngquist was a handicraft expert from *Popular Mechanics* magazine. After its network run, the series continued to air on Chicago TV stations.

## R.F.D. America
Premiered May 26, 1949 on NBC Thursday 8:00 pm; ran until September 15, 1949

Cast: Bob Murphy – emcee
Norman Barry – announcer

As the title implies, this series dealt with topics of interest to rural America. Part of the show was a quiz and other parts purely instructional. As a television series, the program began on a Chicago TV station in January 1949. Early episodes, for example, had guests putting together a giant jigsaw puzzle of a cow made out of plywood and being asked what farm products came to mind when certain song titles were mentioned. The song "Dancing with Tears in My Eyes" reminded guests of onions. Demonstrations of different cuts of beef, a sheep demonstration, and other plant and farm animal-related subjects were presented.

The program had started on radio in 1947 with Joe Kelly of *Quiz Kids* fame as the first host. It was originally a game show with farmers answering questions submitted by listeners. One question and answer caught the eye of staff from NBC and was deleted from the script as being in poor taste.

Question: What do you do to induce a cow to start giving milk after she has decided to be completely stubborn and hold it?

Answer: Usually a cow will hold her milk if she is frightened, or chased by dogs or angered. Any excitement or disturbance interferes with the action of the let-down hormone. Also, if a cow had sore teats or a congested and swollen udder, she will hold her milk. The farmer should check these possibilities. Wiping and massaging the udder with a cloth wrung from very warm water will stimulate the nerves of the teats and cause a cow to produce a chemical hormone – the let-down hormone.

The comment from network staff was "Farmers may know all about these subjects, but the average farmer does not discuss them at the dinner table in front of the women-folks."[105]

Red Barber (left) with major league baseball player Frankie Frisch appearing on *Red Barber's Clubhouse*.

# Sports Programs 21

**LIVE SPORTING EVENTS,** particularly boxing and wrestling, appeared frequently on television in the forties. *Gillette Cavalcade of Sports*, featuring boxing matches, was one of the first network shows premiering on NBC in 1946. Basketball, football, and baseball games were also popular on TV. However, as noted in the Preface, this guide excludes live sporting events and shows reporting sports scores from the series profiled. But several other sports-related shows occupied spots on network schedules in the early days of TV. Such programs are described in this chapter.

### *Campus Hoop-La*
Premiered December 27, 1946 on NBC Friday 8:00 pm; ran until December 19, 1947

>   Cast: Bob Stanton – host
>   Sponsor: U.S Rubber
>   Producer/director: Ernie Colling

Set in a fictional campus ice cream soda shop, this series, aimed at teens, had students singing and dancing to jukebox music, participating in quizzes, and talking about sports. The show also had interviews with athletes as well as film clips of sporting events. The original concept was to report basketball scores. Actresses playing cheerleaders, including a young Eva Marie Saint, created excitement before sportscaster Bob Stanton gave the latest scores. U.S Rubber used the show to promote its athletic footwear particularly Keds sneakers. The cheerleaders had the letter "K" on their sweaters for the name brand Keds. After the basketball season ended, the program focused on baseball and then football. In its second season, the setting of the show changed to a college newspaper office.

## *Sportsman's Quiz*
Premiered April 26, 1948 on CBS Monday 8:00 pm; ran until April 25, 1949

>Cast: Bernard Dudley - host
>Don Baker
>Sponsor: *Sports Afield* magazine

On this five-minute program, radio and television announcer Bernard Dudley asked questions relating to hunting, fishing, and conservation with Don Baker responding to queries using various visual aids like drawings, pictures, and diagrams. Viewers could send in their own questions.

## *Girl of the Week/Sportswoman of the Week*
Premiered September 9, 1948 on NBC Thursday 7:45 pm; ran until December 2, 1948

>Cast: Thelma A. Prescott – narrator/writer/producer/director

Initially, this five-minute series was a documentary called *Girl of the Week*, which profiled topflight professional models, showing how they kept in shape and how they posed for fashion layouts. The initial "girl of the week" was model Dorian Leigh. The premiere episode showed her in a physical education class, on the beach, and in John Rawlings' photo studio being photographed for a *Vogue* magazine cover.

The program's format changed in November 1948 to an interview show with tennis star Sarah Palfrey Cooke chatting with notable women of the sport's world.

## *Sports Album*
Premiered in syndication at various times on different stations in 1948; ran until 1949

>Cast: Dennis James; Bill Slater – narrators
>Producer: Ziv Productions

This package of old sports newsreels was often aired by TV stations right before and/or right after live sporting events like baseball and football games. An episode consisted of three newsreels running five minutes each. Some stations would air just one newsreel for five minutes; others would air the full fifteen-minute program.

The featured newsreels most often dealt with baseball and football. For example, one program showed footage of famous opening days in baseball, the New York Giants in spring training, and the legendary baseball player Ty Cobb. A football-themed show consisted of southern California Rose Bowl classics, Army-Navy games, and Yale-Harvard classics.

Like Dennis James, Bill Slater appeared frequently on early television. In addition to narrating *Sports Album*, he hosted *Birthday Party*, *Charade Quiz*, *Twenty Questions*, *Fishing and Hunting Club*, and *Broadway to Hollywood - Headline Clues*, all described in this book. Actor Christian Slater is the great-nephew of Bill Slater.

## *Identify*

Premiered February 14, 1949 on ABC Monday 9:00 pm; ran until May 9, 1949

Cast: Bob Elson – host
Wayne Griffin – announcer
Producer: William Hollenbeck
Director: Greg Garrison

This fifteen-minute program from Chicago was a sports quiz where a panel of famous athletes tried to identify scenes from the sports world or famous sports stars through drawings, photos, and/or film. During the course of the show, Elson would also interview the athletes.

Host Bob Elson was the play-by-play announcer for the Chicago White Sox baseball team from the 1930s to 1970. Director Greg Garrison would later produce Dean Martin's variety series on NBC.

## *They're Off*

Premiered June 30, 1949 on DuMont Thursday 8:30 pm; ran until August 18, 1949

Cast: Tom Shirley – emcee
Byron Field – race caller

Little is known about this DuMont game show other than that it involved contestants being questioned about historic horse races based on films of such races.

Tom Shirley was an announcer and actor in radio and on television. His last role before his death in the early 1960s was on the daytime drama *Love of Life*.

## *Red Barber's Clubhouse*
Premiered July 2, 1949 on CBS Saturday 6:30 pm; ran until October 1950

Cast: Red Barber – host and commentator

Iconic sportscaster Walter "Red" Barber hosted this quarter-hour series of sports commentary, analysis, and interviews. The show initially aired outside of prime time until February 1950 and then took a brief hiatus. When it returned in September, it was slotted on Tuesdays at 10:30 pm.

*Red Barber's Clubhouse* aired on both radio and television. On the first program, Barber commented on Joe DiMaggio's comeback and the Wimbledon tennis tournament. His guest was Pee Wee Reese of the then Brooklyn Dodgers.

Barber returned with another fifteen-minute series in September 1953 called *The Peak of Sports News*. That program ended in December of that year, but twelve months later Red Barber was back again with his own show titled *Red Barber's Corner* which ran on CBS and then on NBC until January 1958.


## *Practice Tee*
Premiered August 5, 1949 on NBC Friday 7:30 pm; ran until September 9, 1949

Cast: William P. Barbour – golf instructor

Fifteen-minute early evening shows were usually musical variety ones. *Practice Tee* was different. Golf pro William P. Barbour at Sleepy Hollow Country Club in Cleveland presented golf lessons to viewers by instructing a different "pupil" on each week's show, which was a summer replacement for the Friday edition of *Mohawk Showroom*. Barbour's pupils were amateur golfers from the Cleveland area. While the program was geared to amateurs, it was really designed for those with some experience at the game and not for the beginner.

This was the first network series to emanate from Cleveland, Ohio. William Barbour was employed at Sleepy Hollow Country Club from 1939 to 1974. After that he owned and operated Irish Hills Golf Club in Mount Vernon, Ohio.

## *Fishing and Hunting Club*
Premiered September 30, 1949 on DuMont Friday 9:00 pm; ran until March 31, 1950

Cast: Bill Slater – emcee
Bud Collyer – announcer
Jim Hurley, outdoor editor of the *New York Daily Mirror*, Dave Newell, former editor of *Field and Stream*, Gail Borden, former Olympic champion, and author Jeff Bryant – panelists
Producer: Walter Sickles
Director: Jack Rayel

Set in a simulated rustic lodge, experts in hunting and fishing gave tips to viewers on this thirty-minute show. Fish and Game Commissions of many states supplied unusual films of outdoor life for the program. The series started on radio. Its title changed to *Sports for All* on January 20, 1950 broadening the scope of the series.

On a typical episode, host Bill Slater read questions from viewers which were answered by the panelists using a drawing board, film, and live demonstrations.

Jinx Falkenburg and her husband Tex McCrary, hosts of *CBS' Preview*.

# Talk/Interview Shows 22

**IN THE LATE 40S,** talk shows were a fairly frequent occurrence on prime-time television unlike today where they are fixtures on late night and daytime TV but not on prime time.

### *Tex and Jinx*
Premiered April 20, 1947 on NBC Sunday 8:00 pm; ran until September 5, 1949

Husband Tex McCrary, a newspaper columnist, and his wife Jinx Falkenburg, an actress, model, and former "Miss Rheingold" Beer in 1940, had several interview shows on NBC and CBS in the 1940s. Their first show was fifteen minutes long but soon expanded to thirty minutes. Sitting on a living room set, Tex and Jinx interviewed celebrities and showed films of current interest. There were also product demonstrations such as one showing how model trains worked. During summer 1947, the program presented special filmed shows and became known as *The Tex and Jinx Films*.

After the show left NBC prime-time in August 1947, the couple hosted the daytime *The Swift Home Service Club* on that network during the 1947-48 TV season.

In March 1949, Tex and Jinx moved to CBS with a series called *Preview* – a television magazine of sorts where they were presented as "editors" of a magazine that had different departments. A blown-up page or photo, presumably from their magazine called *Preview,* offered a point of departure for introducing the subject of discussion – usually "soft" topics like theater, motion pictures, or books. An early show included the Katherine Dunham dancers, political cartoonist Fred Packer drawing pictures of Winston Churchill who was about to arrive in this country for a visit, orchestra leader Ray Bloch, newspaper reporter Bob Cooke who led a discussion with some college basketball players about an upcoming East/West game, and actor Kirk Douglas plugging his new movie *Champion*.

Commenting on the program, *The New York Times* indicated that, "The camera jumps about at such a breathless pace that the viewer often finds himself waiting to see if anything will go wrong. Too often it does." However, the paper did say that "... the personable Jinx is a true natural for video's cameras. She is "Mrs. Television' in a walk."[106]

### *The Jack Eigen Show*
Premiered October 30, 1947 on DuMont's New York station and thereafter on other DuMont affiliates; ran until February 1951

Cast: Jack Eigen – host

Long-time New York radio host Jack Eigen presided over this fifteen-minute program which aired in the early evenings on DuMont TV stations. On his four-hour radio program which was broadcast from midnight to 4:00 am from the Copacabana, Eigen would play records, answer viewer phone calls, interview celebrities and discuss show business gossip. His television show was much shorter in length but similar in content with Eigen interviewing Broadway and Hollywood stars and presenting show business news.

An experience on his radio program led Eigen to co-write a quirky little book called *Etiquette with False Teeth* after witnessing a noted celebrity at the Copacabana Lounge lose his dentures. The work was described as "A more or less factual volume designed to prevent an individual from banishment from a home, club, clique, or business merely because of false teeth."[107]

### *Tonight on Broadway*
Premiered April 20, 1948 on CBS Tuesday 7:00 pm; ran until December 25 1949

Cast: John Mason Brown – host
Producer: Martin Gosch

John Mason Brown, the president of the New York Drama Critics Circle, interviewed Broadway stars and presented excerpts from Broadway dramas, comedies, and musicals on this program which aired from actual theatre stages. The show started April 6, 1948 on WCBS with producer Martin Gosch as the host interviewing producer Leland Heyward, co-author Tom Heggen, and designer Joseph Mielziner from the Broadway play *Mr. Roberts*. Actor William Harrigan, who had the role of the captain on the ship, did a bit from the play during the second part of the show. Two weeks later, the series debuted on the CBS television network featuring the show *High Button Shoes*.

## *We, The People*
Premiered June 1, 1948 on CBS Tuesday 9:00 pm; ran until September 26, 1952

> Cast: Dwight Weist – host (1948 -1950)
> Dan Seymour – announcer
> Oscar Bradley Orchestra
> Producer: Rodney Erickson
> Director: Ace Ochs
> Sponsor: Gulf Oil

The first regularly scheduled series to be aired at the same time on both network radio and television presented a cross-section of people who were interviewed about important events in their lives. Guests were introduced stating, "We, the people . . . speak."

*We, The People* began on radio in the late 1930s. As *Variety* noted in its review of the television premiere, "In terms of depicting for home viewers how a radio show is run off, it could probably be classed as a success. But to call it a television show is a complete misnomer."[108] As in radio, most guests read off scripts meaning the show was utterly lacking in spontaneity.

Before the start of the premiere episode on television, CBS President Frank Stanton, Siguard Larmon, president of advertising agency Young & Rubicam, and Celment M. Gile, vice president for Gulf advertising held a ceremony that was telecast noting that the program was the first to be simulcast.

The debut featured stories from radio personality Fred Allen, the King Cole Trio with Nate King Cole singing "Nature Boy" along with

Eden Ahbez who composed the song, Mrs. Spencer Tracy describing the work she was doing on behalf of deaf children, "Evil-Eye" Ben Finkle who supposedly could put hexes on sports teams, Maury Dreicer, a gourmet chef, and actors Joe Waring and Martha Greenhouse.

The series moved to NBC in November 1949 with new host Dan Seymour. On a 1950 episode right before Christmas, Ed Sullivan appeared to tell his favorite holiday story about Doc Witten who helped to raise young orphaned boys. The program also included a story related by Edwin Murphy, President of Star Brothers Bell Company, about a church in Okinawa in need of a church bell but that could afford only a cow bell. The company sent the establishment a real church bell. A few years later, one of the company's employees, who had enlisted in World War II and ended up in Okinawa, hid behind the church bell to avoid sniper fire.

Incidentally, Carl Reiner credits an interview of an elderly man that aired on *We, the People*, when Dan Seymour was host as the inspiration for the "2000 Year Old Man" sketch on *Your Show of Shows*.[109]

## *Key to the Missing* (aka *Key to Missing Persons*)

Premiered August 8, 1948 on DuMont Sunday 6:30 pm; ran until September 16, 1949

> Cast: Archdale J. Jones – host and producer
> Val – co-host and investigator
> Director: James Caddigan

This interview series, based on a radio show called *Where Are They Now?*, attempted to track down lost relatives and friends. Archdale Jones talked with people interested in finding a certain person and then asked viewers to phone in any information they may have about the subject. The cases did not ordinarily involved crime so they did not come under police jurisdiction.

"Every year about 200,000 people in the U.S. disappear," Jones told *TV Forecast* magazine in 1948. "Through video we expect to locate many of these people and reunite them with their families. People often don't have the funds necessary to hire private investigators to search for the missing persons, and although they have the facts to conduct a search, they don't understand the techniques and they don't know how to go about finding the lost ones."[110]

One case investigated by the show involved a man named Harry Sewall who was trying to establish the identity of his biological parents. Sewall had been placed in a boarding school at a young age by his guardian and was now trying to find his mother who had lived in Baltimore around 1912. Another case dealt with a woman who was trying to find her sister who had been adopted by another family at a young age.

Initially, slotted on early Sunday evenings, the program moved to prime time on Fridays at 7:00 pm in October 1948 and continued in various prime-time slots until September 1949.

## *Kiernan's Corner*
Premiered August 16, 1948 ABC Monday 8:00 pm, ran until March 30, 1949

Cast: Walter Kiernan
Producer/director: Marshall Diskin

Newspaperman and radio commentator Walter Kiernan interviewed various people around New York City. On the initial episode, Kiernan questioned women at a reducing salon while the women were working with machines designed to lose weight.

As noted in the chapter on game shows, Walter Kiernan also hosted *Sparring Partners, That Reminds Me,* and *Who Said That?* during the forties and fifties. However, he may be best remembered for his newspaper column and radio show, *One Man's Opinion.*

## *Mary Margaret McBride*
Premiered September 21, 1948 on NBC Tuesday at 9:00 pm; ran until December 14, 1948

Cast: Mary Margaret McBride – interviewer
Vincent Connolly – assistant
Producer: George Foley
Director: Garry Simpson

Radio personality Mary Margaret McBride presided over this thirty-minute interview show. McBride started on radio in 1934 on New York station WOR playing grandmother Martha Deane chatting about her fictitious family and giving household hints. Beginning in 1937, she had her own network radio show interviewing celebrated people and talking about almost everything.

Ms. McBride had a "down-home charm" and a "keen and astute interviewing style." "Her voice was 'girlish, hesitant, often bewildered' . . . Her stock in trade was innocence: 'she preserved the air of a little girl lost in the big city,' but managed to draw from the rich and famous revealing anecdotes and warm insights."[111]

On the first episode of her television program, Ms. McBride opened the program by having the camera show the crew, control room, etc., and then she sampled the studio onlookers as to whether or not she should wear a hat on television. Her guests were seven members of the Overseas Press Club and their wives who had recently returned from countries behind the Iron Curtain. They discussed life in Russia and Eastern Europe.

McBride's television series did not last long because she insisted on running her TV show just like her radio series which resulted in a rather static presentation of "talking" heads with inadequate set design and a lot of close-up camera work.

## *Pauline Frederick's Guestbook*
Premiered January 12, 1949 on ABC Wednesday 9:15 pm; ran until April 13, 1949

Cast: Pauline Frederick – hostess

Pauline Frederick interviewed a variety of business, political, and celebrity personages. The program was initially broadcast on the local ABC station in New York City beginning in August 1948. On an early local show, Ms. Frederick chatted with two gentlemen working to establish a Christian university in Japan.

On each fifteen-minute show, the guest or guests would be introduced and sign the hostess' guest book. A November 7, 1948 episode that aired locally in New York had abstract artist and barge captain John von Wicht demonstrate abstract painting and G. Reddy Grubbs and his wife Bippy talk about lip-stick brushes. Impatient with how long it took his wife to apply her lipstick using a lip brush, Mr. Grubbs created one with a guide on it to make applying lipstick easier. On another installment that aired November 28, Ms. Frederick interviewed Metropolitan Opera star Patrice Munsel.

Pauline Frederick was one of the first female news reporters. She began her career with ABC and then covered the United Nations for NBC for twenty-one years. She later worked for PBS.

## *Manhattan Spotlight*
Premiered January 24, 1949 on DuMont on various days of the week; ran until April 20, 1951

Cast: Chuck Tranum – host

Interviews with people who had interesting hobbies and/or talents were the focus of this fifteen-minute program. New York City talk show host Joe Franklin was one of the early guests. The show began in daytime on DuMont and then moved to early evening before settling into the slot between 10:00 pm and 10:45 pm.

A 1951 stanza featured Tranum interviewing Robert Marx of Marxman pipes showing his collection of smoking pipes ranging from those used by Eskimos to ancient stone pipes. The show included a demonstration of how modern pipe makers carve out special bowls with a pipe maker operating a power tool to inscribe a floral design on the briar.

Chuck Tranum later became a talent agent for television commercials.

## *In the First Person*
Premiered January 29, 1949 on CBS Saturday 7:30 pm; ran until October 10, 1950

Cast: Quincy Howe – host

The fifteen-minute *In the First Person* centered on discussions with newsmakers including entertainers, politicians, CEO's, and other interesting personalities. For example, on a November 12, 1949 segment, Quincy Howe interviewed amateur photographer Tom Maloney.

Ned Calmer replaced Howe in September 1950. Some of the people interviewed included Emery Klein, the United Nations television officer and co-author of a book of political cartoons titled *The U.N. Sketchbook* with cartoonist Derso. The two showed sketches that had been done of Dean Acheson and President Franklin D. Roosevelt. A May 1950 installment featured writer Langston Hughes who talked about his book, *Simple Speaks His Mind*, read two of his poems, "Bad Morning" and "Out of Work," and discussed his views about blacks in America.

## *The Wendy Barrie Show*
Premiered March 14, 1949 on DuMont Monday, Wednesday, Friday 7:00 pm; ran until September 27, 1950

Cast: Wendy Barrie – hostess

This interview show, hosted by Wendy Barrie, had several title, network, and time slot changes during its run. First called *Inside Photoplay*, then *Photoplay Time*, *The Wendy Barrie Show*, and finally *Through Wendy's Window*, the series also changed networks from DuMont to ABC to NBC. Originally a thrice-weekly half-hour show, near its end it became a fifteen minute once a week show.

The setting for the show was a facsimile of Barrie's New York apartment where she talked with celebrities and presented show business gossip. In reviewing the show when it moved to ABC in fall 1949, *The New York Times* wrote, "With her own particular form of magic she manages to take the curse off one of those informal interview sessions wherein an assortment of guests wander in and out of the studio. . . . Miss Barrie has a knack for eliciting random information and persuading contrasting personalities to get along together. Certainly for the present she is without rival as television's No. 1 hostess."[112]

In addition to this interview show, Ms. Barrie also hosted *The Adventures of Oky Doky* and the game show *Picture This*. Before her television career, she had appeared in several movies, perhaps best known for her roles in *The Saint* and *The Falcon* mysteries with George Sanders.

## *Maggi's Private Wire*
Premiered April 12, 1949 on NBC Tuesday 7:30 pm; ran until July 2, 1949

Cast: Maggi McNellis – hostess

This weekly fifteen-minute talk show was hosted by Maggi McNellis who interviewed celebrities and other fascinating people. McNellis started her show business career as a nightclub singer but switched to interviewing first on radio in 1943 and then on television. For awhile, she simultaneously hosted this series as well as moderated *Leave It to the Girls*, as described next. After her network TV show ended, she had series on the local CBS and ABC affiliates in New York City.

## *Leave It to the Girls*
Premiered April 27, 1949 on NBC Wednesday 8:00 pm; ran until December 1951

> Original Cast: Maggi McNellis – emcee
> Eloise McElhone, Binnie Barnes, Florence Pritchett, Lisa Ferraday, Ann Rutherford, Dorothy Kilgallen, and Harriet Van Horne – some of the original panelists
> Producer: Martha Roundtree

Created by Martha Roundtree who also developed the public affairs program *Meet the Press, Leave It to the Girls*, which started on radio in 1945, featured female panelists discussing various issues usually related to men with a single male panelist defending his gender. The host would read letters submitted by female viewers, and the panelists would render their opinions on the matter.

The original concept for the series was to have a serious discussion by four professional women of issues sent in by listeners but the show quickly began focusing on topics dealing with male-female relationships.

The television show first appeared on the local NBC station in 1947 with Eddie Dunn as the host sitting at a desk, opening letters, and reading problems such as "Should a man marry a widow or an old maid?" Some of the topics were presented by brief skits. The original panel on the local show included Eloise McElhone, Dorothy Kilgallen, Maggi McNellis, and Harriet Van Horne.

McNellis became the moderator when the series was picked up by the network. An early network episode had regular panel members Binnie Barnes and Florence Pritchett along with guests Faye Emerson, Nancy Kelly, and male guest Paul Winchell with his dummy Jerry Mahoney. Binnie Barnes gave the most outspoken advice on this June 12, 1949 episode, telling a woman who asked for the definition of "love" to go out and meet some guy remarking that there are plenty of bars in town. Concerning a question about men shopping for their own clothes, Barnes responded that since most males are helpless and rely on their wives, there must be some sinister motive for the man to want to go shopping alone.

After the series ended its run on NBC, ABC aired a prime-time version during the 1953-54 season. A syndicated version of the show ran during the 1962-63 season with Ms. McNellis returning as host.

## *Broadway to Hollywood – Headline Clues*
Premiered July 20, 1949 on DuMont Wednesday 8:30 pm; ran until July 15, 1954

> Cast: George F. Putnam – host and newsreader
> Director: Pat Fay
> Writer: Norman Baer

Originally, *Headline Clues* was a half-hour television news program with a home audience quiz built into it. It also featured interviews of celebrities and newsmakers. George Putnam would read International Service reports intermixed with some newsworthy still photos. He would then phone viewers at home and give away prizes to those who correctly answered a news-related question or identified a photo. If the viewer answered correctly, he or she would get a chance at a jackpot prize – a new gas range. The jackpot required a viewer to identify a photo flashed on the screen with a verbal clue from Putnam. The name of the show changed to *Broadway to Hollywood - Headline Clues* in October 1949.

On February 15, 1951, Bill Slater became host of the show with the quiz element dropped and the series devoting itself strictly to regular news stories with a focus on entertainment and celebrity interviews. Conrad Nagel took over hosting duties during the show's final season.

# Public Affairs Shows 23

RELEGATED TODAY MOSTLY to cable news channels and Sunday mornings on network TV, on early television many public affairs shows aired in prime time on the major networks.

## *Meet the Press*
Premiered November 20, 1947 on NBC Thursday 8:00 pm; still on the air today but not in prime time

   Cast: Martha Roundtree – moderator
   Lawrence Spivak – regular panelist

Created by Martha Roundtree and Lawrence Spivak, *Meet the Press* started on radio and for a number of years, up until 1952, aired on primetime television. The program began on October 5, 1945 on the Mutual Broadcasting System radio network. Roundtree partnered with Spivak on creating the program as a way to promote Spivak's magazine, *American Mercury*.

From October 1952 to August 1965, the series aired early Sunday evenings at 6:00 and today, still on NBC, is shown on Sunday mornings. It was simulcast on radio from 1952 until 1986.

The program has always consisted of one or more news reporters questioning a public figure on issues of the day. The very first guest on the program was James Farley, Postmaster General of the United States.

Lawrence Spivak, co-creator and regular panelist on *Meet the Press*.

## Court of Public Opinion (aka *Court of Current Issues*)
Premiered February 9, 1948 on DuMont Tuesday 8:00 pm; ran until June 26, 1951

>Cast: No regular cast members
>Creator/Producer: Irvin Paul Sulds

Focusing on debates of public issues, this program was presented as a courtroom trial with a real judge or attorney presiding and influential people acting as witnesses and counsel on both sides of the same issue. A jury of twelve selected from the studio audience decided which counsel presented the best case. The issue on one early show was whether or not universal military training was necessary.

On a March 3, 1949 installment, the topic was rail travel versus air travel. The former president of the Confederation of Railway Progress acted as counsel for the railroad industry. A former chairman of the Civil Aeronautics Board was counsel for the airlines. Witnesses included Eddie Rickenbacker, then president of Eastern Airlines.

For the series final two seasons, it was slotted against NBC's powerhouse *Texaco Star Theater* with Milton Berle meaning that extremely few people watched it.

## People's Platform
Premiered August 17, 1948 on CBS Tuesday 9:30 pm; ran until August 11, 1950

>Cast: Dwight Cooke - moderator
>Quincy Howe – moderator
>Director: Frank Schaffner
>Producer: Leon Levine

A debate between public figures on important issues was the concept of this series. A discussion about the House of Representatives Committee on Un-American Activities between Rep. Emanuel Celler, Democrat and Henry D. Dorfman, his Republican opponent was featured on the first show. As *Variety* pointed out in reviewing that show, "Rep. Celler, who bitterly criticized the House committee for its alleged whipping up of hysteria, made some sharp comments but had a tendency to mugg in front of the camera.

Dorfman didn't mugg but he was badly confused in his thinking."[113] This description is applicable today to many debates on cable news networks.

*The People's Platform*, developed by educator Lyman Bryson, Chairman of the CBS Adult Education Board, started on radio in 1938 and ran until 1952. Bryson was the original moderator of the radio show. He was replaced by Dwight Cooke.

While the television version of the series left prime-time in 1950, it continued to air on Sunday afternoons until July 1951. Apparently, some of the Sunday afternoon programs dealt with other than political issues. On an October 1, 1950 installment of the program, the topic was "Who Will Win the Pennant?" with guests Red Barber, Lefty Gomez, Carl Hubbell, and Tim Cohane.

## *Operation Success*
Premiered September 21, 1948 on DuMont Tuesday 8:00 pm; ran until June 23, 1949

>Cast: Jack Rayel – host/writer/producer
>Director: Tony Kraber

Produced in cooperation with the U.S. Veterans Administration, this show presented disabled veterans who had been trained for various occupations. The vets were interviewed and then attempts were made to find them employment.

The premiere began with filmed war scenes to remind viewers of the effects of war on veterans. One veteran was interviewed who had learned to become a furniture upholsterer through the VA. Three VA doctors and guidance experts were also interviewed.

Later in the show's run, Bob Pfeiffer became the host.

*Operation Success* was another DuMont public affairs program the network placed opposite the top-rated Milton Berle show on NBC.

## *America's Town Meeting*
Premiered October 5, 1948 on ABC Tuesday 8:30 pm; ran until June 1949

>Cast: George V. Denny, Jr. – moderator

Based on the radio series, *America's Town Meeting* was a debate by prominent people on issues of the day such as "Are We Too Hysterical about Communism?," "Should We Have Uniform Federal Divorce Laws?," and "Is Peace with Russia Possible?" The debate occurred before a live audience. The series was resurrected in 1952 for a brief run on ABC early Sunday evenings.

George V. Denny, Jr. had been a professor and a Broadway actor before he became director of the League for Political Education. In that capacity, he created and moderated *America's Town Meeting* hoping to make citizens more aware of public issues.

Like DuMont, ABC didn't try to compete with Milton Berle's *Texaco Star Theater* deciding instead to air this series.

## *Newsweek Analysis* (aka *Newsweek Views the News*)
Premiered November 7, 1948 on DuMont Sunday 6:30 pm; ran until May 22, 1950

Cast: Ernest K. Lindley – host
Director: Lee Tomalin

Although starting out on early Sunday evenings, *Newsweek Analysis* moved to 8:00 pm Mondays beginning in February 1949. The format of the show was like the news magazine itself with different departments. First, editors of *Newsweek* reviewed current news and then they interviewed leading figures of the day about various topics. The series was a cooperative endeavor between DuMont, always looking for inexpensive programming, which provided the time, and *Newsweek* which supplied the content.

On an episode aired in August 1949, the medical director of the National Foundation of Infantile Paralysis was interviewed about the polio epidemic at the time, the manager of the New York division of the Atomic Energy Commission explained aspects of atomic energy production, and other guests talked about air power and new advances in lighting.

## *On Trial*
Premiered November 22, 1948 on ABC, slotted at various times until March 1950 when it was scheduled on Wednesday at 8:00 pm; ran until August 12, 1952

Cast: David Levitan – moderator
Bob Sabin - announcer

Similar to *Court of Public Opinion*, *On Trial* was an issue-oriented debate series presented as a courtroom trial with a judge, attorneys, and expert witnesses. One counsel was for the issue being debated; the other against. The first episode tackled the topic of prohibiting wire-tapping. Justice Ferdinand Pecora of the New York Supreme Court presided. Lloyd Paul Stryker presented the case for prohibiting wire-taping with witness William G. H. Finch. William B. Herlands was counsel for wire-taping and his witness was Charles P. Grimes.

The audio portion of the show was rebroadcast on ABC radio later the same evening that the television show aired.

The format of the series changed slightly over time with one episode presenting the arguments for a certain issue and the next weekly episode featuring the case against the issue.

## *Meet Your Congress*
Premiered July 1, 1949 on NBC Friday 9:00 pm; ran until October 1949

Cast: Blair Moody – moderator
Producer: Charles Christiensen

Republican and Democratic senators and representatives appeared on this program to debate important issues. The initial show featured Senators James Murray, Joseph O'Mahoney, Homer Ferguson, and Andrew Schoeppel discussing rising unemployment in the United States.

The series, emanating from Washington D.C., was originally seen on Sunday afternoons from March to June 1949. In 1953, the series re-appeared on DuMont, lasting until July 1954. The moderator, Blair Moody, was a former senator from Michigan.

## *Capitol Cloak Room*
Premiered October 14, 1949 on CBS Friday 10:30 pm; ran until September 8, 1950

Cast: Griffing Bancroft

Eric Sevareid
Bill Shadel

A panel of three CBS news correspondents interviewed a political figure from Washington D.C. on this program simulcast on both radio and television.

The series eventually moved to Sunday afternoons in fall 1950 running until January 1951. An episode of *Capitol Cloak Room* was one of the first shows CBS televised in color on closed circuit TV.

Of the panel, Eric Sevareid is no doubt the best remembered as a long-time commentator on the *CBS Evening News*. Griffing Bancroft also began his career at CBS radio and later became a naturalist and author. Bill Shadel was the first host of the CBS Sunday morning interview program, *Face the Nation*.

*Candid Camera's* Allen Funt pictured in a 1949 NBC publicity still.

# Reality Series 24

WHILE NOT LIKE SOME of today's reality series that purportedly document the "real" lives of ordinary people, the 1940s saw the beginnings of certain types of realty programs based on everyday people reacting to unusual situations and based on true-life court cases.

## *Candid Camera*
Premiered August 10, 1948 on ABC Sunday 8:00 pm; initially ran until September 1950

    Cast: Allen Funt – host and creator

This long-running hidden camera show actually began on radio as *Candid Microphone* in 1947. Allen Funt came up with the concept for the program while stationed in Oklahoma during World War II. "He was reading the gripe column in the GI newspaper Yank. It might be interesting, he thought, to record something along this line for broadcast. The problem was that 'ordinary people' often became rigid and tense before a microphone. But what if he could record them on the sly: hide the microphone and let them know they had been duped only after the interview was preserved . . .?"[114]

    The television version of the show began on ABC in 1948 with film shot in a restaurant serving spaghetti showing the different ways customers eat the pasta. Other segments included a woman in a reducing salon being put through some extra exercises; a man in a tailor's shop who was told his trousers had a big rip; a man checking a bag at a railway station being told that everything had to be closely inspected; and Funt, posing as a still photographer, telling a man who wanted a photo of himself with his fiddle that the man didn't look serious enough.

An article in *Televiser Monthly* provided some insight into some of the other early *Candid Camera* gags.[115] A couple in a restaurant is unsettled when their waiter (Funt) advises them that there is nothing on the menu but liver. In another segment, Funt, posing as a doctor, explains to a four-year-old about babies. Using a two-way mirror, the camera shows a girl putting on makeup in a powder room and a man shaving.

In a 1949 episode when the series moved to NBC, Mr. Funt appears before a live audience to introduce his film clips. The audience politely applauds but does not laugh that much. In one clip, Allen Funt poses as a refund clerk in a department store handling customers who return items without a receipt. In another segment, standing outside a brownstone in New York, he pretends he is going to film a big movie star emerging from the house and interviews neighbors who say there is no celebrity living there. Probably the biggest laugh he receives is when he mistakes a man's wife for his mother. In another clip, Funt interviews five-year olds about how to prevent future wars.

Since its premiere in 1948, new editions of *Candid Camera* have appeared on television in virtually every decade from the 1950s through the 2010s –either as a series or a special. After the death of Allen Funt, son Peter took over hosting the show.

## *They Stand Accused*

Premiered January 18, 1949 on CBS Tuesday 8:00 pm; ran until December 30, 1954

Originating from Chicago, this sixty-minute courtroom drama was, in many ways, a precursor to today's judge shows. The unscripted series used real lawyers and judges but with actors playing the parts of defendants and witnesses. Members of the studio audience served as jurors. The cases were fictitious, but the Illinois Attorney General briefed the participants before each episode as if they were taking part in a real case. *Cross Question* was the initial title of the series.

After airing on CBS until May 1949, the show moved to DuMont for the balance of its run. It left the DuMont schedule in October 1952 but was brought back in September 1954 and lasted until December of that year.

An episode that aired late in the series run is an example of the variety of cases presented. The drama involves a custody battle over a five-year-old boy. Tom Roberts' wife Mary remarried after Tom, a news correspondent, had been reported killed in Germany. Mary had married Fred Chalmers, and they had a son named Johnny. Their marriage was annulled when Tom suddenly returned from Europe. Obviously not dead, he had been imprisoned by the Russians in East Germany.

Mary, who is now back with Tom, is asking for full custody of Johnny and wants to take him to Europe with her and her husband. But Fred, the boy's real father, objects. After presenting testimony from Tom, Mary, Fred, and Fred's mother, the jury awards custody to Mary, but the judge disagrees and awards custody to Fred. However, the judge says that if Mrs. Roberts returns to the United States, he will re-open the case.

## *The Black Robe*
Premiered May 18, 1949 on NBC Wednesday 8:30 pm; ran until March 30, 1950

Cast: Frank Thomas - judge
John Green – police officer
Writer/Producer: Phillips H. Lord
Director: Ed Sutherland

Based on cases tried in New York City's Police Night Court, *The Black Robe* was a thirty-minute, semi-documentary series where real people played the defendants and witnesses. Only the judge, dressed in black robes, and the police officer were actors. Each episode dealt with a number of cases. For example, an early episode included several hoodlums brought before the court on assault charges, a small-time con artist selling bogus magazine subscriptions, a man held for manslaughter by automobile, two unlicensed peddlers, and a married couple with a problem of the husband working nights.

Director Livia Granito recalls how the series recruited people to appear on the show:

> We looked for "characters," so you can imagine the kind of people we got! We got drunks off the Bowery – well, at least the guys did. We went on the subway, gave out little cards to people and asked them to come to the storefront that housed our office and rehearsal hall, down the block from the 21 Club, on 52$^{nd}$ Street. A lot of professional actors tried to pass as amateurs,

but we would see right through them. One day, Marlon Brando was passing by the store, came in, and applied – incognito. We went along with the prank and told him not to call us, we'd call him.[116]

Commenting on the use of real characters on the series, *The Billboard* thought, "Too often the eagerness with which one of the alleged miscreants 'confesses' tips the mitt that, let's face it, there's a fin in it, so, what the hell. Similarly, in striving for reality visually, and to bolster it with appropriate dialog, the program goes overboard."

The publication remarked further:

In the show caught (June 15, 1949), two "dese, dem, and dose mugs," one an ex-con attempting to fend off the disruptive efforts of the other is a case in point, involved two supposed ex-cons, one of whom had built up a prosperous business and employed only former inmates, and the other, who was trying to get the employees to hark back to their less legal habits. The exchange of threats, the "dese, dem, and dose" talk and the continual scowling of the offender did more to detract from the episode, rather than giving it the sought after authenticity.[117]

Veteran Broadway actor Frank Thomas, who played the father on the comedy *Wesley*, a detective on *Martin Kane*, and the judge on this series, had to use all of his experience in the theater to keep each episode on track. As his wife, Mona Bruns Thomas noted,

Half of the types who appeared on the show came fortified with plenty of alcohol for their debut. Frequently they departed from their cases and there was the ever-present danger of profanity. Others froze on camera and Frank had to draw out what words he could and fill in to clarify the cases for the audience. There was no effective way of rehearsing or timing the program. My poor husband had to watch his strange casts, preserve order in his fictional court, and see that the cases were solved in time for the program to get off the air.[118]

## *The Crisis*
Premiered October 5, 1949 on NBC Wednesday 8:00 pm; ran until December 28, 1949

    Cast: Adrian Spies – interviewer
    Arthur Peterson – stage director (October)
    Bob Cunningham –stage director (November to December)
    Producer: Ted Mills
    Director: Norman Felton

This series attempted to dramatize peoples' real-life crisis. A person who experienced a crisis in his or her life appeared on each episode and, with the help of interviewer Adrian Spies, began to describe the event. Then professional actors –working without a script – attempted to dramatize what came next with the help of a stage director. The stage director set the scene for the actors, gave them instructions, and called for various simple props.

    In one early script from the Norman Felton Collection at the University of Iowa, actor Thomas Mitchell was the interviewer. The script told the story of Ruth who, at a young age, had been taken into the home of a Mrs. Krunz with a son named Harry five years older than Ruth. When Ruth is in her mid-twenties, Mrs. Krunz asks her to marry her son, but Ruth is really in love with Harry's friend Joe. With Joe about to come by the Krunz's residence, Ruth must make a decision about how she'll respond to Mrs. Krunz's request. At this point, actors do a scene showing how they think Ruth responded.

    Ruth did marry Harry but is unhappy and finds that he is having an affair with another woman. She leaves him only to learn that he had a terrible accident and is crippled for life. Actors play out a scene of what they think Ruth did next.

    Ruth returns to take care of Harry who is more embittered than ever. One day she meets Joe who begs her to divorce Harry and marry him. Joe says he will tell off Harry and Mrs. Krunz and take Ruth away. The actors then perform another scene of what they think subsequently happened.

    Ruth decides to stay with Harry. Joe marries someone else. Three years later Harry dies.

    Another script dated November 23, 1949 is about Francie Masolak who works at the Paradise Café owned by Martin Paradise married to an older, sickly woman. When Martin learns that Francie's father has lost his job and she needs more money, he asks her to move in with him and his wife to be her companion. When Francie meets Florence Paradise, the woman warns her that Martin is a terrible man. Actors play a scene about whether Francie stays or leaves the Paradise home.

Francie stays. Later Martin confesses that he loves Francie and kisses her. Francie then decides to leave the house. Mrs. Paradise drives Francie to the train station in an old truck. Actors do a scene to portray what they think happened then.

Host of the series, Adrian Spies later became a celebrated scriptwriter for myriad TV series like *Playhouse 90, Dr. Kildare*, and *Robert Montgomery Presents*. Producer/director Norman Felton was best known for producing *Dr. Kildare* and *The Man from U.N.C.L.E.* – both on NBC.

# Endnotes

1. Margaret R. Weiss, *The TV Writer's Guide*, New York: Pellegrini & Cudahy, 1952, 95-110.

2. Teedie Burton, "TV Actress Is Visitor in Asheville, *Asheville Citizen-Times* (Asheville, NC), December 19, 1954.

3. John Dunning, *On the Air: The Encyclopedia of Old-Time Radio*, New York: Oxford Press, 1998, 285.

4. Worthington Miner, *Worthington Miner Interviewed by Franklin J. Schaffner*, Metuchen, NJ: The Directors Guild and The Scarecrow Press, 1985, 191.

5. Ira Skutch, editor, *The Days of Live: Television's Golden Age as seen by 21 Directors Guild Members*, Lanham, MD and Los Angeles: The Scarecrow Press and Directors Guild of America, 1998, 59.

6. Ibid., 60-61.

7. "Radio and Television," *The New York Times*, April 30, 1949.

8. Mona Bruns Thomas, *By Emily Possessed*, New York: Exposition Press, 1973, 100.

9. Skutch, *The Days of Live*, 50.

10. Dorothy McBride, Interdepartmental Communication, NBC Continuity Acceptance, November 10, 1948, NBC Collection, Wisconsin Center for Film and Theater Research.

11. Jack Gould, "First Nights on TV," *The New York Times*, March 6, 1949.

12. "Coast to Coast in Television," *Radio Mirror*, July 1949.

13. John Crosby, "'Easy Aces' Succeed in New TV Theory," *Detroit Free Press*, December 27, 1949.

14. "Radio and Television," *The New York Times*, September 17, 1948.

15. "Gosch, DuMont Settle Beef Involving Mostel TV Show," *The Billboard*, October 30, 1948.

16. Herman Scheonfeld, "Off the Record," Television Review, *Variety*, October 6, 1948.

17. Irving Breecher as told to Hank Rosenfeld, *The Wicked Wit of the West*, Teaneck, NJ: BenYehuda Press, 2009, 195-196.

18. Jack Gaver, "Neil Hamilton 'Reunited' with Mamaronek, N.Y.," *The Star Press* (Muncie, IN) April 23, 1950.

19. Edmund C. Rice, "Double Door" script, Edmund C. Rice Collection, American Heritage Center, University of Wyoming, May 7, 1949.

20. "The Borden Theater," Reviews of Teleshows, *The Televiser*, September-October, 1947.

21. McKnight Malomar, "The Storm," adapted by Worthington Miner, Studio One Production Files 1948 – 1955, Performing Arts Research Collection, New York Public Library.

22. Jeff Kisseloff, *The Box: An Oral History of Television, 1920-1961*, New York: Penquin Books, 1995, 229.

23. Cy Wagner, "Vic and Sade," Radio and Television Program Reviews, *The Billboard*, July 30, 1949.

24. Sam Chase, "The Fireside Theater," Radio and Television Program Reviews, *The Billboard*, May 7, 1949.

25. Quote from August 31, 1949 script written by Larry Menkin for "The Hands of Murder" pilot on *Program Playhouse*, Larry Menkin Papers, American Heritage Center, University of Wyoming.

26. Jerry Franken, "Lights Out," Radio and Television Review, *The Billboard*, November 26, 1949.

27. Kisseloff, *The Box*, 211.

28. Lawrence Menkin and Charles Speer, Script 4, "Memo to a Killer," Larry Menkin Papers, American Heritage Center, University of Wyoming.

29. "Anybody Wanna Buy TV Pix?," *Variety*, September 1, 1948.

30. Wesley Hyatt, *Short-Lived Television Series: 1948-1978*, Jefferson, NC: McFarland & Company, Inc., 2003, 11.

31. William Gargan, *Why Me*, Quoted in "Martin Kane," The Thrilling Detective Web Site, retrieved October 14, 2016.

32. Kisseloff, *The Box*, 213.

33. "Plainclothes Man," Television Review, *Variety*, October 12, 1949.

34. "Radio and Television, *The New York Times*, September 29, 1949.

35. "A Unique Twist to The Tele Soap Opera Given by Caples' Man Lewis," *Televiser Magazine*, November-December, 1946.

36. Michael Ritchie, *Please Stand By: A Prehistory of Television*, Woodstock, NY: The Overlook Press, 1994, 148.

37. Mona Bruns Thomas, *By Emily Possessed*, 99.

38. Si Steinhauser, "Real Life O'Neills Inspire Radio-Television Series," *The Pittsburgh Press*, September 6, 1949.

39. "Tele Film Reviews," *Variety*, December 15, 1948.

40. Kisseloff, *The Box*, 276.

41. Jerry Franken, "Arthur Godfrey and His Friends," Radio and Television Program Reviews, *The Billboard*, January 29, 1949.

42. Vincent Lopez, *Lopez Speaking: My Life and How I Changed It*, New York: The Citadel Press, 1960, 350.

43. Ibid., 347.

44. Leon Morse, "The Sonny Kendis Show," Radio and Television Program Reviews, *The Billboard*, September 3, 1949. 45. Jack Gould, "Television in Review," *The New York Times*, June 26, 1949.

46. "Words and Music," Television Reviews, *Variety*, August 10, 1949.

47. Merrill Panitt, "Berle Returns But Show Was a Dud," *The Philadelphia Inquirer*, September 26, 1949.

48. "Al Morgan Show," Television Review, *Variety*, August 23, 1950.

49. "Wayne King Show," Television Review, *The Billboard*, October 8, 1949.

50. "Wayne King Show," Television Review, *Variety*, October 12, 1949.

51. Eddie Condon, *We Called It Music: A Generation of Jazz*, New York: Da Capo Press, 1992, 284.

52. "Penthouse Sonata," Television Review, *Variety*, June 29, 1949.

53. Kisseloff, *The Box*, 110.

54. Jack Gould, "A Pretty Girl," *The New York Times*, May 2, 1948.

55. "Alan Dale Show," Television Reviews, *Variety*, June 9, 1948.

56. Alan Dale, *The Spider and the Marionettes*, New York: Lyle Stuart, 1965, 107.

57. Ibid., 108.

58. Jerry Franken, "The Dennis James Carnival," Radio-Television Review, *The Billboard*, November 13, 1948.

59. Jack Gould, "Programs in Review," *The New York Times*, January 16, 1949.

60. "Sunday Date," Television Review, *Variety*, August 31, 1949.

61. Terry Vernon, "Tele-Vues," *Long Beach Independent*, December 4, 1949.

62. Kisseloff, *The Box*, 305.

63. Quotations from *Texaco Star Theatre* script, show #24, February 28, 1950.

64. "Jack Carter and Company," Television Reviews, *Variety*, March 16, 1949.

65. *The Henry Morgan Show* Script #5, April 10, 1949, NBC Collection, Wisconsin Center for Film and Theater Research.

66. Continuity Acceptance Department, "Continuity Changes," April 1, 1949, NBC Collection, Wisconsin Center for Film and Theater Research.

67. Earl Wilson, "It Happened Last Night," *The St. Louis Star and Times*, April 13, 1949.

68. Milton Douglas, "No Holidays in Show Business," *TV Forecast*, July 8, 1950.

69. Kisseloff, *The Box*, 317.

70. Leon Morse, "The Herb Shriner Show," Radio and Television Program Reviews, *The Billboard*, November 19, 1949.

71. Marty Schrader, "Reviews: NBC," *The Billboard*, December 30, 1944.

72. "Standard Brands Hourglass," Television Reviews, *The Billboard*, May 18, 1946.

73. Judy Dupuy, "Standard Brands' $105,000 Tele Experience with 'Hour Glass,'" *The Televiser*, January-February, 1947.

74. Ira Skutch, *I Remember Television: A Memoir*, Metuchen, NJ: The Directors Guild of America and The Scarecrow Press, 1989, 51.

75. Worthington Miner, 185.

76. "Toast of the Town," Television Review, *Variety*, June 23, 1948.

77. Ed Sullivan, "From the Mailbag," *The New York Times*, July 11, 1948.

78. Sid Caesar, Archive of American Television Interview, March 14, 1997.

79. Kisseloff, *The Box*, 184.

80. Jack Gould, "Programs in Review," *The New York Times*, May 29, 1949.

81. Kisseloff, *The Box*, 113.

82. Alex McNeil, *Total Television: The Comprehensive Guide to Programming from 1948 to Present*, 4th edition, New York: Penguin Books, 1996, 232.

83. Kisseloff, *The Box*, 220-221.

84. Jack Gould, "That Man Godfrey," *The New York Times*, December 12, 1948.

85. "Birthday Party," Review, *The Televiser*, June-July, 1947.

86. John Huster, "Roar of the Rails," *Classic Toy Trains*, November, 1994, 93-95.

87. Ira Skutch, *The Days of Live*, 1.

88. Bob Brown, *Science Circus No.2*, New York: Fleet Publishing Corporation, 1963, 260.

89. Marlo Lewis and Mina Bess Lewis, *Prime Time*, Los Angeles: J. P. Tarcher, Inc., 1979, 57.

90. Lew Lehr, Cal Tinney, and Roger Bower, *Stop Me If You've Heard This One*, Garden City, NY: Halcyon House: 1948, vi.

91. Jack Gould, "Programs in Review," *The New York Times*, August 1, 1948.

92. Sidney Lohman, "The Field of Television: News and Notes," *The New York Times*, July 31, 1949.

93. "Sparring Partners," Television Review, *Variety*, April 13, 1949.

94. Jack Gould, "Programs in Review," *The New York Times*, May 29, 1949.

95. John Crosby, "Auction Show Rates as Dullest on TV," *Detroit Free Press*, November 11, 1949.

96. Ira Skutch, Archive of American Television Interview, January 29, 2004.

97. John Caldwell, "All Home Games to Be Seen on Video This Baseball Year," *The Cincinnati Enquirer*, March 13, 1949.

98. Tim Brooks and Earle Marsh, *The Complete Directory to Prime Time Network and Cable TV Shows: 1946 – Present* (Ninth Edition), New York: Ballantine Books, 2007, 655.

99. "And Everything Nice," Television Review, *Variety*, October 19, 1949.

100. "The Million Mile Traveler," Radio and Television Reviews, *The Billboard*, October 18, 1949.

101. Ira Skutch, *I Remember Television*, 43.

102. Dana Polan, "James Beard's Early TV Work: A Report on Research," *Gastronomica*, Summer, 2010, 25.

103. "Gulf Oil: Schedule Increased with 'You Are an Artist' Over WNBT Added to Sponsorship of the CBS News," *Television Magazine*, January, 1947.

104. "Dancing on Air," Television Review, *Variety*, February 26, 1947.

105. E.M. Guilbert, "Interdepartment Correspondence to Stockton Helffrich," NBC Continuity Acceptance, August 16, 1948, NBC Collection, Wisconsin Center for Film and Theater Research.

106. Jack Gould, "Programs in Review," *The New York Times*, March 20, 1949.

107. Jack Eigen and Gloree Walsh, *Etiquette with False Teeth*, New York: Shelsea Enterprises, 1948-1949, iv.

108. "We, The People," Television Review, *Variety*, June 9, 1948.

109. Carl Reiner, Archive of American Television Interview, March 23, 1998.

110. "'Missing Persons' New WGN-TV Show," *Television Forecast*, October 25 to 31, 1948.

111. Dunning, *On the Air*, 440.

112. Jack Gould, "Programs in Review," *The New York Times*, October 2, 1949.

113. "People's Platform," Television Review, *Variety*, August 25, 1948.

114. Dunning, *On the Air*, 135.

115. Milton Blackstone, "Going Thru Channels," *Televiser Monthly*, November 1948.

116. Ira Skutch, *The Days of Live*, 9.

117. "The Black Robe," Radio and Television Program Reviews, *The Billboard*, June 25, 1949.

118. Mona Bruns Thomas, *By Emily Possessed*, 102.

# Index

**A**
Ace, Goodman  23-25
Amsterdam, Morey  132, 139, 140, 155, 210
Archer, Gene  109, 149
Arnold, Paul  121, 125, 251

**B**
Ball, Lucille  xvii, 18, 208
Barrie, Wendy  196, 215, 268
Bellamy, Ralph  74, 75
Berg, Gertrude  4-6, 39
Berle, Milton  30, 99, 111, 154-57, 160, 161, 171, 220, 273-75
Brand, Jack  101, 102, 242
Bright, Jack  210, 211
Brown, John Mason  209, 236, 237, 262, 263
Bueno, Delora  96, 104, 146, 147

**C**
Caddigan, James  12, 13, 62, 131, 140, 201, 264
Caesar, Sid  175-77
Carter, Jack  132, 155, 159-62, 173, 187
Coca, Imogene  158, 175-77
Coe, Fred  33, 35-39, 41, 54, 56, 121, 129, 169, 170
Collyer, Bud  190, 211, 214, 259
Como, Perry  25, 91, 98, 99, 179
Condon, Eddie  115, 116
Cooper, Wyllis  54, 56

**D**
Dale, Alan  126, 131, 132
Daly, John  72, 216, 218, 219
Dean, James  8, 58
Desmond, Johnny  93, 94, 141
Douglas, Milton  161, 162, 178
Downs, Johnny  102, 129, 136
Dunn, Bob  173, 205, 206, 226
Dunn, Eddie  205, 226, 269

**E**
Edwards, Cliff  107, 180
Emerson, Faye  91, 181, 236, 238, 269

**F**
Fairbanks, Jerry  21, 67, 146, 203, 240
Fates, Gil  211, 223, 224, 236
Fay, Pat  1, 3, 147, 270
Faye, Joey  27-29, 168, 178, 180, 219
Felton, Norman  151, 200, 283, 284

**G**
Garde, Betty  24, 43, 123
Gargan, William  68, 69
Garrison, Greg  68, 110, 221, 257
Givot, George  148, 210
Gleason, Jackie  4, 26, 30, 31, 130, 139, 158, 161
Godfrey, Arthur  91, 99, 100, 179, 188, 189, 224, 252
Goodson-Todman  160, 186, 211, 224

293

Gosch, Martin  27, 28, 262, 263
Grauer, Ben  57, 58, 209, 229, 230, 233

## H
Hamilton, Neil  31, 32, 187
Hartman, Phil and Grace  19-21
Herlihy, Walter  222, 236, 237
Howe, Quincy  267, 273

## I
Idelson, Billy  23, 86

## J
James, Dennis  xvii, 132, 137, 186, 206, 256, 257

## K
Karloff, Boris  60-62
Karns, Roscoe  22, 48
Kendis, Sonny  105, 134
Kiernan, John  245
Kiernan, Walter  213, 216, 220, 221, 265
King, Wayne  111, 112
Klee, Lawrence  54, 74

## L
Lemmon, Jack  8, 31, 32, 202
Lescoulie, Jack 54, 225
Levy, Ralph  93, 134, 137, 144, 180
Loewi, Bob  147, 190, 194, 241
Lopez, Vincent  103, 137, 172
Lytell, Bert  39, 85, 143, 144, 187

## M
MacDonnell, Kyle  128-30
Mansfield, Irving  139, 140, 181, 188, 210
Marshall, Barbara  94, 97, 98, 109
Marshall, Dr. Roy K.  229, 233, 234
Maupin, Rex  101, 110, 145
McElhone, Eloise  210, 211, 220, 269
McNellis, Maggi  133, 134, 268-70
Menkin, Lawrence "Larry"  62, 63, 147, 201

Mildred Fenton Productions  71, 150, 225
Miner, Worthington  4, 6, 11, 12, 41, 42, 171, 199
Moore, Tom  221, 226
Morgan, Henry  160, 161, 215
Morgan, Ray  194, 238
Morse, Carlton  23, 86
Mostel, Zero 27-29
Mottola, Tony  93, 94, 102, 107

## N
Nagel, Conrad  50, 218, 219, 270
Nelson, Ralph  6, 7, 177, 227

## O
Ochs, Ace  93, 263
Oboler, Arch  51, 56
Olson, Johnny  185, 186, 225

## P
Parks, Bert, 207, 208, 214, 223
Parrish, Judy  3, 65

## Q
Quinlan, Roberta  94, 97, 98, 106, 107, 114

## R
Rayel, Jack  259, 274
Reiner, Carl  134, 138, 139, 180, 264
Roberts, Ken  27-29, 210
Ross, Lanny  92, 93
Roundtree, Martha  269, 271
Rubin, Benny  145, 146, 210
Russell, Connie  119, 179

## S
Schaffner, Frank  11, 12, 42, 273
Seymour, Dan  172, 263, 264
Silvers, Phil  137, 158, 219
Simpson, Garry  233, 265
Skotch, Ed  100, 117, 225
Skutch, Ira  37, 121, 129, 232, 247
Slater, Bill  194, 208, 229, 256, 257, 259, 270

Stang, Arnold  29, 30, 141, 160
Stanton, Bob  106, 122, 233, 255
Stearns, Johnny  17, 18
Stearns, Mary Kay  17
Steele, Ted  94, 96
Sullivan, Ed  99, 103, 105, 137, 155, 161, 166, 170-72, 264

## T
Telford, Frank  50, 173
Terkel, Studs  151, 152
Thomas, Frank  11, 69, 83, 281, 282
Thomas, Frank Jr.  54, 86
Thomas, Mona  11, 12, 83
Tillstrom, Burr  192, 197, 198

## W
Wallace, Mike  68, 227
Waring, Fred  104, 105, 172
Whiteman, Paul  113, 184, 189
Wolf, Ed  85, 173, 190, 214
Wood, Barry  102, 103, 105, 111, 114, 123, 134, 180
Wood, Peggy  6, 8, 41, 177
Wrightson, Earl  97, 113, 129, 134
Wynn, Ed  163, 164

## Z
Ziv Productions  24, 25, 239, 256

www.ingramcontent.com/pod-product-compliance
Lightning Source LLC
Chambersburg PA
CBHW060110170426
43198CB00010B/837